Praise for Sacred Fire

Sacred Fire is the story of a marriage, but also a reflection of life together in a society that often enables us to grow in different directions. How can two people who are very different stay married for life?

This memoir provides some of the answers, and a lot of inspiration to kindle your commitment to marriage. Uma Girish is an expert weaver of this tale of love, commitment, and values that really matter.

- **Daniela I. Norris**, author of *On Dragonfly Wings*

Sacred Fire is a powerful testament to love, individuality, and commitment within marriage. With raw honesty and heartfelt wisdom, it reveals how two souls can honor their unique paths while remaining deeply connected. This inspiring memoir illuminates love's resilience and its capacity to endure and evolve through life's challenges.

- **Anita Moorjani**, New York Times best-selling author

This story invites readers into the complexities of love, identity, and personal growth within an Indian marriage that spans continents. It explores a woman's journey from an unforgettable wedding day to the emotional turmoil of loss and self-discovery. Uma's heartfelt narrative captures the coexistence of grief and joy, as cultural traditions collide with modern realities. Through moments of turmoil and catharsis, the story highlights resilience, peace amidst chaos, and navigating the quiet spaces between lives shaped by shared memories but tested by time. It will resonate with anyone who has faced relationship challenges or struggled with personal evolution. Uma's honest reflection and beautiful prose make this an unforgettable journey.

- **Melissa Kaplan**, Somatic therapist

A beautifully written and insightful portrait of a marriage and the unforeseen consequences of the decisions we make. Uma didn't want an arranged marriage, but living alone and working in a city far away from her beloved family ultimately made her reconsider. Her story depicts how a woman can navigate the tumult of being called to a spiritual path not shared by her husband. A must-read!

- **Paula Robinson**, author of *The Healing Home & Garden: Reimagining Spaces for Optimal Wellbeing*

SACRED FIRE
Memoir of a Marriage

By

Uma Girish

Soul Spark
—PUBLISHING—

Other Works by Uma Girish

Understanding Death: 10 Ways to Inner Peace for the Grieving

Losing Amma, Finding Home: A Memoir About Love, Loss, and Life's Detours

Lessons from Grace: What A Baby Taught Me About Living and Loving

SACRED FIRE
Memoir of a Marriage

By

Uma Girish

Soul Spark Publishing™
An imprint of Soul Spark Enterprises
soulsparkpublishing.com

This is a work of nonfiction. Nevertheless, some names, identifying details, or characteristics of individuals have been changed. Additionally, certain people who have been listed are composites of a number of individuals and their experiences.

Sacred Fire: Memoir of A Marriage, First edition 2025
ISBN 978-1-964445-13-7 (paperback) 978-1-964445-14-4 (ebook)

Book Cover and Interior Formatting and Styling by Lucie Ward
Mandala graphics by TitikBak
Editing by Michelle Ireland

To G, who's writing this story with me

PART 3

Prologue

I t's 7:30 A.M. May 19, 1991. My wedding day. Already it's a blow-dryer-on-max-heat kind of day. The temperature is expected to touch 112 degrees Fahrenheit.

I feel drunk as a bee; a part of me wants to heave. The heat is doing a number on me.

Six yards of silk sari in a calming shade of forest-green bordered with maroon *zari,* wrap around my body like a scorching trap. The heavy rose garland around my neck is an itchy albatross. Throw in chunky gold bracelets and bangles, necklaces with thick pendants, and heavy gold earrings that weigh down earlobes, and all a bride can do is swoon.

I do. It's my wedding day and the very first thing I do is faint. The only saving grace is it happens in a private bridal room, far away from the invitees whose hungry eyes will soon begin to follow my every move. As I slouch in a chair, limp as a rag doll, my sister fashions a rolled-up newspaper fan and waves it over me. Someone rushes off to bring me a cold drink. Draping a cold compress over elaborately made-up eyes is not an option, minutes before the priest beckons me to ascend the wedding *mandap.*

Having forced a quick recovery, I climb the steps of the *mandap* minutes later. Festooned with garlands of marigold, jasmine, lotus, and lily, it evokes a garden vibe. The musicians announce my entry with the *nadaswaram,* a reed wind instrument which is integral to every festive occasion. The drums start up, and the violins complete the orchestra.

Two Hindu priests, their bare chests striped with holy ash, sit across from each other and fan the flames of the ceremonial fire. They are waiting for me to take my place beside the man who will soon become my husband.

It has only been eighty-four days since G and I met for the first time, but I've longed for this moment to arrive. My heart is a vast green meadow in balmy sunshine.

I cross my legs, sit down in front of the holy fire, and tuck the sari folds as elegantly as I can. I turn to G and smile, then take a moment to gaze at the crimson patterns of *henna* on my hands that bear motifs of birds, leaves, twirls, and curlicues. Earlier, the henna artist had asked me to spot the "G" she'd buried somewhere in the design, and when I did, popped a *mithai* in my mouth, its sweetness filling my entire being.

I look up and see a sea of beloved faces, here to bless our union: grandparents, aunts, uncles, cousins, distant relatives, and friends of the family. Some smile and wave; I nod and smile. Colorful as a flock of macaws, the women are decked in shades of flaming orange, turquoise, and parrot-green, and drip with gold, diamonds, and gemstones that set off their saris.

Sanskrit *slokas* and chants fill the air as the priests set about the business of getting us married. Platters of fruit, silver bowls of turmeric and sandalwood paste, betel leaves, coconuts, more flowers, incense, and holy water occupy the space between them. A roaring fire guzzles large containers of *ghee* to keep going.

Someone hands me a glass of lime juice or cold buttermilk at regular intervals to ensure that I survive the heat. After all, an Indian wedding is an epic saga.

The chants and blessings and prayers and rituals go on for hours, until we're both exhausted. During a short break when the two priests are huddled in consultation, G leans over and whispers to me: "I feel thoroughly married to you."

It's time for a sari change. This time, it's nine yards of maroon-and-gold, for the climactic moment of the wedding. This sari is draped in a particular way, a style I'm ignorant of. So I stand still, mannequin-like, as two elderly aunts circle me, grabbing handfuls of sari, twisting and tucking until it's wrapped around me.

On the wedding *mandap,* G and I make seven circles around the fire, him leading the way. I follow, the pads of all five fingers of my right hand joined together in a *mudra* held in the palm of his hand. *Saptapadi. Seven steps.* The fire burns, a sacred witness to the vows the priest speaks out loud. G repeats after him. A promise made with every trip around the fire. To provide food and nourishment and care for the family; to remain loyal and faithful, thus deepening the bonds of our commitment; gathering resources to sustain the family; respect and commitment toward both sets of families; to stand by each other at all times; a blessing to invite progeny to preserve the lineage; a commitment to love and respect one another and walk together through grief and joy, good times and bad.

Next, Appa sits in a chair placed beside the sacred fire, and I sit in his lap. G faces me standing up. The priest instructs Appa to bring together the outer edges of his palms together and hold his hands open. He asks me to nestle my open palms in my father's. G is guided to place his open palms right below my father's. The priest pours holy water into my hands that flow over into Appa's. A moment later, the priest instructs Appa to pull his palms away and my palms settle into G's. A transfer of responsibility. *She was born to me. I raised her, cared for her. My responsibilities are now over. From this moment on, she is yours. It is your duty to protect her and ensure her well-being.*

The priest's chants grow louder, and the drum beats reach a crescendo, heralding the auspicious moment of the day. A gold chain is placed in G's hands. A cluster of women lift up my ornamental braid and the rose garland away from my neck to make room as G fastens the chain around my neck. A shower of rose and marigold petals, and turmeric-stained rice grains rain down upon us, carrying the fervent wishes of the elders gathered to bless the occasion.

We are now man and wife.

The rose petals that rained down upon us will naturally fall off our clothes, wither and fade. It will be much harder to shake off the fears and insecurities that will creep into our union and challenge our intention to build a life of happiness and harmony.

PART 1

Kindling

HEAT

Arranged marriage is not for me.

My teenage self arrives at this conclusion having witnessed a marriage where my father has struggled with alcoholism for several years, and my mother, a submissive human, feels utterly powerless. They were strangers who committed to a life together after walking around a sacred fire. Now my mother chooses to honor her marital vows and continue to love and support her husband, no matter what life dishes out.

My fantasies involve the arrival of a man who will awaken a tsunami of passion within me, instead of being a good wife to some random stranger I must learn to love.

Born and raised in southern India—the land of astrology,

horoscopes, and complex rituals—I break out in hives when I hear the words *arranged marriage*. I cannot conceive of hitching my life to that of a complete stranger like my parents did. I cannot trust the pronouncement of a random astrologer that my natal chart and *his* (whoever the prospective groom may be) match together and promise marital bliss.

I have no desire to end up like my mother whose days are defined by domestic drudgery, the size of her ambition circumscribed by the perimeters of the home we live in. My role models in eighties India are the suave and sophisticated TV news anchors on Doordarshan, India's first broadcasting service. Neethi Ravindran, Gitanjali Aiyar, and Minu Talwar in their crisp and colorful handloom saris represent sartorial elegance and worldly wisdom. Their perfect hairdo, makeup, and British-school accents awaken my desire for a well-charted career path, independence, and financial freedom.

So, I, the product of a lineage of chartered accountants, found myself a fancy job in advertising. Friends and family barely understood what I did. "I write the words you see on billboards," I used to offer by way of a simple explanation. "Oh," they'd say and nod abstractly, which told me the conversation had reached a dead-end.

Life in the advertising world was fun and filled with variety. I left the parental nest to work in Bombay and Calcutta for a year each. An assortment of friends made for a busy social life. Although I went out to dinner and movies with male friends, there was a complete absence of chemistry. I failed to magnetize the love of my life, as I'd secretly hoped to. Two years of freedom which included living in a company-owned apartment somehow wasn't satisfying enough.

Opening the door to my empty apartment night after night, a wave of loneliness would hit me. The foreboding of that emptiness was so intense that I stayed in the office longer and longer, and rarely returned to my apartment before bedtime. The casual and carefree vibe of the agency meant enough folks were hanging around after hours racing against impossible deadlines, prepping for presentations, or just kicking back with a beer.

Truth be told, I didn't enjoy wasting my time in a cubicle filled with the stale smells of day-old sweat and cigarette smoke. I longed to come home to a welcoming hug, the smells of dinner cooking, and someone who was interested in hearing about my day. When it got too lonely, I quit my job and headed back to my parents' home in Hyderabad.

⚜

A memory from my college days.

Marry for love, my heart often whispers.

It's a balmy morning in Hyderabad. As I walk into the college building I see the girls swarming around nineteen-year-old Nazneen, giggling and nudging her.

Nazneen and I are second-year students.

"Tell us, how did the wedding night go?"

"Was he gentle?"

"Did it hurt?"

"Did you... go... all the way? Does that even happen the first time?"

The last question presumes that a virgin is not always able to consummate the marriage on her wedding night. If her man is patient and kind, he's usually willing to wait.

The girls huddle closer, eager to squeeze every last detail of Nazneen's virgin-to-wife graduation story.

I stand a safe distance away, not entirely comfortable with this invasion of privacy. If I were completely honest, I'm hungry for all the juicy details. Only two of my friends have boyfriends and they meet on the sly. The consequences would be severe if their families found out. One of them tells me how mortified she feels when her boyfriend gropes her because her god and religion do not permit premarital physical intimacy. She confesses that he's eager to get on with it but she fobs him off—and he's slowly losing patience.

The rest of us have no clue what that realm of life is about. As for sex education, we depend on what we can glean from trashy romance novels. Hearing a first-person account is a big deal, so I'm as eager as the next girl, even if I'm happy to let them do the prying and digging.

A faint pink blush creeps up Nazneen's alabaster skin. Her brown kohl-laden eyes sparkle, flitting from one face to the next, as she gauges how much to say. A sudden wave of shyness overwhelms her and she stuffs a corner of her emerald-green chiffon *dupatta* into her mouth and smothers her embarrassed giggles.

Raised in a conservative Muslim family, Nazneen was groomed to set her sights on making some man a good wife. She grew up hearing the words, *The day you become a wife is the most important day of your life.*

Six months ago, she rushed up to me clutching a 5 cm by 7 cm photograph of the groom her parents had chosen for her. I was sitting on a wooden bench in the college canteen, munching peanuts. "Here he is. My *miya*," she said, darting the photo in and out of my line of vision and making me dizzy.

"Nazneen, stop. Here, let me see." I tugged the photo out of her fingers. Fat cheeks, dark greasy hair, pale skin, and brooding eyes framed by square glasses.

"Do you know this guy?"

"He lives in Dubai. My parents tell me he's tall," she said, gazing at his picture with complete adoration.

"Have you spoken to him?"

"Not yet. I will when he calls. But we'll only see each other on our wedding day. It's tradition." Her fingers traced the edges of her *miya's* photograph.

"Don't you want more out of life?"

"What can a girl want more than a good husband?" Her eyes were dreamy and faraway, her words a soft whisper.

I could hardly believe what I was hearing. I'd want to know what books my man read, his taste in movies and music, and what happened in his heart when he opened the morning papers and read about dowry deaths, rape and caste crimes, the injustices women live with.

At nineteen, Nazneen knew as much about men as I did about life in Antarctica. Yet, she seemed unconcerned about throwing away a college degree to link her destiny with a total stranger. When I saw her turn the pages of an Economics textbook with a dreamy look in her eyes, her mind unconcerned about the midterms, it was obvious to me that she was simply going through the motions. She would marry a man she'd see minutes before her wedding ceremony, relocate to Dubai and morph into an obedient wife, producing meals and babies on demand. My heart rebelled at the very thought, but Nazneen was as cool as the pastel chiffons she wore.

Over the next months I watched her excitement build to fever-pitch. She'd search me out during break, bright-eyed and heady with love, and whisper that Salim had called or sent her a gift. She was beginning to fall in love with the idea of being in love. It was unfortunate that it was the only way a Muslim girl from a conservative background who was expected to marry in the traditional manner could introduce romance into her life. She fueled her long-distance passion with photographs, letters, and transatlantic conversations. In one photograph she showed me, Salim leaned against a Subaru, his eyes expressionless.

Dubai, to a nineteen-year-old, must have seemed like a slice of paradise. Glittering malls, dazzling lights, and air-conditioned high-rises. Nazneen's present reality was the oppressive heat and the hot dusty streets of Hyderabad. No wonder she saw Salim as her Prince Charming, the man who would transport her from a mundane life to a magical one.

At the engagement ceremony that preceded the wedding by a few hours, Nazneen looked like a princess straight out of Arabian

Nights. Coppery curtain of hair shining like silk. The artistic maroon of *henna* on her palms and feet, intricate motifs of flowers, stars, and the moon weaving a romantic tale. Gem-studded bracelets, necklaces, and earrings that made her earlobes sag.

The bride and groom sat in different rooms in observance of the custom. The girls who sat around Nazneen gasped every time one of Salim's many gifts arrived throughout the evening—a box of almond chocolates, a bouquet of red roses, a bottle of Eternity.

A thin gold veil covered Nazneen's face. According to the Muslim tradition, the bride, on her wedding day, must look no one in the eye until she sets eyes on her husband. Friends and relatives lifted her veil and commented on her beauty, but Nazneen's eyes remained downcast, chin dropping to chest as soon as the viewing was over. Groups of women sang and danced around her; the air alive with boisterous festivity.

When the *mullah* pronounced the auspicious hour, Salim arrived at the wedding *mandap* escorted by his friends and took his place in front of a thin white cotton sheet, a makeshift screen, placed between the two. The *mullah* started to chant in a singsong voice. The sheet was lifted at the appropriate hour and a family elder positioned a mirror between the bride and groom angled in such a way that their eyes met for the first time. Soon, Nazneen was overcome by shyness and her chin dropped to her chest as Salim's hungry eyes devoured her creamy skin.

Nazneen was back in college a week later after a whirlwind honeymoon. And here she was, being pestered by the girls to recount every last sensual detail of her first night as Salim's wife. I crept away, leaving behind the secretive glances and shy whispers. I just couldn't bring myself to listen. I never knew what was shared in that intimate circle.

My feet moved in the direction of the tamarind tree, my favorite thinking spot. Were Salim and Nazneen right for each other? Only time would tell.

Is falling in love the magical solution? Apparently not. Not if you know Sushma and Anoop, my friends who fought to marry each other after a magical courtship. Their marriage lasted a short two years.

Is it possible to marry a man you don't know, then begin to love him? I guess it is. All the several-decades-long arranged marriages in our lineage prove it.

Marriage is a gamble, my mother once told me. Some pick the right ticket and hit the jackpot. Some think they've won the lottery and later discover their numbers were all wrong.

I never saw Nazneen after we left college. We went our separate ways, but I often thought of her. I offered a silent prayer for the girl who had walked into her future as Salim's bride, the man she laid eyes on minutes before she became his wife.

FLICKERS

I know the conversation is coming, but I'm not prepared for it when it happens.

It's a still night; not a single leaf moves. Standing in the narrow balcony adjacent to the second-floor bedroom, I try to distract myself with the goings-on below. Cars and buses crawl in thick bumper-to-bumper traffic on the streets of Hyderabad. Pedestrians take advantage of stalled traffic and dart across the road with scant respect for personal safety. Hot pink neon signs wink and flash, advertising the neighborhood shops and restaurants. People walk in and out of buildings. Everyone is in motion, preoccupied and purposeful. And here I stand, an island amid it all.

Tears rush into my eyes. A fist of loneliness pounds inside my chest. Inside the apartment, my parents are busy. They are sitting across from each other under the white glare of a tube light, sifting through a pile of envelopes addressed to my father. They work as a team. Amma slits the letter open and passes it to Appa who reads it, then tosses it into one of two piles: Potential or Reject.

I stare at the night sky and ponder my fate. A half-moon is tangled in the trees. *How did I get here?* After twenty-three years of living in a family of seven (the number reduced to six for the last eight years after my beloved grandmother, Thaathi, died), I'd left home and lived on my own for two years before ending up back here in my parents' home. I'd earned decent money, made good friends, tasted independence, but my life was empty and alone.

I'm almost twenty-six, but haven't found love.

My parents, convinced that I'm about to be forgotten on the proverbial shelf, have taken it upon themselves to find me a husband. "You have two sisters in line to be married after you," Appa said. "We allowed you to go and work and live in Bombay and Calcutta. You had all the freedom, but you didn't find anyone. So now I have the responsibility to find a good husband for you."

He wasted no time in placing an ad in the matrimonial columns of a national newspaper. *Alliance sought for slim 5'5" graduate from a Hindu Brahmin family.* Details of my natal chart were included. Families of prospective grooms were invited to write to a P.O. box number.

That was two weeks ago.

Well, it's all my fault. I'm not good enough for Cupid. My best bet is a family astrologer now invested with the authority to make the most significant decision of *my* life.

"Come inside and read some of these letters." Appa's voice drifts into my consciousness. "See who you might want to meet."

Nobody. I don't want to meet anybody in a stupid fake 'girl-seeing' ceremony. I don't want to read those stupid letters. Just leave me alone.

But I drag my feet inside and disinterestedly thumb through a few letters, making sure my sullen face is on display the whole time. The formally-written letters offer highlights of the prospective groom—education, job, height, weight—and also contain a natal chart and a passport size photograph. One guy is clean-shaven and wears thick glasses. Another is light-skinned and has beady eyes. A few have the studious look of engineers, accountants, or researchers.

My stomach clenches. *I can't do this. I can't. I can't. I can't.*

My mind conjures up the scenario and makes me cringe.

No, I can't. I can't. I can't.

I cannot sit in my parents' living room dressed in a silk sari while Amma serves hot coffee and crispy savories to the potential groom's family. I can't listen to them discuss complicated family trees, delight spreading on their faces when they discover common friends and distant relatives, their shared lineage connecting them all back to some unheard-of village.

I can't subject myself to the torture of fixing my gaze on the floor tiles or furniture for inordinate lengths of time just so Mr. Maybe and I don't have to look at each other.

I can't live through an eternity of shifting glances and awkward smiles until the adults in the room finally run out of conversation, the crispy savories now soggy under the whirring blades of the ceiling fan.

I can't bear the thought of The Question: *Would you two like to talk to each other?* And the embarrassing getaway to the nearest balcony or rooftop terrace where we will continue to be unduly interested in the color of the sky and the trees until one of us is able to come up with the ice-breaker question.

He may ask me what my hobbies are, what kind of music I listen to, whether I enjoy cooking (an indirect way of making sure there's no danger of starvation in the marriage, because I will be expected to produce all the meals). I'll clam up, my insides seething, for I'll be damned if I'm going to share my likes and dislikes with some random guy I barely know.

In the meantime, the elders are waiting, secure in their fantasy that a lifetime of common dreams are being exchanged in the ten minutes of conversation between two people who are encountering each other for the first time ever. It's the biggest joke.

As we both reenter the room, our Q&A session abandoned after a few fumbling attempts, all eyes will be upon us. Chairs will scrape back. Awkward coughing and throat-clearing will fill the air. *Do we like each other,* will be the million-dollar question on everyone's mind, the response to which will be exchanged by both sets of parents on the phone, a few hours later.

Even as every cell in my being screams. *No, don't do this,* a part of me knows I have to.

What are my choices? Being lonely or settling for an arranged marriage. I've had enough of empty apartments.

Maybe, just maybe, it's time to give Mr. Maybe a shot.

MR. MAYBE #1

I am on holiday in Kerala with my parents and siblings when Thaatha, my maternal grandfather, calls from Chennai where my grandparents live. He informs Appa of a 'prospect' in Chennai and suggests we cut short our vacation and return at the earliest so that the prospect and I can meet.

The potential groom is an Indian-American from California on a bride-hunt. He's fair-skinned (a big hit with color-obsessed Indian parents), well-educated, and holds a good job.

There is a rush to book tickets on the overnight train and we arrive in Chennai the following morning. Grandma, Aunt, my cousins, and siblings cannot stop smiling. They laugh and joke and take digs at me. I can't see what the fuss is all about. I'm a little irritated at the abrupt end to our holiday and can't summon any excitement for the meeting.

Will you wear a sari or a salwar kameez?

Turmeric yellow sets off your skin.

No, orange is a better choice.

Oh, I have just the right pair of turquoise earrings and bangles to match if you choose an outfit in that color.

Closets and wardrobes are riffled through in search of the perfect outfit and accessories. Grandma beams as she hands me a bottle of *Estee Lauder,* her jealously guarded perfume. I'm exhausted by this effervescence around me. Who is this guy? What kind of a life does he live in America? How will I know if he's the man for me? Anxious thoughts cram my head, leaving little space for the flutters the family expects of me.

"He's coming alone, his parents are in California. He'll be here at five-thirty," says Grandpa. "And he'll take you to Marina beach. You can have a chat there." The times, they are a changing. From balconies and private terraces, we've progressed to meeting suitors on the beach.

But … go to the beach with a man I've never met? The very thought is enough to make my palms clammy.

I somehow survive the hours in between. My family is in a state of fever-pitch excitement. I'm dressed and ready by five. Nothing fancy. Just an orange-and-blue salwar kameez with a matching pair of bangles and ear studs, kohl in my eyes, the traditional *bindi* in the middle of my forehead, and a touch of lip gloss. Once ready I fidget, pace, sit, stand, and crack my knuckles. Five o'clock comes and goes. So does five-thirty.

By six o'clock, Grandpa's fingers start to drum on the dining-table. He peers at the clock every ten seconds and then walks out to the balcony to see if he can spot a car or taxi bearing the prospect. He walks back inside, picks up the phone, starts to dial, then brings his finger down and disconnects the call. Being overanxious is never a good sign for a girl's family.

The waiting is painful. I can feel everyone holding their breath every time they hear the elevator groan. *This time it must be him.*

What kind of a man is this, I wonder. His first supposed 'date' with me, and he doesn't even have the good grace to call and let us know he's delayed. Or maybe he's chickened out; he's not coming at all. He gets a big fat zero from me on first impressions, not a great way to start off an alliance.

And finally, the man does arrive. It's now twenty past six.

When the doorbell sounds, I want to flee, to be anywhere but here. Grandpa rushes to answer it. It's The Man.

"Hello, Vasant," says Grandpa.

I look everywhere and at everyone, so that I don't have to look at the man. I'm trying to read their expressions. They look infatuated, like the last man on earth just walked into our living room. They beam, grin, make eyes at each other, and send silent messages.

I muster up all my courage and drag my eyes to Vasant's face. His eyes are grey; his skin has seen little or no sun, and the white skin exaggerates the pink of his lips. A thin sprinkling of hair on a glistening scalp. He's short and is dressed in jeans and a white t-shirt. We offer each other a thin smile but no words.

"Sorry I'm late ... bad traffic," he mumbles, and I catch a nasal American twang.

Grandma and Amma have disappeared into the kitchen. They return, moments later, with a tray full of steaming mugs and plates of fried delicacies. The fact that Grandma has pulled out all the stops doesn't escape me. In a household where coffee is always served in the traditional silver *davara-and-tumbler*, coffee mugs languishing in a china cabinet have been retrieved in honor of the American suitor.

Ten minutes of banal chatter. Then, Vasant looks at me and says, "Whenever you're ready," as if eager to escape my family's appraising glances.

"Sure," I say, and get up to leave.

As he shifts gears in the car, I notice his fingers are long, his nails well-rounded and clean.

On the drive, we stick to neutral topics–weather, traffic, the growing number of high-rise buildings, and the changing city skyline.

The beach is not as crowded, being a weekday. We find a spot on the sand and sit at a respectful distance from each other. I cup a palm full of sand, let it fall through my fingers. A lonely gull wheels overhead. A few feet away from us, a mother rushes to stop her toddler who is trying to eat a fistful of sand.

Vasant stares at the ocean. He is possibly wondering how to get this session off the ground. He seems as lost as me in navigating the arranged marriage turf. Didn't you find a nice blue-eyed, golden-haired woman to love in America, I want to ask. I'm a little surprised that he has traveled continents to find himself a bride.

"So, you grew up in Chennai? Vasant has landed on the conversation-opener.

Over the next fifteen minutes he quizzes me about my education and hobbies, taste in music and movie stars, and my family. He tells me he works with his dad in the family business and is close to his mom. I notice he says *maahm* like they do in America. My antennae perk up as I recall that saying about men and mama's apron strings.

"You wouldn't mind moving to the U.S., would you?" he asks, needing to get that information out of the way.

"I wouldn't be here talking to you if I didn't mind leaving India, would I?"

A peanut vendor walks up to us, pauses hopefully to assess whether we'll buy, and seeing no inclination, moves on.

"Yeah, I guess. It's just that my entire family lives there ... my elder sis and her family too ... and I'd like to settle down there. I don't plan to come back ... to India."

I feel we're getting ahead of ourselves, talking of a possible future in the U.S. when we hardly know each other.

"Tell me about your family," I say, picking up a broken shell half-buried in the sand.

An ice-cream cart stops in front of us. The man tinkles a bell and looks at us expectantly. When we show no interest, he moves on.

"Well, I'm a modern sort of guy but my mom is kinda traditional. I know she'll expect her daughter-in-law to join her in doing the *puja*, temple visits, that sort of thing..."

My skin prickles.

"I'm not a traditional person. I believe in God, but... my connection with God is very personal."

"Hmm... but I'm guessing you'll have to flex a bit for her. As for me, I love traveling and books and we can... I mean, if we're okay with each other, that is... do a lot of fun stuff. So, I guess what I'm saying is, life isn't going to be an endless round of tradition."

The sky is streaked with the palette of dusk: indigo, peach, and soft gold. Another vendor, another cart piled high with slivers of raw mango dusted with red chilli powder and salt, passes by. My mouth waters as it remembers the pucker of sour mango, the salt a pleasing counterpoint to the tang.

"So ... you want me to be a certain kind of person for your mom and another kind of person for you to do the fun stuff with?"

"Yeah, you got it."

A mental shutter drops. "I don't think that's possible."

I feel the wind whipping my hair and taste ocean salt. A beautiful dusk drops gently down on the horizon. Lights flicker to life. I am seized by a sudden urge to live, to see, to smell and breathe, to walk and talk, and be free.

"I think we should go," I say.

"Oh, okay. So ... what do you think? That ... we won't work out?"

"What do you think?"

"I guess not."

"I have to agree."

Vasant drops me off outside the building gates and doesn't bother to see me to the door. I'm mighty relieved. The moment I ring the bell, the door swings wide open and my entire family is right behind it, unable to hide their excitement.

"No need to get your hopes up. It won't work out," I say.

I hear a collective exhalation of disappointment. They want every detail of the beach visit.

"Three vendors walked by. He didn't even buy me an ice cream cone, you know," I say, appalled at the man's lack of manners.

"Looks like he wants a split personality," Grandpa guffaws when I tell him the whole story. He isn't too disappointed that his first attempt at finding a suitor for me has fizzled out faster than a shooting star.

How many times will I have to go through this charade until I meet Mr. Right? I don't even want to think about it.

For now, I'm just happy this one didn't work out.

MR. MAYBE #2

This time, the setting is our home in Hyderabad.

It is a cold January morning. I'm already breaking out in goose bumps at the thought of the upcoming meeting. Appa is in a distinctly cheerful mood. Last week, he received a letter from a potential suitor's father. The man said his son was visiting Hyderabad on business, so could he use the opportunity to combine it with a 'check-out-the-girl' session. Appa, of course, wasted no time in dashing off a response in the affirmative.

I glance at our modest living room. A sofa, a couple of armchairs with comfy cushions, a center table, an old TV, and a dining table off to the side. The wall cabinet shelves hold figurines of dancers expressing a *mudra*, assorted birds, and books, their colorful spines adding a dash of liveliness. Not exactly the epitome of elegance, but at least everything is dusted and pleasing to the eye.

My knees hadn't turned to jelly when Appa handed me Jagan's photograph a couple of days ago. A software engineer who lives and works in Bangalore, his unsmiling eyes behind square framed glasses give him an academic look. Dark wavy hair neatly combed to the side. Bristly mustache.

And now, the big day is here. Jagan is expected to arrive at our home around lunch time after clearing his morning commitments.

"I'll be home for lunch," says Appa, whose office is only a couple of kilometers away from home.

"Will he stay for lunch?" I ask, trepidation rising.

"No, he only has half an hour to spare. He said he'll come back in the evening and take you out for a longer chat."

I bristle. I chide myself. *Why are you doing this when you believe in roses and candlelight and moonlit walks?* More and more, the idea of opting out of this marriage circus seems very appealing. But the part of me that loves the idea of sharing my life fights back. I'm no lone wolf and can't see myself rattling around an empty apartment. I naively, foolishly believed Love would find me effortlessly, but now it looks like I'll have to accept the idea of learning to love someone. Just like my parents and grandparents and great-grandparents did, the people whose marriages, I'm often reminded, lasted fifty and sixty years.

Unbidden, a memory floats up. I was perhaps sixteen years old and home sick. It was a time when I was interested in all things partners and partnerships. Amma had just stepped out after a bath, her wet hair still wrapped in a thin white cotton towel.

"Amma, what was it like to marry Appa, a man you barely knew?" I ask.

"I didn't have any say in the matter," she said, smoothing her face with Vicco Turmeric paste, the smells of sandalwood and turmeric dancing in the air.

"Your grandfather and Appa's elder brother negotiated our marriage. I was standing on the balcony the day Appa arrived at our home to 'see' me. I peeked from the balcony and saw how pink his face was and knew he was the one," she said, her eyes softened by nostalgia, as if she was seeing into that moment right now.

"Pink?!" I repeated, failing to understand how a pink-faced man could be considered attractive, shaking my head at this inexplicable Indian obsession with fair skin.

"Then I came downstairs wearing a silk sari and gold jewelry that your grandmother had selected for me. There was fresh jasmine tucked into my braid. Your aunt who was only fourteen years old walked downstairs with me. I stared at the floor; didn't look up at all. I was so shy."

"You stared at the floor? When your pink-faced man was right across the room?" I giggled.

"Those days were different. We were not so bold, like you. Appa's family asked if I could sing. My grandfather asked me to sing a song, so your aunt and I sang together." She capped the tube and picked up a packet of *bindis*. Peeling off a bright maroon *bindi*, she peered into the mirror and pressed it into the middle of her forehead.

"You had to *prove* that you could sing?! Perform on demand?" I knew I'd never be able to get her to understand the self-righteous indignation I felt on her behalf, all these years later.

"That was the custom, Uma."

"Then what happened?"

"The elders on both sides of the family were pleased. Appa's horoscope and mine matched well. Appa's family liked me, and my family liked Appa. So, they proceeded with the wedding planning."

"What about Appa? No one asked him if *he* liked *you*?"

"Appa had told his older brother that he was not in favor of 'seeing' and 'rejecting' girls. So, he was going to say yes to the first girl he saw and trust that she was the one God had chosen for him."

A warm feeling of respect flooded my heart. Appa had found his own way to skirt the male-chauvinist patriarchal rules of the times. "That was really sweet of Appa."

"He was also very handsome," Amma added.

"Of course. Let's not forget the pink-faced hero!"

Amma swatted at me playfully. "And the next time I saw Appa was on our wedding day."

"Your wedding day?! Didn't you want to know him before you became his wife?"

Amma unwrapped her towel and a cascade of wet hair fell well around her shoulders. "The elders would never allow such a thing. So, we didn't even think about such things. The elders told us what to do. We listened and obeyed."

Amma and Appa have been married almost thirty years. Good times and bad have rolled through their lives, but their marital foundation is solid, unshakeable.

I'm chasing love in the nineties, a time when so much has changed with regard to women's roles and choices. My interior landscape looks nothing like my mother's. I want so much more than she did, and I don't believe it's wrong to want it. Financial freedom, the ability to use my voice, and a man who will love me for who I am.

I want a different kind of man, one whose inner life I know and love.

When I slip between the covers and turn off the light at night, I allow myself to dream about this man. As facetious as it sounds, someone who speaks good English is high on my list of priorities. I want him to share my love of words, to feel poetry in his bones, to read a paragraph of my prose and glimpse my soul. Having grown up with a father who knows his way around the kitchen (and hating how most men I know believe it's their birthright to simply holler at their wife when they need a cup of coffee or can't find their glasses), my idea of a sexy guy is one who sautées and sizzles with practiced ease.

The charade I'm putting myself through is a far cry from that dream.

❦

I'm tossing a tangerine *dupatta* over my shoulder when the doorbell rings. My tummy ties itself up in knots. I walk to the door, every step a heavy weight toward a possible future. A tall, lanky man is on the other side. Wavy hair and small eyes framed by glasses. Dressed in a formal blue shirt and navy trousers, he looks like he just stepped out of a boardroom. He extends his hand and I shake it, hoping he's distracted enough not to notice my damp palm.

"Please ... come in," I say, as Amma hovers in the background.

We settle down on the living room sofa and I silently implore Amma to talk so that he and I won't have to. Not one who's ever had starting trouble, she obliges on cue and asks Jagan all the usual questions: about his parents, childhood, education, and career. Jagan rations his words, probably scared to use them all up for fear he'll have nothing to say to me. Having set the ball rolling, Amma makes a discreet exit so we can get started on the Q&A.

"So ... what do you do? Working somewhere?" he asks.

"Yes, I'm a copywriter. I freelance for a couple of ad agencies." I play with a corner of my *dupatta*.

"What kind of music do you enjoy?"

"Well, mostly film music, though I don't know much ..."

He raises an eyebrow. "Not South Indian classical?"

"No. I mean, it's all around me, but I'm not particularly..."

I tell him my favorite television show is reruns of *Three's Company*. He's never heard of it. This confession confers a 'westernized' image on me, one that definitely isn't working in my favor.

The doorbell rings again. Appa's arrival at this point provides a welcome diversion. He looks pleased that the two of us are 'having a chat.' I can almost see thought bubbles in his head filling up with wedding garlands, guest lists, and elegant invitation cards. He shakes hands with Jagan. "Hello, Jagan. Nice to meet you." And walks into the bedroom, leaving me utterly abandoned.

Over the next few minutes, I learn that South Indian classical music is Jagan's big passion. He attends concerts whenever he has time to spare. A few moments later he glances at his wrist, mumbles something about a meeting and asks to take leave of my parents.

I call out to Appa and Amma.

Appa stalls him. "Would you like to meet her in the evening?"

I cringe. *Just let it go, please.*

"About…seven?" Appa persists.

"Yes, sure." And Jagan is gone.

I exhale slowly.

"So … what do you think of the young man?" Appa asks.

"I … I don't know … I hardly know him … to like … or dislike."

"Yes, but first impressions?"

I offer a non-committal shrug.

"At this rate, you're never going to get married." Disappointment is clearly etched on Appa's face.

I turn on him.

"So that's the agenda here. Get me married, no matter what, so it's one down and two more to go. Is that what I am, a burden? Someone who has to be married off and then your responsibility will be over."

My throat hurts with unshed tears.

Amma looks at me. She still finds it hard to believe that a child who came out of her womb is capable of hot, fiery words.

Appa turns to her. "Talk to her. She can be so stubborn."

Amma takes one look at my face, decides that silence is her safest option. She serves lunch. We eat, wrapped in tomb-like silence.

Much against my wishes, I'm dressed and waiting at half-past six in the evening. I feel hollowed out. I'm waiting for a man Appa has hunted down through a national newspaper, not feeling the anticipatory rush of a date I want to go on. We're planning an evening out because our natal charts tally. *God, get me out of this somehow, anyhow, because my heart isn't in it. I want this to happen naturally, to fall in love, to watch the sunrise with the man I love, to walk and talk and share. Maybe it won't happen next week or next month or even next year, but it will happen. Won't it?*

Appa is back from work early that evening. He seems excited about this get-to-know-each-other scenario. Maybe he should go instead of me.

It is now 7:15, fifteen minutes past the time Jagan was supposed to be here. I've eaten off all my lipstick.

What is it about me that makes guys want to stand me up? Am I scary? I stand in front of the mirror and pull ugly faces. I shake my head and my earrings dingle-dangle a No. Then I smile a confident smile and tell myself these guys don't deserve me. I find myself sinking deeper and deeper into relief as the minute-hand creeps further and further away from the time he said he would show up.

By a quarter to eight Appa is at the end of his patience. He pulls out a bunch of business cards from his wallet and quickly scans them.

"He's staying at Hotel Kamath," he says.

The hotel is a five-minute walk from our home.

"I'll go over and check if he's there." He slips his feet into sandals.

My jaw is tight, my heart pounds inside my chest. I can't believe that my father wants to chase after a man who stood me up.

"Appa! You can't do that!"

"Why not?"

"You're being desperate. There's no need to."

"I'm simply going to check if he's planning to come or not."

"Don't you understand what he's doing?" I'm losing control over my voice. "If he was keen on coming, he would've called. He would've explained if he was held up somewhere. Don't you see?"

"Maybe he's stuck in a traffic jam. Maybe his business meeting went on too long ..."

"I don't like this, Appa."

I stalk off to my room and peel off my clothes. I slip a nightie over my head, walk into the living room and stare defiantly at Appa. I need to show him I still have the final say.

His confusion delights me. "Why have you changed into your night clothes?"

"Because I'm not going anywhere."

"I told you I'm going to check ..."

"... and I don't want you to. You think I'd want to marry a man who stands me up? Who doesn't even have the basic courtesy to call and say he doesn't want to go out with me? I'm sorry but I have no opinion of such a chicken."

The loudest sound in the room is the ticking of the clock.

Appa grabs his keys and strides towards the front door. I grab hold of his arm.

"If you *must* go, please just do one thing. For my sake. Check at the hotel's front desk if he's in his room or not. You'll have your answer. Without embarrassing anyone."

Ten minutes later, Appa returns home.

"I called his room from the lobby phone. There was no answer. But the front office told me his keys were there ... so he is in his room."

A part of me is relieved, a part of me is disappointed, and a part of me is confused.

Saying anything at this time would be like rubbing Appa's nose in the mud. To be fair to him, he let me travel out-of-state for work, as far away as Bombay and Calcutta, and find someone I wanted to spend my life with. *I* didn't find anyone. Now, he's simply doing his parental duty, aligning with the tradition he was raised in. Enough is enough.

This time, I'm sure. I will do this no more. I'm beginning to think I can adjust to the idea of an empty apartment.

SLOW BURN

Over the next weeks, I seethe and have furious arguments in my head. I am the judge and the jury. My father is the convicted criminal. I bristle at being treated like a prize cow in a bazaar, prospective bidders gawking at me. I am a woman of deep sensitivities, desires, and dreams. But to Appa I'm the eldest daughter whose well-being must be entrusted to my future husband. His efforts at acquiring a good alliance will be a marker of how well he honored his parental responsibility. Given his past reputation in the family, his desire for this accolade is understandable.

❧

The seesaw of my affection for Appa has been swinging wildly since I was six years old. One of my earliest memories of him is seared into my mind and body.

Appa is leaning over his bed, vomit gushing out of his mouth, saliva strings beaded with puke clinging to his lower lip. Grandma scoops up the vomit into a basin, tears running down her wrinkled face. Amma stands frozen at the doorway, her face a mask of confusion.

That was the day a combination of fear, mistrust, and sadness rushed into my unformed insides and filled me with questions I daren't ask anyone.

For the next sixteen years, I found myself in a race with the bottle for Appa's time, attention, and affection. My anger led me to negative attention-seeking. I slacked off studies, even failed a few math tests. When I sniffed alcohol on his breath, I guilted him with angry eyes and watched him squirm as he tried to convince me that he hadn't been near a bar. I backchatted and argued. But the bottle won every time. For reasons I never understood, I lacked the lure it held for Appa.

Late at night Amma maintained a vigil by the window, her constant worry growing that Appa would crash the car. As the world outside the window grew darker and more mysterious, her anxiety at Appa's absence deepened by the hour. She watched every approaching car with increasing hope until it drove right past our home. Then she'd phone a few bars Appa frequented. When that turned up nothing, she'd call a few of his colleagues.

I'd burrow deeper into the sheets and press my palms over my ears, my shame a large spreading stain. How did she not realize that she was broadcasting Appa's failures to the entire world?

Sometime later, I'd hear the familiar slap-slap-slap of her footwear. I'd shut my eyes tight and feign sleep the moment I spotted her from the corner of my eye. She'd call my name, softly at first, trying not to awaken my siblings, and then more insistently when I didn't respond. When that didn't work, she'd shake me awake.

"It's twelve-thirty... Appa's not home yet."

"What do you want *me* to do?" I'd snap back.

"I've called Silver Swan and Nanking. He's not there. I don't know where to call next."

"Why call anyone? Why do you stay up for him anyway? Wasting your sleep. Please ... just go to bed." I'd turn over and drag the sheet over my head.

But the white noise in her head was so loud she wouldn't even hear my words.

"Shall I call Uncle Martin next door?"

"Call whoever you want. Don't bother me. Don't wake *me* up. I don't want to waste my sleep on a man who doesn't care for his family," I'd growl.

Not that I got a wink of sleep, anyway.

Lacking the courage to wake up our neighbors, she'd finally fall into an uneasy sleep sitting up, startling at every night sound.

When Appa's car eventually pulled into the shed where he'd park, headlights throwing dancing shadows on our bedroom walls, something in my body would unwind. Appa's journey from the shed to the front door took forever. He'd lean on the wall, trip over a potted plant, grab hold of the gate and steady himself, shrugging off Amma's helping hand while I watched through the window. Tanked up on whiskey he'd stagger in and sprawl on the nearest sofa. Amma would cry softly as she held a glass of buttermilk to his mouth hoping it would sober him up. Most of the buttermilk would dribble down, forming a wet patch down the front of his shirt.

Amma's role in this nightly drama baffled me. She stood by Appa, through all the lows of his alcoholic life. I knew she'd call his office the next morning and lie on Appa's behalf – *he's running a fever, but he'll be at work in the afternoon.*

Later in the day, she'd enter the puja room and join her palms together in a posture of deep servitude. Facing the framed pictures of the gods that lived in our *puja* room, she'd get down on her knees dutifully and mop the floor of the puja room, dust the photo frames, dot each picture with wet sandal paste and vermilion, then place banana slices and a silver bowl of milk, the deities' daily diet.

It was remarkable, her belief that unwavering devotion would secure Appa's redemption.

The idea of an alternate life, a life without being married to Appa was unfathomable to her. Docile and submissive by nature, she'd been raised to believe that serving her husband and family came above all else. As much as I wished she had the courage to choose another life, I knew that we, her four children, were the reason why she couldn't leave. Amma had never worked outside the home a single day of her life and that tied her to Appa. Walking out simply wasn't an option.

Frightened and frustrated by Amma's fragility, I swore I would never be anything like her. When my relatives remarked that I had my father's stubbornness, a warm glow of pride spread through my chest. I'd watch Amma, a chronic people-pleaser, spinning in confusion when, without meaning to, she offended one relative even as she pleased another. She never quite figured out the formula to get everyone to like her all of the time.

I, her eldest child, had slid out of her womb speaking my mind.

The one trait I did inherit from Amma was my sociability. She loved people, could start a conversation with a complete stranger in minutes—and so can I. Sadly, the shame and secrecy of Appa's alcoholism had caused us to shrink ourselves and be wary about how much we shared with folks in our neighborhood. Except for Uncle Martin, the person we reached out to in desperation, because we needed his help to lift a drink-sodden Appa out of his car.

Unable to imagine a way out of this life, or a possible healing of the situation, we had resigned ourselves when a magical moment presented itself in the form of Uncle Austin—an Alcoholics Anonymous sponsor—who opened his heart and embraced Appa. He gathered the shattered pieces of Appa's life, pieced the broken man back together, and led Appa back home to himself first, and to us, next.

Appa has been sober for five years now. But while he was busy wrestling with his demons, I'd grown into a young woman who was beginning to taste financial freedom and autonomy of thought.

When he sobered up and reentered the stream of family life,

Appa sometimes forgot that leadership is earned, not demanded as the man of the house. Especially when you were stepping back into a territory where others had grown used to leading in your absence. As the first-born, I rebelled against his attempts to force obedience. You don't get to take off the mantle, toss it to the side, then pick it back up, and demand to be honored as the head of the family.

Every time I returned home late from the advertising agency trying to meet a tight client deadline, Appa and I got into it. I was twenty-two, earning my own money, and I now had curfew hours?!

Over the next months and years, Appa wove his life into the A.A. tapestry, rewired his emotional landscape, and began to evolve into a new man right before my eyes. He became something of a local hero in the A.A. community. It was not uncommon for our landline to ring late at night, Appa speaking in soft whispers because his family was sleeping. I'd hear the car pulling out of the garage and know he was on a mission to save a struggling-to-stay-sober alcoholic. Other nights I'd hear him counsel an alcoholic teetering on the cliff-edge of temptation, using gentle words to get the man to step back to safety by reminding him of what mattered. At meetings we attended as a family, the wives of newly sober men touched Appa's feet, tears of gratitude running down their faces. The genuine respect he awakened in me soon deepened into admiration and love.

I listened to him share on open-mic nights, giving voice to his shame and guilt at being an absent father, an irresponsible husband, a human whose personal pain had overtaken everything that made life worth living. I blinked back tears as he spoke of the amends he was making, the forgiveness he sought, and his commitment to surrendering his addiction/sobriety to a Higher Power.

Appa stitched the ragged pieces of our family fabric back together with humility and honesty. Every evening the six of us would sit around the living room as a family and share about our days over hot cups of Brooke Bond Red Label tea and Marie biscuits. He supported my career choice of advertising and set up a meeting with an old friend in the industry. He stepped back and gave me space to move to jobs in Bombay, then Calcutta, and discover myself and learn the value of independence. He surprised me by showing up unannounced at my Bombay ad agency and took me out to dinner. He arrived in my Calcutta apartment and stayed for an entire week, waking up early to pack my lunch every day of that week.

What became the thorn in our relationship was his need to prove his paternal responsibility by securing my hand in marriage with a man who would lead me to a safe and happy life. After years of struggling with a reputation that caused people in our extended family to cringe when his name was mentioned, commandeering the operation of his eldest daughter's wedding was the perfect way for Appa to reinstate his integrity.

And I, his eldest daughter, was standing in the way of what could potentially be his resurrection project.

⁕

A part of me was gripped by a very real fear. What if I married a man who turned into an alcoholic? If it had happened to Amma, it could happen to me.

The stories of my parents' early married life sounded magical. Appa had been the model husband caring for Amma, feeding her, and braiding her hair, when she'd come down with dengue fever two months after I was born. He'd changed diapers and rocked me to sleep, fully present to the responsibilities of fatherhood.

But then the devil in the bottle had lured him away and the magic had morphed into misery. What if Amma's fate befalls me?

A couple of weeks after the no-show by Mr. Maybe 2, there is a surprise development. G's parents reach out to mine and moot the idea of their adult children meeting. G's family and mine are related on my father's side.

Mutual interest in seeing their offspring settled in marital land motivates both sets of parents to put their heads together and hatch a plot. G's oldest sister and brother-in-law will chaperone me to New Delhi where G lives. Amma and Appa are completely on board, excited about the idea.

Although we're technically related, G and I have never met, but random mentions of him by family members have stirred my curiosity. I've overheard tidbits. *He plays the guitar. He was in a theater group and has acted in a few anti-apartheid plays.* And this one got me really invested. *He is totally against the idea of an arranged marriage.*

With this new door that opens, Appa wastes no time in finalizing my travel dates and arranging tickets.

A few nights before I'm due to travel, Appa circles back to the matchmaking topic at the dinner table. He looks at Amma, then at me. "So, shall we start looking at some more horoscopes?"

The tangy *rasam* and rice I'd been savoring a moment ago turns to mush in my mouth. I get his line of thinking. *What if she rejects G? At least we'll have a few more horoscopes to fall back on.*

The idea is to have Plan A, B, and C in place so that if one falls apart the next one can be activated.

Amma looks at me. She remains silent.

I somehow manage to swallow the food in my mouth, then say, "No."

Appa's face hardens. "You want to argue again?"

"I don't want to argue with you, but...something tells me I must wait until after my Delhi trip."

What's *something*? I don't know. It feels like a deep knowing that I need to meet G before we make any further plans on the matrimonial front.

Appa turns to Amma with questions in his eyes. When she still says nothing, he raises his eyebrows as if to question, *So, what do you think about her bright idea?*

Amma's eyes dart between me and Appa. "I think we can wait till she comes back," she says in a voice that carefully straddles caution and compliance.

Appa shrugs, non-committal. I read it to mean *Okaaay. This doesn't sound like the brightest idea but have it your way. I'll let you win this time.*

I cheer internally at my small but significant victory. If nothing, I've just bought some time.

PART 2

Igniting

GLIMMERS

Faded blue jeans.

Pale blue T-shirt with thin horizontal stripes.

Ivory sleeveless sweater.

Scuffed sneakers.

The blue jeans cause a small jolt of joy in me. Denim is cool, so very cool. His cool-guy reputation immediately ratchets up a notch.

A thick head generously sprinkled with salt, but more pepper. Neatly trimmed lush beard.

G grayed early, they warned me ahead of time, shoring up my possible disappointment just in case my mental image of him included raven locks.

The train has just pulled into Nizamuddin Station, the smell of coal smoke and human sweat drifting in through the metal-barred windows.

I feel the heat on my cheeks as I get busy retrieving my suitcase and bag from under the seat. I think of the one letter he wrote, welcoming me to New Delhi and his home, a cordial and carefully worded invitation. My heart swelled as I lingered over his sentences, the words chosen from a diverse and healthy word-bank. His descriptions of the capital city's history and the sightseeing opportunities the trip will afford impressed me.

I'm using my human shields, Gita and Ronnie--G's sister and brother-in-law--to delay the moment when I'll have to look into his eyes and say my maiden hello. I sense his awkwardness too as he rushes around, hauling our luggage off the train and hugging his family before he turns to me and puts out his hand. "Hello."

I take his hand. "Hi." I smile, acutely aware of every detail of my disheveled appearance: the raccoon-eyed kohl smears, crow's nest on my head, and crushed clothes following a thirty-six-hour journey from Hyderabad.

"Welcome to Delhi," he says, sounding like a tourism-office guide.

"Thanks."

I take note of his clipped accent. He speaks the Queen's English.

And off we go, meandering through masses of people arriving and departing, goodbyes and welcomes, until we get to the parking lot. I notice the blue Maruti Gypsy. I've never been inside such a fancy jeep. He stows the luggage, hops in the driver's seat, makes sure everyone is settled in, and drives out.

On the drive he points to interesting landmarks and offers tidbits of historical information, his voice a soothing auditory backdrop to my buzzing thoughts. *Is this the guy? Could this work? Maybe not. No tingly vibes yet. Sigh!*

Third-floor apartment, no elevator. We grab our bags, trudge up the stairs, and walk into what's possibly the most well-maintained two-bedroom bachelor apartment. *This is a bachelor pad?! Really?*

We enter a small-sized living room with a few functional pieces of furniture. But my eyes are instantly drawn to the framed fabric painting of Kali that hangs on a cream-colored wall. This, and a Kathakali face mask, with its exaggerated eye make-up and bold striations of primary colors add a touch of tradition. He isn't all American music and anti-apartheid plays. A white Chinese lantern centers the living room ceiling and a braided rug in jewel tones is a splash of color on the floor. Not a thing is out of place. *This guy knows how to clean.*

I take a bath, wash off the grime and dirt of Indian Railways, my hair and skin restored to their healthy glow. I'm famished. Off to the side in the living room is a table that holds a homely meal. Fluffy white rice speckled with roasted cumin and green peas; a bowl of bright yellow dal; a dish of mixed vegetables; and crispy savories. I eat with undisguised relish, quieting my deep gut rumbles. Spices and seasoning blend on my tongue, waking up my train-food-weary tastebuds into familiar sensations of pleasure.

If the best way to a woman's heart is via her gut, he has me.

I've always admired the ease with which Appa navigates the spice cupboards and steel utensils in Amma's kitchen. On the days that Amma, prone to bouts of asthma, woke up with a bad wheeze, Appa made and packed our school lunches. If she was unwell on a festival day when a feast was in order, he made sure we ate a delicious meal that included my favorite dessert: a *payasam,* rice pudding garnished with cashews and black raisins fried and plumped up by the ghee.

G can cook. This stuff is sooo good. Brownie points for cleanliness and culinary prowess. A couple of his friends join us for lunch, and everyone tucks in, chewing and crunching the only sounds in the room.

I wash my plate and stack it in the drying rack, then return to the living room. Most of the seats are taken. All except one spot on the three-seater sofa. G is sitting on one end of the sofa and his friend occupies the other end, so I move in and settle into the middle space between them. G springs up and crosses the room, preferring to stand.

Shame colors my face pink. Why on earth is he behaving like his pants are on fire? I wasn't trying to sit in his lap.

Thankfully everyone is busy chatting, so G's escape and my discomfort slip by unnoticed. He skips right past this moment of awkwardness, and pretends that everything is normal.

Later that night, I lie in the dark and wonder what my future holds. I'm sleeping in the spare bedroom. The single bed is comfortable and I'm grateful for privacy. G has taken the living room couch, letting Ronnie and Gita use his bedroom.

Ronnie's gift of finding humor in every situation is such a relief. Gita is always game for fun but seems a little preoccupied on this trip. I don't know either of them well enough to share my innermost thoughts and anxieties, so I hold it all close to my chest. The long journey and the excitement of the day soon take hold and I slip into deep sleep.

Monday morning, G goes off to his job in the city. Over the next three days, Gita, Ronnie, and I hang out together. We set out after lunch for a bit of shopping and sightseeing. We walk past shops that sell antiques, books, art, and a variety of fabrics. When we meet up with G at dinner time I notice that he avoids walking on my side of the road, or next to me. Most of his conversations are restricted to his family.

Does he not want me here? If that's the case, why write a letter inviting me? Being ignored on a trip, the express purpose of which is to get to know each other, seems like the grand irony. No matter how much I try, it's hard not to take it personally.

Ronnie tries his tactics of gentle encouragement. "Why don't you take her for a drive and pick up some dinner?" he suggests one evening.

G doesn't respond. I'm on embarrassment overload. The silence in the room grows heavier by the minute. The shrill ring of the land-line cuts through the awkwardness. I seize the phone like a lifeline. The operator puts me through to my friend in Bombay. G grabs his jacket and car keys and runs out the front door.

Next morning, I overhear an exasperated Ronnie. "Why is your brother acting so strangely?" he says to Gita. "I feel sorry for that poor girl. If this is going to continue, we should pack our bags and head home."

I don't know what to think. Confusion, anger, and shame blend a nervous cocktail inside me. I wasn't expecting fireworks and flutters, but I didn't imagine it would be such a damper. I guess this means we'll just go home, and I'll be back to square A on the prospect hunt.

Not wanting to dwell on this despondency, I choose to hold on to a tiny spark of excitement. We're driving to the hills tomorrow. Even if I seem to be hitting another wall on the marriage front, I decide that I will enjoy my trip to Ranikhet, a tiny hill station best known for its views of the Himalayas.

Tonight, a friend is picking me up. We're going to an amusement park, Appu Ghar, then dinner. My heart is happy at the prospect of going out with someone who actually *wants to* hang out with me.

My inner kid has a blast at the amusement park. I scream my lungs out on the Ferris Wheel, buy a bounty of scarves, skirts, and blouses from bargain shops, and eat the best street food, a mélange of tangy, spicy, and crunchy: fried potato, piping hot samosas, and cilantro-mint-tamarind chutneys sprinkled with chilli powder, cumin, and *garam masala*.

I arrive home pink-cheeked and pleasantly tired, weighed down by my bags.

"Wow. Looks like you cleaned out the shops." I'm taken aback that G actually makes a comment when I walk in the door.

He follows it up with, "Let's see what you bought."

It's a miracle that I don't drop the bags and fall over them myself. It throws me for a loop, this sudden interest he shows me. I empty my bags on the floor, pick up each piece, and hold it up for him.

"Can you believe I got this for twenty-five rupees?!" I say.

"Twenty-five?"

"Yeah. Such a steal." I swirl the scarf, running my fingers over its silken texture.

"That's a good color."

I notice he doesn't say *on you* but I'll take the compliment.

"I got these two for forty each." I hold up two skirts, one magenta, and the other turquoise.

"I like that one," he says, pointing to the magenta skirt.

After fifteen minutes of this, the tension in my bones begins to soften a little. Maybe this thaw will crack open to reveal a caring heart. Maybe something new is blossoming here.

SPARKS

The Maruti Gypsy winds its way through the crowded streets of New Delhi, towards the snow-capped mountains in the charming hill station of Ranikhet. I've never seen snow, not even from a distance. I'm so ready for my first sighting. At this moment I have no idea that the universe will bring me much more than the magic of snow.

G has been behind the wheel for most of the nine-hour drive. Ronnie is in the passenger seat. Gita and I are in the back.

As the vehicle negotiates the steep hairpin bends and climbs toward an altitude of 6000 ft., G's face takes on an ashen look. His queasy gut finally forces him to pull over and let Ronnie take the wheel. I hop in the passenger seat beside Ronnie while G climbs into the back seat and curls up, hoping to quell the rising waves of nausea.

Darkness drapes over the hills as the jeep swallows the miles. As light leaches from the sky, I ponder G's silent treatment of me. *Why does he clam up with me? Did I make a mistake by saying yes to this trip? Maybe he has a girlfriend no one knows about.* He refused every snack I offered him on the day-long drive: salty peanuts, almond biscuits, and spicy fried lentil munchies.

Except for the night when I returned home with bags of clothes from my shopping expedition, his silence has been a theme since we arrived in Delhi five days ago. I'm frustrated by his extreme introversion. Granted, this contrived situation is awkward for both of us. Although everyone's trying to pretend this is just a regular vacation, there is an underlying urgency. G and I have a ten-day timeframe to get to know each other and decide whether we want to spend the rest of our lives together. Clearly this has amplified his discomfort, but I'm a player in this strange drama too. And I'm the one visiting, and totally out of my comfort zone.

I'm here because I am twenty-six and my parents are nearing panic mode. In the Indian context, an unmarried daughter of my age represents a crisis.

G's parents are also in a similar quandary, but with a significant difference. An unmarried twenty-nine-year-old man in a patriarchal culture may be somewhat of an oddity, but an acceptable one. He doesn't need 'looking after.' So, it's safe to assume that his parents are not perched on the edge of the cliff like mine are. His clock isn't ticking; mine is. My father repeatedly reminds me that my "unmarried" status could seriously compromise the matrimonial prospects of my two younger sisters; that I may want to hitch my wagon to a Mister soon.

As far as I'm concerned, none of the above are *reasons to get married*. Love is the only reason. My fantasy includes a rush of tingles, sweet nothings, and lots of heat when my man walks into the room.

And now here I am, Gita and Ronnie acting as my chaperones, driving to the hills for a three-day trip, a vacation that G planned for us.

The jeep lurches to a stop and wrenches me from my mental meanderings. We've pulled up at the guesthouse. A short man wearing a dark sweater and a beanie rushes out, folds his palms in a *namaste,* picks up our bags and beckons us to follow.

We follow him into a room that's icy. My skin prickles in goosebumps and my teeth chatter. Thankfully, Ronnie, who's no stranger to surviving in the cold, pokes at the logs in the fireplace and soon gets a cozy fire going. Within minutes I feel warmth creeping back into my blood and bones.

Exhausted by the bumpy ride, G falls into bed. What happens in the next few moments is certainly the choreography of a cosmic force, for I am simply moved like a marionette. I pick up a woolen blanket, walk over to his bed, and gently lay it over his sleeping body. It is an intimate act, something I'd never have had the courage for if my mind had suggested the idea.

When steaming bowls of soup arrive from the kitchen, I carry a bowl over, tap G on the shoulder and say, "I think you'll feel better if you eat something hot."

He sits up in bed, takes the bowl from my hands, and helps himself to mouthfuls of the spicy broth. "Thank you," he says, his eyes meeting mine with an openness I haven't seen before.

Something rearranges within me in that instant. I don't have a name for it, but it feels like a veil of tenderness draping over me.

Morning arrives in misty light. I am excited to dive into the day, but loath to give up my toasty warm bed.

"Good morning." G's cheery voice greets me from the doorway. We have adjoining rooms, separate beds. He's dressed in jeans and a soft blue sweater.

Sensing my reluctance to emerge from the cozy covers, he says, "I'll make you a nice cup of tea. You'll warm up in no time." Clearly, I'm not the only one who experienced an internal shift the previous night. This is the friendliest he's been on this entire trip.

A few minutes later, I'm sipping tea and standing in front of my open suitcase, pondering how many clothes I need to wear to stay warm.

"Here, let me help you. It's best to dress in layers," says the veteran who has survived a decade of winters in northern India.

Patiently, he explains to me the order in which layering can offer me the most comfort from the cold. I shower and dress following his suggestions, snug in three layers of increasing warmth.

I step outside the room and step into a magical winter land. A thick topping of pure white snow on the distant Himalayas is nothing short of a mystical experience. Wisps of cloud float low, flirting with the mountain ranges. Delicate and wobbly silver dew-drops glisten on the leaves.

It's a crisp morning, the sun pouring all over the courtyard, so we choose to eat breakfast outside. One of the kitchen boys runs out and sets up a table. He drapes a cheery red gingham tablecloth over it, and proceeds to load it with bowls, cups, saucers, and silverware. Fresh fruit, hot toast, eggs, butter, fruit preserve, and a giant pot of tea. Ravenous, we tuck in.

I'm on my second cup of tea when Gita says she and Ronnie are setting off for a walk. The significance of the moment is not lost on either of us. *Let's give these two time alone.*

Thanks to the energy shift of the previous night, we ease ourselves into a natural conversation, from the schools we went to, growing up in southern versus west-central India, favorite books, G's boarding school experiences, our careers, and the common ground we occupy: our resistance to arranged marriage.

Ninety minutes dissolve like mist in morning sunshine. I detect disappointment in me when I spot Gita in my peripheral vision, evidence of how much I've enjoyed sharing my story with G. Gita tells me later that G pulled her aside and whispered fiercely: "Couldn't you have taken a longer walk?!" Clearly, I'm not the only one who felt a connection.

We grab our jackets and head into town to buy a few supplies. For the first time on this trip, I slide into the passenger seat as G takes the wheel.

I've been blowing on my hands every so often prompting G to ask, "Do your hands get cold?"

"I don't know why, but my hands and feet are always cold."

"Let's buy you some mittens then," he offers.

His casual use of "Let's" feels warm and inclusive, like we're becoming a unit. I find a lovely pair of beige mittens and G insists on paying for them.

The next day we stroll through the deep, dark woods, the filigreed gold of sunshine spilling all over the forest floor. A cocoon of silence drapes itself around us. It's so still we can hear each other breathe, every twig that snaps beneath our shoes, the distant call of a myna, and the soft rustle of wind moving through the trees. Today I feel safe enough to open up about Appa's struggles with alcoholism, and how I had to be an adult even as I was moving through the bewilderment and confusion of my teenage years. He listens attentively, and I feel layers fall off my shoulders.

Somehow, we find ourselves standing in front of an old church. There's not a soul in sight. As we walk around the modest white building it becomes clear that this place of worship hasn't been in service for a few years. Curtains of cobwebs brush our faces as we peer into its dark interiors. Dry, crackly leaves litter the ground.

I plop down on a mound of leaves and G finds a spot beside me. I'm beginning to feel something spark in the air between us. Is it trust? Safety?

My mind checks the boxes. *Family pedigree. Similar background. Common relatives.* As I sift through these considerations, my consciousness serves up an idea with compelling clarity. *I want to spend my life with him.*

Not a shred of doubt or confusion rattles me. In fact, I've rarely been more certain of anything in my life. I want to be with this man. I can see us building a life together.

Stop it, I still my heart. What if this is a one-way street? I don't know how he feels about me. I have no clue what he's thinking, whether the ice floe inside him has thawed enough to let me in. I sense that he likes me and has grown comfortable in my presence over the past three days. In the land of arranged marriages, that is an entire era. But is that enough for him?

With all the wisdom of my twenty-six years, I plunge into land-mine territory: the conversation about love.

I sneak a glance. His eyes are closed, face turned toward the sun. I hate to pop his peaceful bubble, but I need some answers.

I clear my throat. "I... I've been thinking."

He opens his eyes, turns toward me. "About what?"

"About you," I say, looking away, not ready to read his eyes. "About us." I pick up a crisp leaf and crumble it between my fingers.

Drumbeats reverberate inside my ribcage.

"I don't know about you, but... um... I've made up my mind about you."

I'm taking the lead and putting him on the spot. All the fanta-sies I've nurtured about a romantic proposal from my perfect guy vanish in a puff of smoke.

G looks away from me.

My heart is about to burst out of my chest. "I'm ready to commit to a life... with you." *There. I've said the words out loud.*

Suddenly I'm a hot sweaty mess under all those layers.

This is the moment when the guy looks deep into the girl's eyes and says, "I feel the same about you. My God! How did I get so lucky! I'm going to make you the happiest woman on the planet."

This is what G says next. "You hardly know me. We saw each other for the first time only five days ago."

I remain unfazed. I have no idea where my next words come from, but they surprise me with their profound wisdom.

"Two people can spend an entire lifetime together and never really know each other. I like what I've seen of you so far. And I trust it."

Silence sits between us, a solid physical presence.

After what seems like a long time he says, "That makes sense."

The wind has picked up. I wrap my arms around me and blink my watery eyes.

"You're cold. Shall we go?" he asks.

"It *is* getting chilly. Ronnie and Gita must be wondering where we are."

My thoughts are a jumble as we traipse back to the guest house. He hasn't said yes. He hasn't said no, either. I want this to work. I want to be with G. What if he says no? Will I be able to handle the disappointment after all that I've been through? I can't bear to think about starting over.

We're both quiet on the walk back to the guest house. I'm not sure what he's thinking, but I'm completely absent to the mystery of the woods. The yeses, no's, and maybes of our situation are dancing in my head.

Whereas the thoughts racing through my head are disorienting, a deep knowing cradles my spirit. It's a space within that whispers *all will be well*. It asks me to just trust. I don't know why, but I do.

STARBURST

It's the following morning, the day we drive to our next destination, Nainital. The suitcases are stowed in the trunk. I cast one last look at the quaint guest house in this magical hill station. With no idea how this tale will end, I hold tight to the visceral knowing that landed in my body the moment I placed the blanket on G.

The mean girl who lives rent-free in my head pipes up. *Aren't you forgetting something? He hasn't said yes. Stop with all these foolish romantic notions.*

The Wise Self who's been living in my heart since the moment I took my first breath smiles, closes her eyes, and sighs a deep, peaceful sigh. She has no desire to argue with the mean girl or convince her of anything. All she says is, *Patience, my dear. All in good timing.*

"Hey, dreamer," G's voice nudges me back. "Ready to go to Nainital?" Everyone is in the car waiting for me. This time, Gita and Ronnie are seated in the back. The passenger door is wide open. I catch Ronnie's wink. His message is clear: *That's where you belong. Get in there.*

It's only a couple of hours to Nainital, but we take a few detours for scenic views of tattered clouds drifting by, sparkling streams of water gurgling their joy, and the verdant spread of green like a never-ending emerald quilt.

Everything in me feels soft and open. The rhythm of my breath is an intentional accordion. Conversations between G and me ebb and flow, and I find myself wading further into an ocean of deep feelings for him. He laughs more easily and seems to have settled into his being, a far cry from the awkward, introverted person I met in Delhi.

An indigo sky of twilight has settled over Nainital when we pull into the guesthouse where we're booked to stay. Gita and I share a room; G and Ronnie take the other.

As I'm putting my bags away, Ronnie approaches me. "G wants to have a chat with me. You know, man to man. Commitment is a scary thing for guys, darling. We're going to the dining room for a drink."

A tiny bird of hope flutters her wings in my chest. If G has approached Ronnie to talk things over, it's a positive sign. He must be closer to making a decision. If it was a no, he'd have told me by now. My heart whispers, *please say yes, please say yes, please say yes.*

I can only imagine what the mean boy who lives rent-free in G's head is up to. Maybe the noise up there is so loud he can barely hear his thoughts. Even as I'm buoyed by this development I feel shaky inside. Hanging in the limbo space was easier than this.

I barely taste my dinner. Gita curls up in bed with her book and is soon immersed in it. I lean against the headboard and read the same sentence over and over half-a-dozen times, not registering a single word.

My Wise Self has gone on vacation and my mean girl is sitting on a gem-studded throne, a fake tiara sparkling on her head. No matter how hard I try I'm unable to tune out her shrill high-pitched voice. *He's terrified. Terrified men don't say yes. They run away. Your foolish romantic notions are about to be dashed.*

I sneak a glance at Gita who's still lost between the pages of her book. Voices drift from outside, bits of conversation and laughter from residents strolling past our room after dinner.

What if he says no?

What if he's not convinced by Ronnie's advice? Do I really want him to choose me because someone encouraged him to?? No.

What if this whole trip was a big mistake?

The door swings open and Ronnie bursts into the room. I scan his face for a shred of hope. He regards me for a long moment, then smiles knowingly, and nods. "You'll be in the family, my girl. We're still talking. I just came by to get a bottle of whiskey."

Sparkles explode inside my chest.

He grabs the bottle, says "More later," and leaves the room.

I have a million questions, but now is not the time.

"I guess you can relax now," says Gita, briefly emerging from the covers of her book. Damn, that must be a good book.

Forty-five minutes later, Ronnie returns, G following behind. G smiles at me, then beckons me outside. I walk over, unsure of what's coming next but breathless with anticipation. As I get closer, he opens his arms out to me and I walk into them. It feels like coming home to a safe harbor after months of being lost at sea. He holds me for a long minute, then steps back, goes down on one knee and speaks the words I've been longing to hear.

"Will you marry me?"

I hadn't imagined a romantic proposal in the hallway of a guest house, but I'll take it.

"Yes. Yes, I will." I'm laughing and crying, unable to believe that this is really happening.

He takes my hand, then leads me out into the moonlit night. We walk toward a bridge. The night chill creeps into my bones. It's pitch dark, but mother moon lights our path.

"I'm sorry, but I needed some time to think things through. It's a big decision. It is for you too. But things like responsibility and commitment are a big deal to guys. Ronnie helped me clear up some stuff in my head. I just wanted to be sure I was doing the right thing...and I know I am."

That is a big speech coming from this man of few words.

He takes my face between his hands. "I love you." Then he kisses me under that milky moonlit sky with such tenderness that I weep.

"I love you too."

Now we're both shivering. He holds me tight, and I burrow into the warmth of his jacket. "Shall we go back where it's nice and warm?"

And off we go, hand in hand, feeling the flush of real love, the stars above guiding our path to a new life together.

TWIN FLAME

G and I are getting engaged."

The words spill out of my mouth the moment Appa answers his phone. We're back in Delhi and I can't wait to give Appa the news he's been waiting to hear.

G and I are getting engaged.

The six words I'm still getting used to saying and believing. I savor every syllable, roll the words around my tongue. Words I never thought I'd say, for I'd come to believe that love had passed me by, that I would have no choice in my own engagement.

Appa's subdued sniffles come through the phone line. "So... happy. God bless you... and G," he manages to get the words out through the chokehold of emotion.

We're out in the city later that day when the others manage to sneak into a jewelry store and pick out a ring for me. Our formal engagement ceremony will come later, choreographed and blessed by elders on both sides of the family, so this little ring exchange will do for now.

Ours is a two-person engagement: just G and I. My Wise Self is smiling and nodding. I recall her words: *Patience, my dear. All in good timing.* My inner rebel has found her home in the heart of a man who is a champion at honoring our independent natures.

Our simple engagement ritual happens at the Krishna temple in the neighborhood. The place is virtually deserted in the middle of the day except for a flock of crows scavenging for bits of coconut, jaggery, and rice dropped by the devotees from their offerings to the deity.

Making our way inside, we sit on the cool stone porch outside the main sanctum-sanctorum. The ebony stone form of Krishna emanates an inner radiance, reflecting a golden gleam cast by the tall oil lamps. A medley of fragrances hangs in the air, remnants of the morning puja: incense and rose, oil-drenched wicks, burnt ash, and camphor. The smells of the divine, the sacred, of Amma's puja room in every home we've lived in.

Gratitude warms my heart. Gratitude for a man who gets me, a man I feel safe with. Gratitude for how easily we seem to weave into each other's being. Gratitude for the blessing of intimate love.

It's over, the long and awkward parade of prospects, the feelings of increasing dread because none of them were right for me.

It took a while, but here I am, sitting beside the man my soul knew was waiting for me.

We sit in silence, lost in our own thoughts. A prayer feels in order, but Amma is the prayer-person in our family and she's not here. I rake through my memories trying to extract a few Sanskrit *shlokas* to offer to the gods. Waking up to Amma's early-morning *shloka*-chanting is a favorite childhood memory. The few prayers that are lodged in my memory are purely by osmosis. My prayer language, however, has mostly been English. Speaking to God in a language that is familiar and conversational always felt more intimate, comforting. Although a sacred and poetic language, Sanskrit has always felt foreign to me.

G recalls the Lord's Prayer, a throwback to his Catholic boarding school days, but he's lost in Hindu prayer-land. So, I settle for a few simple words that rise up straight from my heart.

Thank you, God, for hearing the desires of my heart and bringing this beautiful man into my life. My heart is so happy. I promise to be faithful and love him with all my heart.

Almost on cue, G takes my left hand and slips a simple, unfussy gold band on my third finger. Looking into my eyes, he says, "I love you. I promise to do everything I can to look after you and keep you happy."

I smile. "I love you. I'm so grateful we found each other."

We sit for a while, arms wrapped around each other, soaking in the peace and contentment of the moment.

An Indian engagement ceremony is replete with a sacred fire, flowers, incense, gold jewelry, and sixty-nine rituals! But this is exactly how I visualized *my* engagement would go, and it's perfect.

It wouldn't be an exaggeration to call this my favorite temple moment. Temples with their codes and rules usually make me hypervigilant. I've mostly tiptoed around religious practices and priests, afraid to make a wrong move or mispronounce a Sanskrit word. What we just did to honor our commitment to each other feels heart-led. None of it was circumscribed by any religious framework.

I twirl the ring on my finger; the newness of my status as G's fiancée still feels surreal.

That evening, we host an impromptu celebration party to which a few of G's friends arrive, bearing acoustic guitars and musical voices. Ravi, a software engineer, tries to fade away into the wall, but when he starts to sing everyone is transported. I notice Sid's tic of constantly sweeping away an unruly mop of hair that falls over his forehead. Dan is at home, a true party animal.

It's a casual, happy scene. Guys pulling on beer bottles, easy banter, and music, lots of music. When G picks up the guitar and strums, it's the most sensual thing I've witnessed. Eyes closed and brows furrowed, he plucks and picks, the air pulsing with melody.

As much as I'm trying to enjoy the music, it's the first hint of how different our worlds are. There are specific song requests, and the guys oblige, taking turns at the guitar. Someone suggests a song named "Hotel California" and everyone cheers. That's followed by another called "Teach."

Am I the only one who's never heard of these songs? Raised in the conservative South, the bastion of classical music, I've never been exposed to western music. G went to school in Bangalore, a party town where he and his buddies grew up on jazz, blues, and rock. I'm the outsider looking in.

Gita serves a fabulous fragrant *biryani* and everyone digs in hungrily. More drinking and music follow. As the night grows long, things get louder. Sid, emboldened by the booze, gets a little aggressive, stirring awake the trauma that sleeps in my bones.

I need to escape. Quietly I leave, slip into the bedroom, lie down, and close my eyes. Minutes later I feel G's fingers stroking my cheek. "You okay?"

"Yeah. No...I just...I still struggle when...I just needed to get away for a bit."

He lies down beside me, tucks a strand of hair behind my ear. "I'm sorry Sid is being an ass."

"It's not your fault. It's just hard on me."

"I understand. Anyway, they're wrapping up. They'll be gone soon."

I smile, grateful for his understanding.

"Want to go for a drive?" he asks.

After a frenzied day of planning the party and getting through it, the thought of some alone time with him sounds delicious.

"I'd love that," I whisper, braiding our fingers together.

Driving out at midnight is a thrill I can't even describe. I've had curfew hours most of my life. Being out late meant worrying about the arguments that would erupt the moment I walked through the front door—even if I had a legitimate excuse. The impossible deadlines imposed by the advertising agency clients made no sense to my chartered accountant father who worked sane hours in a regular office.

This is the bliss of pure freedom. I no longer have a curfew. We can stay out as late as we wish, and we have no one to answer to.

"Go freshen up if you need to," says G. "Let's say bye to them and head out."

Ten minutes later, we're driving down the deserted roads of New Delhi well past midnight. Freedom never tasted sweeter.

SMOLDER

Nizamuddin Station is teeming with a sea of humans struggling with an assortment of shoulder bags, suitcases, and backpacks, threading their way through all manner of obstacles: carts, food stalls, and stray dogs. The PA system periodically blares arrival and departure announcements. Coolies dressed in red tunics carry heavy suitcases on their heads, cushioned by a coiled cloth. Vendors wheel carts loaded with mounds of roasted peanuts, potato crisps, and deep-fried samosas.

I'm blind to it all. My heart is leaden at the thought of saying goodbye to G and returning to my parental home in Hyderabad. I'm wondering at the mystery of how one week has rendered me so dependent on his love when I spot him walking towards me, a biscuit packet in hand.

"I don't want to go," I whine.

"I don't want you to go either. But think of all the excitement there will be in Hyderabad when they see you. You have so much to share."

He hands me the biscuit pack, then takes my hand.

"It went by so fast," I say, tracing the oval of his nail.

My throat hurts, the tightness of unshed tears. I'd marry him and move into his apartment right this minute if I could. But that's just wishful thinking.

Choosing the wedding day is a parental prerogative. Amma and Appa will pick an auspicious date in consultation with the family astrologer. All the stars must align perfectly, and the cosmic weather be favorable for our marital union to get off to its best start.

G and I have tossed ideas back and forth about our wedding. The wedding is usually held in the bride's city of residence. As Hyderabad is hellishly hot during summer months, we're both leaning in favor of a November wedding—subject to parental approval, of course. The very thought of draping myself in a silk sari, wearing a ton of jewelry, a heavy rose garland around my neck, and chanting vows in front of a roaring fire for more than three hours in hundred-degree weather makes me nauseous.

We're in the first week of March. November is a good eight months away. How can we possibly stay apart for that long?

"When will I see you next?" I ask.

"Don't worry. We'll think of a way to meet somewhere. I could wangle a work trip to Bombay and maybe you can come too."

A shrill whistle cuts through our conversation. The train is ready to depart.

G gives me a polite peck on the cheek. "I want you to know that all your problems are *my* problems now. I want to know what you're thinking and feeling. Promise me you'll write?"

"I will." I try to smile, let go of his hand, and get on the train which starts moving within minutes. "I love you. I'll miss you."

"I love you too," he blows me a kiss and waves.

With that I turn around and head to our coach. It will be a long journey of solitary, unfinished thoughts, and fragmented dreams.

৵৵

My siblings corral me the moment I walk in the front door. "We want to know everything. You dare not leave a single detail out," they threaten. Questions come at me quicker than I can respond. *How did you know he was THE one? Did you kiss? Were you nervous to say yes?*

The narrative of how G and I knew and said yes to each other is the most anticipated story of the hour. My siblings who are twenty-three, twenty, and nineteen, have a ringside view of this love story unfolding in real time. In a country where arranged marriages are the norm, stories of love marriages often involve real pain: secret dalliances, irate parents, and a whole lot of heartache.

Our story has a fantasy feel to it. I don't take that blessing lightly.

Now that I'm home, and fifteen hundred kilometers away from my love, letters are our lifeline. We don't have a landline, but Appa's workplace is only a ten-minute drive from home, so he occasionally lets me use his work phone to call Delhi. I have to wait until late evening, though, for the office to empty, and call when G is home after work. Sometimes I have to wait weeks to hear the sound of his voice.

The arrival of the mailman is the highlight of my day. I rip open G's letters and lose myself in the pages. G writes about the minutiae of his regular life: weekend activities, guitar classes with Gussy, and shares lyrics from his favorite bands—Grateful Dead, Queen, CSNY—and musical legends like Dylan and Clapton. He patiently opens me up to a whole new world of music I didn't even know existed. His letters usually contain a paragraph devoted to the meals he made, and all the places he wants to introduce me to. He never fails to let me know how exciting life seems now that I'm on his horizon. I feel cherished by his words.

The missives flying between Delhi and Hyderabad create a fever of anticipation. Cool November weather is no longer a pressing consideration. *I can endure one day of hot weather*, I convince myself. *I'll be on such a high that I won't even feel it.* Lucky for us, the astrologer points to an extremely auspicious date in May. That's less than two months away. Quick phone consultations between both sets of parents, and the date is confirmed. May 19, 1991. I can't wait to become this beautiful man's beloved bride.

SEARING

I just can't seem to write a half-decent slogan today," Sameera moans, rolling her eyes. A junior copywriter at the ad agency where I freelance part-time, Sameera's warm smile and friendly manner sparked an instant friendship between us.

Within weeks of our budding friendship, Sameera announces her engagement to a young man chosen by her parents. One afternoon I walk into the copy department to the sight of celebratory henna-stained palms, her alabaster skin aglow.

I hug her, then stand back and regard her. "Look at you. Did you know there's a halo around you?"

She giggles, then mock-punches me in the arm.

"I'm happy for you. Are *you* happy?" I ask. "I mean, you're so young."

"Twenty-two is hardly young. Twenty-four and not being married is old in our community. Anyway, this is how it happens. I can't even think of falling in love with someone. That only happens in Bollywood movies."

"As long as you're happy and sure of your guy. That's *all* that matters."

As her wedding day draws closer, Sameera's excitement is fizzy. Some days I catch her between work breaks chatting on the phone with her fiancé. Sameera has only met him a couple of times because he lives and works in San Antonio, Texas. But she's giddy and giggly and can't wait to be married.

"Don't you miss your fiancé?" she asks about G one morning, as I'm stapling a stack of papers. "You live so far away from him."

"Of course, I do. I'm so glad our wedding is only weeks away."

"I can't wait to be married! My guy is a total romantic. He sends me flowers and cards and calls me every day."

I'm a dyed-in-the-wool romantic, but something about this young girl's fascination makes me uneasy. I can't quite put my finger on it, so I let it slide and go about my day. Love does show up in many flavors and fads.

When Sameera returns to work after her wedding and a two-week honeymoon in Goa, she seems a bit jaded. She's definitely missing the new-bride glow. I give her a welcome-back hug. Her megawatt smile which usually lights up the room is gone. I also notice her swollen lower lip, like a botched Botox shot.

"How did everything go? Looks like the wedding and travel took a lot out of you."

"Oh, it was fine." She doesn't say more.

Not wanting to be nosy, I grab a copy pad with the day's items marked on it and head to my desk. Sameera was supposed to turn in the first draft of copy for a brand of perfume the agency is pitching next week. As her copy chief I have to approve of her draft before we can adapt it to flyers, billboards, and a TV jingle. But as the day drags on, Sameera looks more and more distracted.

I put the notepad away. "Okay, if you haven't written anything for me to review, can you have something for me by tomorrow? Unable to dismiss my big-sister concerns, I tread gently. "Is something bothering you?"

Sameera's eyes squirrel the room. Her voice drops to an angry whisper. "It's such a sham, the whole damn thing. The build-up, you know."

Confused, I wait for her to unpack her train of thought.

"I don't know how to say this..." she begins. She pauses to gather her thoughts, as she draws circles on the desk with the stapler.

"This whole... first night thing."

I know that phrase. *The first night. The night when a woman loses her carefully preserved virginity in the marital bed.*

"Did something happen?" I want to be sensitive. "Something you... maybe... you didn't like?"

"Look at my lip, Uma." She sticks out her lower lip and I now see crimson welts close to her gum line, like it was chewed on. "It was as if he couldn't hold back. I was like a... a... a piece of meat. Those Bollywood scenes are a bunch of lies. The real thing? It's nothing like that." Unshed tears pool in her eyes.

My heart breaks for this young bride whose dreams of tender beginnings to intimacy are shattered. "I'm so sorry this happened to you." I reach for her hand.

"I feel exhausted, Uma. That didn't feel like love." She looks away, her right hand cupping her chin. A long sigh, and she turns to me. "I had so many dreams... but you know what? It was a relief to return from that honeymoon."

Words crowd my head, but it doesn't feel right to offer any. If this were a boyfriend, I'd have told her to dump him. She's talking about her husband of three weeks. The innocence with which a virgin enters the sacred portal of marriage, and her dreams about the gentle unveiling of her body have been violated.

Why didn't she say no to being treated like a piece of meat between the sheets? Couldn't she have refused him? Maybe she didn't want to make a scene. Most girls are raised to please, please, please. Did that belief bind her, hold her down?

"I feel awful," I feel lame. "I mean, I don't even know what to say."

"What am I going to do? Tell my parents and have them worry?" She closes her eyes and shakes her head.

I'm twenty-six years and seven months old—and a virgin. Would I, a rebel who rooted for love, have broken the cardinal rule and given myself over to passion—if the right guy had shown up?

Perhaps. Maybe not. I'll never know.

It's a milestone, the marital threshold, the transition from girl to woman. Every girl dreams of it. I'm no different. I dream of a gentle lover, his hands and lips sighing over my skin. Does it hurt the first time, I often wonder. No one in my circles even whispers about anything related to sex. All I have to go on are the Mills & Boon romance novels I devoured as a teenager, books that featured western men who are often portrayed as chiseled, muscled, and macho. I don't know too many Indian men who fit that description. The other ongoing source of sensual education is the Bollywood cinema screen. But we just know that the heroine's sighing and moaning and gasping are far removed from real life.

It's an irony that sex is a taboo topic in the country that gave birth to the epic of erotica. The sculptures in Hindu temples are voluptuous goddesses entwined around male gods in evocative poses, making the secrecy and fake modesty that surround sexuality laughable.

I haven't ever looked between the pages of *Kamasutra*. I wouldn't even know where to find a copy, and it's not as if you can ask around. But my primary resistance to an arranged match is exactly because of this. The very thought of a stranger's hands roaming my body makes me break out in hives. Even as I consented to Appa's matrimonial ads, I found myself hatching elaborate plots in my head on how to reject every potential suitor until I was too old to be married.

The aliveness of desire is a novel experience. Every part of me is drawn to G. I want to be with him, and I want him. My whirlwind trip to meet him and return to Hyderabad—three days after our bohemian engagement—gave us no time or space to share our thoughts on matters of intimacy. Yet, no part of me believes that my first sexual experience will be anything like Sameera's. Having overcome his extreme shyness in the beginning of our relationship, G has been sensitive to my every need.

A conversation we had one day slides into my mind.

We were walking down Janpath, a bustling urban market in the city. "Why did you behave like that with me?" I asked.

"Like what?"

"Not talking to me, crossing over to the other side of the road so you didn't have to walk next to me, refusing every snack I offered you on the drive to Ranikhet..."

"I didn't know what to say." He shrugged. "Here you were... so beautiful. Too good for me is what I said to myself. And we were supposed to get to know each other... it was awkward."

"*I* made you feel awkward??"

"Well, let's just say I was intimidated."

"Intimidated?? By me? I've never thought of myself as an intimidating person."

"You were *meditating* every morning. Boy. That was intimidating."

I laugh out loud and smack him on the arm. I did begin my mornings by trying to sit in silence, although the inside of my head felt more like rush-hour traffic on one of Delhi's arterial roads.

Just thinking about that conversation makes me smile. I feel certain that a man who's intimidated watching me sitting in lotus pose isn't going to maul me on our wedding night.

STOKE

Amma frequently bemoaned my lack of interest in all matters related to housekeeping. Top of this list was my deficient enthusiasm when it came to cooking. A prospective bride's expertise in the grind-chop-mince-and-marinate routine was a huge attractor in the marriage market—and a cause for serious concern in my case.

"Don't worry, Ma," I consoled her. "I have a feeling the guy I marry will be a fabulous cook."

"It's not a joke, Uma," Amma said, as she chopped a bunch of cilantro. "You must know how to cook at least a few items. Wherever you go, you have to eat."

"Oh, I'll eat, Ma. I just don't know about my husband." I giggled.

Amma shook her head in despair.

My sisters whined that I often found a way to dodge kitchen chores.

"I'll go do the grocery shopping. Please, just make the meals," I'd negotiate and dip my head back into the mystery novel that had me in its clutches.

"Your poor husband. We feel sorry for the guy," was a common refrain in our home.

Clearly the universe was on my side. I'm marrying a man who knows his way around a kitchen. Even so, with less than ninety days before I become a Mrs., I'm driven by a desire to shore up my culinary know-how, so I make a project of it. I sit beside Amma every evening, a navy journal in hand. While she folds laundry, slices onions for the evening meal, or rolls wicks for the oil lamps in her puja room, she reels off survival recipes.

I write the name of the dish at the top of a fresh page. As Amma recites the ingredients, quantities, and prep method, I write detailed notes. My recipe book includes a combination of easy-to-moderate South Indian meals. It will serve as my trusty guide as I navigate unfamiliar culinary waters in early married life. To this day, this navy journal with its yellowed pages occupies pride of place on my kitchen shelf.

❧

The value of being a virgin on my wedding day is ingrained in my bones, something I intend to honor. So, when G and I make good on our plans to meet in Bombay, I gladly accept a friend's invitation and stay at her place. I do want the freedom to come and go as I please, so I steer clear of relatives and am thrilled when my friend places a set of spare keys in my palm.

G works all day, but we spend evenings together. We continue to share our dreams for married life. While in Bombay, G buys me a cassette tape of the Eagles. During the day, I play the tape over and over tasting the words, learning the lyrics, and immersing myself in the music that makes my man come alive.

It's a windy afternoon and we're sitting on the patio of the Taj Palace Hotel in Colaba, sipping delicious cups of Darjeeling. "Do you want kids?" he asks me. "I don't mean anytime soon—but...you know, whenever you're..."

"I definitely want kids," I cut in. "Not immediately, of course. But yes, before I hit thirty."

A cool breeze blows in from the marina. Boats bob on the tranquil blue surface of the bay.

"I'm glad you feel that way." He cups his left hand over a cigarette and flicks a lighter, blowing a thin stream of smoke. "But it's entirely your call."

"I want to have babies."

"I'm sure a baby is a big responsibility. So, if you'd rather work for a couple of years...you're free to do whatever you want."

"I've always wanted to be a stay-home mother. I want to raise our child full time."

"I'm glad we're on the same page about this. My mother went back to teaching school after taking a twenty-five-year break to raise the three of us." He tips crumbling ash from the cigarette. "What about now? When you come to Delhi? Do you want to go back to work right away? I'm fine with whatever you decide. Want to stay home—do that. Want to go to work—that's fine too."

"I'd like to stay home for at least six months. Learn to be a good wife," I smile. He laughs. I can't believe I said that. It almost makes me laugh.

I'm quick to clarify. "Actually, what I mean is—get used to life in Delhi. And then I'll look for a part-time job."

Our conversations flow easily. The deep sense of safety and freedom I feel when I'm with him make me long for our wedding day. I love how we're beginning to shape our lives by marrying traditional values with what's right for us.

Our Bombay trip ends too quickly. Saying goodbye all over again is hard but the bright spot is, our wedding is only a month away. I'm not the only one who's keen on getting married and moving to Delhi. Tired of my endless moaning about how much I miss G, my parents and siblings can't wait for me to be married, either.

DESIRE

We've been married for twenty-four hours.

I think back to the oppressive heat, swirl of silks, and the Sanskrit shlokas that threaded us together. I am a wife. It feels like the largest slice of good fortune, yet it's so new and real.

I'm still levitating in la-la land when news from the outside world pierces my euphoria. Wrapped up as we are in the bubble of marital bliss, we haven't glanced at a newspaper or turned on the television in our hotel room.

"Appa called," G says, when I step out of the shower. "Rajiv Gandhi was assassinated thirty minutes ago."

India's youngest and most charismatic prime minister cut down in the prime of his life. He was only forty and represented the hope of transformative political leadership in a country that has been traditionally dominated by septuagenarian leaders.

"Oh, no. Do you know who...why...?"

"He was addressing a rally in Sriperumbudur...and was killed by a Sri Lankan suicide bomber. There's complete chaos everywhere," G says, fiddling with the knobs on the TV set.

Our honeymoon destination is five hundred kilometers away from where the assassination happened. We have bookings in Ooty, a charming hill station in southern India.

"Does this mean we can't travel?" My head knows the answer, but my heart begs. *Please say no, please say no, please say no.*

G takes me in his arms. "I'm so sorry, sweetheart. There's rioting everywhere. I don't think it's safe for us to travel."

My heart plunges to my ankles. A part of me is mourning the death of our prime minister; the uncharitable part of me is wondering why he had to go get killed today. Immediately I feel remorse wash over me.

G steps back, looks at me. "I know you're disappointed about Ooty. We'll do something, I promise. You'll have your honeymoon."

The news worsens as the day wears on. The entire nation is in mourning, but also enraged at this dastardly terrorist act. Mob violence, police firing, and curfews force the decision out of our hands. We have no choice but to cancel our air tickets and resort bookings.

It seems selfish to claim our personal bliss when there are larger issues at stake, like the safety of our country and innocent civilians caught in the crossfire. My body is heavy with a multitude of emotions. The grief of this gruesome murder. The loss of hope that India will no longer be led toward a new vision, a new future. Anger that our honeymoon has been rudely snatched away by forces beyond our control.

The plan is for us to fly to G's parents' home. My honeymoon will begin with my in-laws.

❧

A tingle runs up my spine every time G says the words "my wife." This possessive pronoun has never sounded sweeter. Equally I love the words "my husband" and say them over and over, relishing their newness in my mouth.

A few days into our stay at his parents' home, G devises a plan and makes a booking at Bamboo Banks, a resort at the foothills of the Nilgiri mountains. It's a hundred-odd kilometers from his parents' home, so we borrow his nephew's motorbike and head there. On the way we brave an unexpected cloudburst and a mildly scary encounter with a wild tusker which shows up on our path. This elephant does not feel like a gentle giant as it regards us with undisguised curiosity.We stand still to let him know we don't pose a threat and wait until he lumbers away.

Our three-day stay in a secluded cottage on a forty-acre property turns out to be the perfect honeymoon. Except for a few horses grazing in the distance, there's nothing but endless miles of farmland outside our cottage window. Idyllic and pastoral, it's the perfect setting to begin the voyage of discovering each other. Now that we feel comfortable and safe with each other, we begin our gentle travels into physical geography.

I'm a twenty-six-year-old virgin, a fact that's more common than not in our culture. I'd accepted the sacred mandate of only giving myself to the man who married me.

But now that the moment is here, I'm overcome by waves of shyness. The only person I've been naked with is me. I'm a novice in the area of somatic pleasure and pleasuring.

As my new husband traces the topography of my body, it feels like a wild adventure, equal parts thrilling and scary. The geography of my body is an unexplored mystery that G opens me up to. I soon discover what a powerful aphrodisiac tenderness is.

His fingertips form the compass that guide me to where pleasure lives. We're finally able to open to sexual pleasure in our late twenties within the safe framework of a committed relationship. It feels sweet and safe, infinitely tender, and worth every moment of my twenty-six years of waiting.

Touch becomes a whole new vocabulary. Crescendo is the musical experience of the body. This rapturous bubble I find myself in makes me wonder how we lived without each other's gentle loving. We've been two halves floating alone in the world, until we found each other and melded into a whole. All I want to do now is touch him and smell him and merge with him. The world outside our bodies fades away.

For the rest of our honeymoon, we're two humans drunk on love and cocooned in a world where only pleasure exists.

A few days at my in-laws', then we're on a plane flying to Delhi to begin life as newlyweds.

The plane lands on time. I step out on the airfield and a wave of hot air whacks me in the face. *Welcome to my first Delhi summer.* We grab our bags, flag a taxi, and arrive in G's apartment—now *our* apartment—where our story began. Traipsing upstairs with several suitcases, we're out of breath when we arrive on the third floor. G unlocks the front door. Then he turns around, picks me up, and carries me over the threshold to begin our new life.

It's well past lunch time. I'm famished. G comes up with an instant meal idea. "It's something I make when I need a meal in a hurry," he says, grabbing a couple of onions from a basket on the kitchen counter.

"What are you making?" I ask.

He turns around, picks me up, and sets me down on the kitchen counter. "There. You just sit here and look pretty, and I'll have your meal ready in no time."

Expertly he minces onions, a stick of ginger, and a couple of green chillies. Hot oil in a wok. He throws in a teaspoonful of mustard seeds, then adds the chopped items and sautés it. A pot of rice is cooking on the side. When the rice is done, he mixes cold yogurt into it, adding in the onion mixture, curry leaves, and salt.

It's one of the tastiest quickie meals I've ever eaten but watching my man and his spatula-wielding moves in the kitchen is, by far, the bigger turn-on.

TENDING

I wake from a deep, dreamless sleep. The air is heavy with the earthy, woodsy scent of *khus* mats, the aromatic grass curtain in the air cooler on our bedroom window. Cool, fragrant air fills the room, the water pumps working hard to bring mild relief from the hundred-degree day outside.

I glance at the wall clock. 3:20 P.M. Afternoon naps have never been my thing, but I'm exhausted from making a fresh meal in the sweltering heat of our third-floor kitchen. Cook, shower, eat, and pass out for two hours: this is my new routine, thanks to my eagerness to show off my culinary skills to G. I make a fresh, hot meal every single day, the week's menu sparkling with variety.

Even though my navy recipe journal has been a lifesaver, my

nose has been a reliable gastronomic guide on this adventure. I open my recipe book and faithfully follow Amma's instructions, but it's the well-categorized smells in my olfactory folder that let me know whether the vegetables need to be sautéed longer, when to add the garnish, and how much longer I must boil the tamarind stew.

G smacking his lips in appreciation and holding out his plate for seconds is rich reward and the impetus to try another new recipe. I cook the kind of meals our mothers served us through our growing years. G's boarding school life had taken him far away from these home-made tastes. As expert as he is at cooking North Indian food, the meals I now serve him are a throwback to his childhood.

The contentment I feel living this simple life of domestic bliss takes me by surprise. Here I am, the doting wife kissing her husband and waving goodbye as he sets off to work, briefcase in hand. My days are a happy haze of trying out a new recipe, washing dishes, and folding laundry. After evening tea, I turn on the music, G's book of lyrics in hand, trying to learn the words to the songs he loves.

When G returns home in the evening, he asks, "How was your day?"

"Oh, the usual."

"I still want to hear every detail." He settles down beside me on the couch, his entire attention focused on me. "Tell me. What did you do?"

I offer a boring inventory of the humdrum chores that shaped my day, and my husband hangs on my every word as if I were recounting the saga of a thrilling adventure.

Our two-person universe is a self-sustaining organism. We're very protective of our precious bubble. We have no need for friends. We've lost the desire to be social. Most weekdays we set out for an after-dinner drive. Weekends we go to the cinema, try a new restaurant, or wander in one of Delhi's numerous urban markets or bookshops. On rainy Saturdays we enjoy long, slow, lazy lovemaking and stay home with good food and music.

❧

A couple of months of this routine, and I begin to feel a little homesick. G lived a mostly solitary life and has had to make the adjustment to engaging with another human. I have the opposite problem. My environment has suddenly gone from five chatty people to just one who craves silence after a day of being peopled out. My social self feels somewhat starved. I miss the boisterous dinner table conversations, laughter and teasing in the air with three siblings who always had plenty to say.

My family has relocated from Hyderabad to Chennai after our wedding. Appa quit his job in Hyderabad right after our wedding to take up a new position in Chennai. It's the first time I don't know what my parental home looks like. I hate not being able to visualize my favorite people in their favorite corners of the home.

G picks up on my melancholic mood one evening. "What's wrong, sweetheart? Is something bothering you?"

I hesitate. I don't want him to feel like he's not enough, that our life together isn't enough. "It's just...I'm very happy here with you, but...I do miss my family."

"Why don't we call them?"

It strikes me then that I haven't even considered the possibility of calling home, given how expensive direct-dial calls are.

"Is it too late?" I wonder aloud.

"It's only 9:45."

Amma answers the phone. Hearing her voice on the phone line is like warm honey in my veins. The person who has the family grapevine on tap, she fills me in on weddings, new babies, and job transfers. Everyone takes turns to talk, and my heart feels nourished.

༄

Six months into married life, the idea of perfecting the role of a housewife starts to lose its shine. Serving up meals and staying on top of laundry have become drudgery. The urge to create, to self-express stirs within me.

One morning, I spot an ad in the newspaper for a part-time copywriter. *A sign from the universe.* The position is at a small two-person advertising agency with a tiny client portfolio, but I welcome the opportunity to prime my right brain. The compensation isn't exciting, but it will be a much-needed diversion. I interview for the position and get the job which requires me to do three half-days a week.

A few months into this job, I'm craving a bigger canvas: an agency with a larger client portfolio, a creative department, and the hunger for new business. Everest Advertising hires me, and it's everything I dreamed of. The healthy paycheck I bring home; a young team buzzing with creative ideas, energy, and fun; and the chance to build my own social circle. I'm back in the adrenaline rush of campaign fever and draconian deadlines.

G and I drive together to work and back. He's patient on the evenings when I have a late meeting or presentation. On the days he packs lunch, I find sweet little notes tucked into the napkin: *I love you. I'm thinking of you. Hope you're having fun.*

The fun advertising gig lasts a whole year. But a new dream, a bigger dream begins to tug at me, one that I'm unable to ignore.

STARRY

The day after I quit my job at Everest, I'm staring at my positive pregnancy test result and crying tears of joy. The timing couldn't have been better if we'd plotted it on a calendar. My beloved who has taken to calling me his queen believes this is his invitation to treat me like royalty. He cooks to satisfy my crazy hormonal cravings. He won't let me do a thing around the house when he's at home. And he buys me more fruit than I can ever eat.

I take naps at the oddest times and eat like an elephant. When I suggest traveling to Chennai to spend a few weeks with family, my doctor suggests that I wait out the first trimester before flying. When my three-month ultrasound looks good, she gives me the all-clear to book my ticket.

My first morning in Chennai. The sun is all bright light and blinding glare. It's barely 9 A.M. and I feel a trickle of sweat tracking a path between my breasts.

I'm sitting on the floor, my eyes still heavy with sleep, my suitcase open in front of me. I arrived at my parents' home late last night. Too tired to tackle a bulging suitcase that contained two months' worth of clothes, I stacked it in a corner of the bedroom I'll share with my youngest sister Maya. I hate unpacking, but staring at the suitcase won't magically unpack it.

Amma is sautéing onions in the kitchen, an aroma that usually excites my salivary glands. Now it makes me want to heave.

It hasn't even been twenty-four hours since I flew out of Delhi, but I can't stop thinking about G. He'd never have let me unpack. I hear him saying: "You put your feet up and just talk to me while I take care of this." I can't believe how spoiled I've become.

In the twenty-two months that we've been married he's become the person who knows me best: how I like to wake up (s-l-o-w-l-y), my favorite Grateful Dead song ("Ripple"), and the consistency of my morning porridge (milky). My eyes become misty as I remember his tenderness, his little acts of kindness that weave such ease and care into my life.

But here I am, and these blouses, skirts, jeans, maternity outfits, and inner wear need to be sorted and stored. I'm overwhelmed just thinking about it. Why on earth did I pack so many clothes for an eight-week stay?!

I pick up the blouses that are right on top, place them on the floor, then slide my hand under a fuchsia pink top when my fingers find a piece of paper artfully tucked between the sleeves. I open the note. *Miss you already. G*

I smile, breathe in his love that rises up from that sweet little note. I can feel the tears coming. I breathe deeply and dig into the suitcase again. Another note appears from under a brown skirt. *You're even more beautiful now. G*

I'm in full ugly-cry mode now. Greedy for more, I start to pull out my clothes higgledy-piggledy, making a complete mess. Love notes pop up from every corner of the suitcase and make me want to apparate to Delhi.

When we were newly-weds, G used to tuck love notes in my lunch box. The first time I chanced upon one, Babs, a fellow copy-writer had giggled and mock-gushed: "Awww, how sweeeeet!!" Within minutes everyone in the office had crowded around me and my exposed lunch box, hands flying to hearts exaggeratedly.

As I find surprise notes in every compartment of my suitcase, I'm reminded of that special moment.

My fingers suddenly curl around something hard and square. It's a mixed tape of all my favorite songs. "Ripple." "Witchy Woman." "Hotel California." Songs from the first bands he introduced me to during our brief courtship.

My youngest sis Maya walks into the room and catches me sniffling. "What ha...?" she starts, then spies the notes scattered on the floor by the whirring ceiling fan. Crouching low, she reads one, then drapes an arm around my shoulder. "Missing G already?"

I feel bad. My parents and sisters have been waiting for me to arrive. It hasn't even been twenty-four hours and I'm already gooey and sentimental for my husband.

She squats beside me. "Here, let me help you." She gathers a pile of clothes, heads to the closet. "Aren't you hungry? Growing a life inside you, and all?"

With Maya chipping in, we get the unpacking done in no time.

Later that evening, we're settling down for dinner when Maya teases me. "She's already pining for her beloved husband." Turning to me, she asks, "Are you sure you're going to be able to survive for eight weeks without him?"

My sister Vidya, Amma, and Appa join in, and we banter back and forth. Suddenly it hits me. I've missed these dinner table conversations. With two parents and four siblings eating together and talking a lot, this was our connection time. Sometimes it used to get downright raucous with Maya, the family mimic, performing for us and the rest of us egging her on for more.

When I play the mix tape after dinner I get all choked up again. I've always been a crier, but now the baby hormones have my tear ducts on overdrive. Sixty-three days before I see G again.

INCITED

I don't want to go," I whine to G for the umpteenth time. "I want to have the baby here, with you."

A first baby is born at the mother's parents' home. That is tradition, pure and simple. This involves me flying to Chennai before I begin my third trimester and staying at my parents' for, at least, six months—the entire last trimester and until the baby is three months old. No one will let me get on an airplane with a newborn. My heart hurts just thinking about being away from G for that length of time.

I've rarely been one to bow to tradition, much to the bane of family elders who place great value on unquestioned obedience.

My parents want me in Chennai in time for a religious ceremony performed to invoke blessings on mother and child. Forty days after the baby is born is considered a sacred window: time to rest, recuperate, and learn how to care for a newborn. That's when the elder women—Amma, Grandma, and my aunts—will guide me on how to bathe and nurse and swaddle and hold the baby.

I'm six months pregnant. My belly walks into a room well before I do. My travel window is getting narrower by the day.

"Sweetheart, listen to me," G uses his best cajoling voice. "We're new parents. We don't know how to do this. Think of all the support you'll have at Amma's."

"I don't care. We'll figure it out. But I'm not going."

"You know I'll be there when the baby comes," he tries.

"For a week. And then you'll have to head back for your work."

My total defiance makes G sigh.

I flew to Chennai to be with my family when I was three months pregnant. I stayed with them for two-and-a-half months, and it was the most homesick I've ever been—for my husband. Separation anxiety from a spouse is a new thing I've invented.

Hormonal emotions flood my being, washing away all logic. Anytime we start a conversation on where to have our baby all my insecurities rise up within me reducing me to a messy emotional wreck in minutes.

"If we have the baby here, I'll still have to return to work soon. And then what? You're going to be home all by yourself with a new baby. It'll be much easier in Chennai. You can hand the baby over to Amma and catch a break."

"I can't argue with you, but I can't bear the thought of being away…" I'm a puddle even before I finish the sentence.

"Okay, okay. Calm down." G holds me. "I don't want you getting upset over this." He rubs my back. "Shall I make you a nice cup of tea?"

Distraction and denial are my best friends, but we do have to circle back to the topic because there are logistics to consider. I have to find an OB-GYN in Chennai. We need a baby cot and baby clothes and diapers. It's only fair that I give my parents time to prepare for the baby's arrival. The very thought makes me distraught all over again.

Sick and tired of the emotional roller-coaster, our baby decides to take matters into its own tiny hands. I wake up one morning and feel that something isn't quite right. An emergency appointment with my OB-GYN confirms my suspicions. The baby's head has descended into my birth canal. I'm only thirty-one weeks pregnant. It's way too early. My doctor sends me home with strict instructions. *Don't leave your bed except for bathroom visits and showers, until you're at week thirty-six.*

This is an unexpected situation, but the wicked part of me rejoices. This is sure to help my cause. I'll get to have the baby in Delhi. G fusses over me like a mother hen. He serves me breakfast in bed. He makes my lunch, leaves bottles of filtered water and flasks of tea on my bedside table before he leaves for work. I have strict orders not to shower until he's home.

Much to our relief, Amma arrives in Delhi two weeks later, and we get to the shore of Week 36 safely. My doctor rules out travel at this late stage in my pregnancy, so it's decided that we will have our baby in New Delhi. I cannot stop smiling. I just know this baby and I will get along famously.

༫

October 29, 1993. My waters break early in the morning. G helps me get dressed for this moment we've been preparing for while Amma fills a flask with hot coffee.

We're ready for our baby to arrive. Cotton swabs are cut and folded into small squares, cabinet drawers are stuffed with cloth diapers and burp rags, and there's plenty of antiseptic, baby lotion, and wipes.

With no contractions, I'm chatty on the drive to the nursing home we booked months ago. G and I fell in love with Spring Meadows the day we took a tour of the place.

We pull up, get registered, and settle down for the wait. Two hours later I'm still sitting around with my big belly, as calm as the Buddha, so they start an IV drip to induce labor. Works like a charm. Waves of crushing pain squeeze my belly within minutes and leave me breathless. As I breathe in and out, the contractions power-ing through me, the room resounds with Amma's and G's voices saying the Serenity Prayer over and over again. All those years ago when Appa joined A.A., I never imagined that his grand-daughter's entrance would be heralded by the prayer that has sheltered our family through every storm.

The pain doesn't let up. "Please...rub," I moan, pointing at my swollen belly. G starts to do palm circles to ease the pain but something about the motion just doesn't feel good. I push his hand away and beckon to my mother. "Amma, please." The instant she places her hands on my belly, something in me relaxes. Her gentle and instinctive circular rubs, I know, will soothe my baby's passage.

Dads are not allowed into the delivery room. It's hard not to have G by my side at the finish line after sharing every moment that led up to it. It feels like all of eternity, but ninety minutes after my contractions begin our beautiful baby girl's lusty cries fill the room. Naïve, I celebrate my easy first birth; I have no idea what is to follow.

Nobody tells you the gender of your baby beforehand, but we've already picked out a girl name. Rukmini. My womb-sense let me know that I was carrying a girl. Rukmini was G's maternal grandmother and my aunt. A lady of extraordinary grace and beauty. When the nurse lays the swaddled baby in my arms, I call her by the name that easily springs from a part of me that knows: Ruki.

Ruki, Ruki. I speak her name. She's tiny and sweet and feels strange in my arms. As much as I have longed for her I don't know what to do with her now that she's here. Am I supposed to be responsible for this tiny being? A terrible feeling of inadequacy swallows me. When the nurse takes the baby from me, I happily let her. I watch with utter relief as she whisks the baby away to run a series of tests.

Getting this baby out of me has decimated me. I search within but can't find those first-moment magic feelings that mothers typically gush about. All I want is sleep. Sleep for the next few weeks and wake up magically morphed into Marvelous Mum.

But, of course, that's not what happens.

The baby is gone. And I'm still here, my feet in stirrups, my body drenched in sweat, and my mouth parched. I ask for water, but I'm denied. Again, and again.

"Doctor, please. I'm so thirsty," I beg.

"Not yet, Uma. It'll be a few more minutes. I'm sorry," Dr. M says, still poking and prodding between my legs.

"Just a few sips." My lips feel like rawhide.

Every muscle hurts. I just want my legs off these damn stirrups. "How much longer?" I moan. "I'm so tired."

At some point, Dr. M moves off to the side of the room and begins to confer with a couple of other white-coated people. I watch them huddle and consult in whispered tones. Then, she walks up to me.

"So, this is what is happening. I'm having trouble stitching you up after the episiotomy because you're bleeding everywhere I touch. Your veins have enlarged during the pregnancy," she explains.

"I'm so tired. I can't do this for much longer," I argue.

"You've been very cooperative. And I know how tired you are. So, we'll do this under general anesthesia. You'll go to sleep. You won't feel anything. And I'll stitch you up."

Knock me out. Send me to the place of no pain, God bless you, Dr. M.

A white-coated gentleman holding a syringe materializes beside me. "How are you feeling?"

Just give me that shot and get me out of here, I want to say.

"Okay, can you count to ten for me, please?" He picks up my limp arm and gently slides the needle in.

"One, two, three..." and I float away.

When I wake up I'm woozy and my stitched-up episiotomy is on fire. I have no sense of time. Later, I will learn that the doctors worked on me for close to two hours. I'm on a gurney going somewhere, every bump of the ride a mini tremor in my body. I'm wheeled out of the delivery room to my private room. When they pick me up and move me from the gurney to the bed, I hear someone sobbing loudly. Suddenly someone's head is on my chest and the sobs grow louder. I force my eyes open and see G.

"Oh, sweetheart, I'm so happy you're out of there," he hiccups the words. "I was so worried. I couldn't bear the thought of losing you."

Foggy and having lost the ability to string words together, I pat him on the head.

"They brought the baby out hours ago...but you...you were in there for so long." He sniffles. "I didn't know what was happening." Amma hands him a towel. He wipes his face, then turns to me again. "How are you feeling, my love?"

"I'm in...a lot of pain," I say, sounding like a drunk. It's as if my words have to push past sludge.

"Don't worry. You're here with me now...and I'll take care of you." He strokes my cheek, then kisses my forehead.

"So tired..." and I drift off again.

I wake up much later. Amma is reading in a chair next to my bed. I look around the room, then ask her, "Where's G?"

"He went out to buy your medicines. How are you feeling?"

I try to move and wince. "Still hurting." A sharp pain shoots through my nether regions. "I need a painkiller."

"He'll be back soon," she says, setting her book down. "I've never seen him break down like that, Uma. He was so worried."

A ray of gratitude bursts through the dark cloud of pain that grips my body. It's killing, but I can get through this. I can get through anything as long as I have G by my side.

∽

I'm brown, but my baby is born yellow. A high bilirubin count, they tell me. Jaundice, in layman's terms. She's getting phototherapy inside an incubator in the neonatal unit. I tear up when I see the blindfold placed over her eyes. Stuck in that tiny box, she looks unbearably tiny and alone while a bright light pours over her body to bring her bilirubin count to healthy levels.

We go home three days later. The luxuries we'd enjoyed at the hospital—the nursery in particular—are now painfully missing. There are no nurses to whisk the baby away for a bath or diaper change. It's my job to care for her.

I used to talk and sing to my watermelon belly, impatient for the moment when I could hold my baby. When this little swaddled bundle was delivered into my arms, nothing maternal and magical surged up within me. Guilt rises up every time my mind loops back to that moment. Friends who became first-time mothers and the mothers in books and movies sparkled and glowed; why don't I?

When I first held my baby girl, I felt like a failure. *How am I supposed to take care of you and keep you safe? I don't feel up to the task at all.*

I've wanted this baby for months and months—even as far back as the time when G and I met in Bombay and chatted about me staying home with our kid(s) full-time. I was ecstatic when I got pregnant and brought a religious fervor to living by the rule book: no coffee, no spicy foods, daily walks and vitamins, afternoon naps, and regular doctor visits.

Why then do I feel a muted grayness when a rainbow of colors is supposed to swirl in my heart? What's wrong with me? Am I broken in some way? Maybe I'm not made for motherhood, and this was all just a foolish fantasy. How will I care for a baby I can't seem to bond with?

Letting these thoughts swim up to the realm of consciousness brings up a truckload of guilt. Especially because G has magically morphed into Best Dad of the Year even if he's only been a parent for less than a week. An expert swaddler, he can fashion a cloth diaper firmly around her baby butt with a few quick flips. He picks her up with such exquisite tenderness it makes me weep. He cushions her wobbly neck in his palm and carries her as if it's the most natural thing in the world. He lays her down in the tiny pink tub and dribbles warm bathwater over her soft skin and speaks softly to soothe her through her watery wails. How does he know to do all this?

As for me, her mother who's supposed to 'know' how to be one by pure instinct, things get worse. Nursing is a nightmare. She won't latch on and wails in hunger. When she finally manages to, she's so exhausted she falls asleep. It's only been four days since she arrived here, and I already feel like a colossal failure.

"Hold her gently. Be careful. Look, her neck isn't supported."

"Try the other breast."

"She looks uncomfortable. Try moving that pillow under your arm."

My husband's endless stream of apparently well-intentioned advice grates on my already-raw nerves. I want to scream. *Why don't you try breastfeeding her? Maybe you'll have better luck.* I fall back on the pillows wondering what woman on god's blessed earth romanticized the notion of a baby and mother curled into each other as the little one suckled and slept while the mother gazed in adoration.

My nipples are raw and cracked, and all I want to do is protect them from my baby.

❧

It's Diwali, the festival of lights. Blooms of colors light up the late-evening November sky. Oil lamps sit in pretty rows upon windowsills. On a night that's all about light and color, my world is a monotone of gray. As the winter sky darkens, a hollow ache snakes into the pit of my belly. My womb is bare, my arms are full of baby— and yet, a nameless emptiness gnaws at me. *It's over, it's over, it's over,* the words echo inside my head, an endless metronome. What's over? I don't know. But my life seems to have hit a dead-end. After forty weeks of momentum and anticipation, I've delivered my purpose.

The baby's here, all ten fingers and toes. A healthy seven-pounder who has aced all her early milestones.

Everything, and nothing, makes me weep. No one knows how to console me because no one—me included—knows what ails me. It's the early nineties and post-partum blues is not even a fancy phrase in India, leave alone a diagnosis. If it is, no one talks about it openly.

Guilt guillotines me.

What's wrong with you? Why are you crying? Nobody died. You just delivered a healthy baby. Shame on you. Instead of being grateful for your good fortune, here you are sighing and sobbing into your pillow.

It doesn't help that the baby starts to wail, like clockwork, at 10 P.M. Her ear-splitting colicky cries fade with the pale gray light of dawn. We've tried everything from gripe water and fennel seeds to rocking, shushing, and rubbing.

I'm sore and raw, so G walks the length of our bedroom trying everything he can to comfort her, but she won't let up. Her incessant wails pierce the stillness of night. He swaddles her and cradles her. Amma asks for the baby, but he won't hand her over. It's obvious how possessive he is, reveling in his new role as pro dad. *This is my territory. She's my baby and I'll handle her.*

I can tell Amma is sensitive to G's possessiveness. She simply hovers on the periphery of our bedroom, trying not to rock the boat.

Nothing works. The baby won't stop wailing. Yet another dawn sky paints soft pink streaks outside our bedroom window. Amma finally breaks down and holds out her arms. "Here, let me try." G makes a show of tucking the baby's blanket extra carefully, taking his sweet time before handing her over.

Who knew the baby was just waiting to be pillowed in Amma's experienced arms. Her rigid, agitated body softens within minutes. The cries slow to a whimper. Blissful silence drenches the room. Maybe the arms that have rocked and cradled and soothed many babies come coded with safety.

Amma whispers to G, "Why don't you sleep? I'll take her to my room for a while." I could kiss her feet in sheer gratitude. But G's paternal possessiveness kicks in. He wants the baby to be with us— in our room. He's peeved that the baby has chosen to calm down in her grandmother's arms. A terrible act of betrayal.

My frustration has reached its limits. "Please," I say. "Let her sleep with Amma. I can't have her waking up and screaming again."

He opens his mouth to say something, but I silence him with another "Please, let it go."

Babies don't have preferences, I want to say, but I'm beat. Just an unsettled nervous system finding safety in experienced hands. Given the weight of all that I'm dealing with I could've done without a resentful son-in-law situation.

I'm no good at nursing my baby. My episiotomy still hurts like crazy, so I let her dad bathe and change and rock her to sleep. The only thing I crave is the hypnotic numbness of sleep. The ache in my bones carries a story that's deeper than birth pains. Nothing on earth prepared me for this.

And then there's G, the competent dad who dotes on his

darling daughter, takes care of me, and sacrifices sleep with heroic selflessness.

A sudden emotion engulfs me, washing over every barrier I've tried to erect, and floods me with shame. It is the emotion no mother wants to admit to, much less feel.

I'm on the outer periphery of a circle. In the middle of the circle is the tender and beautiful story of a father-daughter bonding.

I am jealous. This jealousy burns in me.

I'm the forgotten one. I've done my job, handed them the prize. Now she's the princess and the attention that was lavished on me as a mother-to-be has been abruptly yanked away. Even shaping these offensive words on the page, allowing them life, makes me cringe. Post-partum blues have turned my safe, happy world into a place of unspeakable sadness. I'm trapped inside a deep, dark well, swimming in the waters of self-loathing.

I've lost the love of my life to the little human who ought to be the new love of my life. In place of the nourishing love of motherhood lurks the acid of bitterness.

What happened to the bubble of love G and I once cocooned in? *I didn't realize how addicted I am to his love and find it unbearable that I have to share that love now.*

Parenting suits him while I languish in my misery. He's working so hard to make everything comfortable for our baby girl while I secretly seethe with bitter contempt.

I recall our romantic trip to the hills when we first opened our hearts to each other. Since then, I've shared my heart and soul with

G. But the thoughts that march through my head these days are so awful I have to bury them in the depths of my own darkness. How can I bear to give voice to the strange meanderings of my mind without owning that I'm a monster, not a mother?

Between Amma and G, they have the baby's needs covered. I'm just a prize cow needed for the hourly milking.

The baby is five weeks old when Amma returns to her life in Chennai. Appa and my sisters have been managing home, hearth, and work and they'll be glad to have her weave back into the family fold.

G has resumed work, so it's just the baby and me all day long. I've been dreading this time, wondering if a tiny thing with survival needs can be trusted to my impulsive moods.

What I fear turns out to be exactly what she and I both need.

As I massage warm olive oil into her skin, something cracks open inside me. Her bitty foot with its half-moon nails fits inside my palm. Lying in a pool of sunshine she stares up at me with deep, trusting eyes. Dark eyes that tell me know she knows I can do this, take care of her. As I change her diaper, she smiles and coos at me. She's tiny, but she knows me, my voice, the smell of my skin. It's comforting to her. I'm comforting to her.

As she sleeps I watch her belly rise and fall, and a fierce, violent love takes over my being. It's a love I've never felt before—and likely will never feel again. It's been a while coming, but when it does, it's a force. A one-of-a-kind love that is beyond all words and emotions.

Over the next weeks this feeling spreads, deep and wide, inside me. It seeps into every cell of my being. I was born to be a mother. There's no other job I'd rather be doing than the mundane and magnificent job of raising a human. Soiled diapers and burp rags begin to feel like the holiest of holy assignments.

FIRESTORM

Sunday morning unfurls with the slowness of honey dripping from a spoon. Everything feels deliciously slow. We're in the bedroom, G, Ruki, and I. Sections of the morning paper, books, coffee mugs with their lip-drips running down the rim, baby toys and blankets form a happy scatter. The air cooler sprays misty air, the fragrant breath of khus wafting over us.

I hear the phone ring in the living room, but I'm loath to move my lethargic limbs. Before my body can respond to my brain's command, G is already speaking to someone on the phone. The murmur of conversation drifts into the room, but I don't catch any words. I'm watching eight-month-old Ruki repeatedly bang her favorite yellow rattle against her baby cot. She shrieks and waves her hands when G walks into the room a minute later.

The look on his face triggers uneasiness within me. "Who was on the phone?" My bones already know it's not good news.

"That was Mahesh's friend from Bangalore," he says.

Why is my brother's friend calling on a Sunday morning?

"Appa was in an accident this morning. He's in hospital."

Sunshine blasts into the room, blinds me for a moment. I squint at G.

Appa is *in hospital?*

"Why is Mahesh's friend calling?" I ask. "Where's Mahesh?"

My brain circuits feel jammed. Everything is misfiring. All order has been instantly dismantled.

Ruki starts to whine. "Mahesh is on his way to Chennai," G says, picking her up.

"But what happened? How's Appa?"

"I don't know anything more. This guy, Mahesh's friend, doesn't know much either."

On a recent phone call Amma had mentioned that she was going to be away at an out-of-town wedding this week. *Does that mean Vidya and Maya are at the hospital with Appa. Which hospital? How do I reach them?*

"I'm going to call the travel agent and look at some flight options," G says, leaving the room. Ruki starts to fuss again, and he grabs a teether to hand her.

"We can't go," I say, suddenly getting to my feet. "Ruki is only eight months old."

I'm not thinking straight. Ruki is not a high school sophomore prepping for her final exams. An adequate supply of diapers and baby food to last a plane journey to Chennai—and she'll be just fine.

Can I bring my brain back online and start to pack her stuff?

I hear Ruki talking to herself. Having recently discovered the power of her voice, she verbalizes every feeling that enters her field. I wish I could shrink myself into the safe cocoon of an eight-month-old's world where the most frightening event is the frenzied barking of the dog next door.

Tickets? Flight? When are we going? Do we need to go? How do I pack up an eight-month-old's world into suitcases at such short notice? How are we going to pack up our lives for the next few weeks or months and head out in a few hours? What about all the food in the fridge? How will the maid know we're gone when she shows up tomorrow morning? How do we let her know when we'll be back?

Questions and doubts swirl in my head. My brain feels incapable of computing basic information.

"Ruki's the least of our problems. Amma needs us. Your siblings need us."

I think of Vidya who's not quite twenty-seven, and Maya who's only twenty-four. I see Amma wringing her hands and turning to them, her eyes full of questions. What if Appa's injuries are serious? What if there are complicated medical decisions to be made? *Stop. Stop. Stop.* I can't go there. Not yet.

Where do I begin? What started out as a languorous Sunday now crackles with the static of crisis.

G lays Ruki down in her cot. He turns to me and wraps his arms around me. "Don't worry, sweetheart. I'll take care of everything. Let me call the agent. Just make a list of Ruki's stuff. Everything we need to take."

I stand frozen, every nerve numbed. Make a list. Sludge clogs my neural pathways. *Toys.* My mind whirls back to Chennai and my young sisters. Are they doing okay? How are they handling this crisis? *Diapers.* Has Amma got on a train to Chennai? Or is she taking a taxi? *Clothes.* Mahesh must have reached Chennai by now. *Feeding bottles.* Why does a random Sunday morning have to fall apart in such spectacular fashion? Shit, shit, shit. I'm such a selfish person. The rest of my family has been plunged into making decisions that are hard and heavy and I'm whining about my Sunday? *Shampoo and baby oil.* I'm so lucky to have G's calm strength and efficiency to lean on.

Slowly, life returns to my limbs. I move like an automaton, feeling so much, feeling nothing, registering something, understanding little. I stand in front of a yawning suitcase and will my fingers to fold tiny baby things: cloth diapers, bibs, pajamas, and thin cotton tops.

A long-ago memory wakes up.

Sunday morning. The sound of the front gate creaking on its unoiled hinges. My siblings and I rush to grab the grocery bags from Appa's hands. We scatter the contents on the floor, then chase onions and tomatoes that try to run away. The smell of spring-green curry leaves and fresh cilantro explodes in the dining room. Sorting the vegetables into separate piles we

slip them into paper bags and stock them in the refrigerator.

Appa regales us with stories of his morning encounters: the penny-pinching coconut-seller; the grimy little boy who clutched his feet and let go only when Appa parted with a 25-paise coin; the cilantro seller who sat behind a hillock of the herb and always handed him an extra bunch at no cost.

Soon a debate ensues about the day's menu and poor Amma is spinning by the end of it. Dry stalks and mud from the vegetables litter the room until one of us brings a broom and sweeps it all away. Amma inspects the fresh produce in peace. Soon, pungent mouth-watering smells of tamarind water spiced with pepper and curry and turmeric powders fill the room.

"The tickets will be delivered in half an hour." G and the reality of the crisis we're in shear my pleasant reminiscences. "We're taking the three o' clock flight. Need to get moving."

People who say there is comfort in a pair of busy hands certainly know what they are talking about. As I drag my mind back to the here and now and insert soft toys and teethers into the suitcase, and count out the diapers for my in-flight bag, the pain loosens its grip on my heart. I'm grateful for the temporary reprieve, grateful to lose myself in the nothingness of mundane routine.

I pick Ruki up from her cot. Her chubby fist curls around my finger while she babbles to a crow perched on our balcony railing. A tsunami of maternal love rushes over me. I crave safety and comfort, yet a fierce instinct to protect my little one takes root in this moment of terror.

A few hours later. We're strapped into our airline seats. The stewardesses—every hair and sari pleat in place—flash lipsticked smiles and oblige requests for a drink or blanket. They saunter up and down the aisles, settling bags in the luggage hold and people in their seats.

When I was younger, my dream was to be an 'air-hostess' as they used to be called those days. Traveling to exotic lands and living a good part of their lives in the clouds seemed to me a wonderful way to live.

In this moment, I envy the orderliness of their lives. Mine has been turned upside down by a ringing telephone. A delightful giggle announces Ruki's arrival in the arms of a stewardess. Her right cheek bears pink lipstick imprints, and she proudly holds up a stuffed white kitten her cuteness has earned her.

The air inside the aircraft smells of trapped desperation. I thankfully accept my child and bury my face in her milk-scented shoulder.

Soon the flight is ready for take-off. I fight down an urge to run screaming to the doors begging to be let off because I've changed my mind about flying to Chennai. I'm terrified of what's ahead, at what we will have to face.

Dusk is beginning to drop her indigo veil over the city as our taxi pulls out of Chennai airport. I stare out the window. It's the usual chaos. Blaring horns, trucks bullying motorcyclists, a fog of exhaust fumes, and an angry driver shaking his fist at a cow that is crossing the road at typical bovine pace. Office buildings, residential apartments, and restaurants whiz past as we drive toward the beginning of a crisis.

My head is a buzzing beehive of angry, fearful thoughts. My body feels strangely untethered, cut off from my head. I've taken up residence in Head Central as if it's a safe zone where I have control. If I think hard enough and come up with the right solutions, we will all be safe.

Soon after my wedding, my parents and siblings had relocated to Chennai where Appa found a secure accounting job. But Appa's deep desire to serve suffering alcoholics resurfaced. That dream had manifested when he was hired as the resident warden at a reputed research and rehab facility. Free accommodation on the premises. While Appa organized recovery classes and A.A. meetings, Amma found her groove in the Al-Anon fold. My brother had moved out of state for work while my two sisters stayed with my parents.

It was only a month ago that my parents and two sisters had moved into the apartment attached to the rehab facility. It couldn't have been more perfect, I'd thought to myself. The girls will marry and move away. Appa can wind down into retired life with the opportunity to hang up his hat whenever he wants.

And now this, a cruel cosmic joke.

The uncertainty created by the missing parts of the story causes my mind to spin out a variety of threatening what-ifs.

What if Appa's injuries are worse than we suspect?

What if he never recovers from this?

What if he loses his job?

What if he...?

My brother, Mahesh, works for an international engineering firm based in Bangalore. Vidya has a secretarial position and Maya recently accepted a new job offer but will now need time off to manage this domestic crisis. I have an eight-month-old baby and live two thousand kilometers away.

Sensing my inner turmoil, G reaches for my hand and squeezes it. "We'll get through this. I'm here for you, for all of you."

His words enter my being like a miracle drug and calm my anxiety. With my husband by my side, I can face this storm. I can face any storm. I squeeze his hand back, hold a sleeping Ruki tight, and offer up a quick prayer that all of us, especially Appa, survive this storm.

ॐ

Our bags take up a lot of room in the modest and overstuffed one-bedroom apartment. My sisters usually sleep in the living room. Now there are three more adults--me, G, my brother—and a baby here. Even as I'm shifting suitcases and bags around, trying to create space, I realize that staying busy is my strategy. I'm avoiding the moment when I'll have to go to the hospital and see my father.

It's 9:30 P.M. Mahesh is on hospital duty. Amma and my sisters are holding the fort at home.

As if he can read my mind, G says, "I'm off to the hospital. You take it easy. I think it's best you see Appa in the morning."

I want to see him. I don't want to see him. Not yet. I'm trying to

138

decide what to do when Ruki's loud wails reach me. Moments later, Maya walks into the room and hands her to me. "She wants her mama. She's staring suspiciously at all of us, wondering who we are."

Ruki is understandably disoriented by the unfamiliar surroundings and won't let me out of sight. She springs out of Maya's arms and clings tight to me. How am I going to leave her and head to the hospital? I'm the only grounding, comforting presence when her father leaves the room. A small part of me is grateful, relieved even, that the inevitable—my first sight of Appa—is delayed by at least twelve hours.

I've been watching Amma since we arrived a half hour ago. She looks eerily calm, doing the dishes, then setting the table for a late dinner. When she disappears into the kitchen to warm some milk for Ruki, I corner Maya. "Amma seems way too calm. How's she really doing?"

I've managed to piece together the barebones of what happened.

It was a perfectly ordinary Saturday afternoon. After his siesta, Appa had decided to visit his sister who lived three kilometers away. Maya decided to accompany him. As Appa kickstarted his Kinetic Honda and Maya hopped on behind him, they had no idea that life would never be the same, once when they turned the corner.

Two guys on a motorbike hit Appa's scooter from behind and knocked him down. Appa hit his head—Maya remembers the crack of skull hitting the tarmac—and lost consciousness immediately, frothing at his mouth and bleeding from his ear. Maya's shouts for help caused a small crowd to gather. Someone called an ambulance.

Fortunately, the accident occurred right around the corner from the rehab facility and an ambulance was readily available. Appa was rushed to the nearest hospital and wheeled into Intensive Care.

When you strip away all the medical jargon, what remains is this: *head injury*. More tests are being run to determine the seriousness of his injury and the extent of damage to his brain. The situation is grim. Even more reason why Amma's face, like the surface of a lake on a summer's day, is unnerving. Amma had to rush back home from a family wedding she was attending in a nearby town.

"I'm not sure," Maya says. "I think it hasn't registered yet, the seriousness of Appa's diagnosis."

I didn't know back then what I now know about the human brain and neuroscience. How the brain will do everything it can to protect us from shock, 'bubble-wrap' itself against pain which will eventually follow, given enough time.

I make palm circles on Ruki's small back to soothe her. "Amma is someone who feels things. She cries easily. This is so strange, seeing her go about her life as if this is an ordinary day."

"As of now we need to focus on Appa," Maya reminds me. "He's not out of danger yet." Her eyes are pools of sadness.

The gut punch of those words. *Not out of danger yet.* Will he survive this? I shake loose the terrible thought and pull my attention back to the present.

An hour later, G returns from the hospital looking exhausted.

He pulls me aside, rests his hands on my shoulders. "The doctors say the first forty-eight hours are crucial. They don't have any further updates yet. Hopefully, we'll know more tomorrow. We have to trust."

I hold on to him. "How does Appa look?"

He drops his hands and looks away. "It's hard to see Appa like this."

"Like what?"

"You'll see him tomorrow. I don't want to put ideas in your head."

"No, I *want* to know. Please. Tell me."

"He has no external injuries. When you look at him, you wouldn't say this man was in a serious accident. But his eyes look unfocused."

"What do you mean *unfocused*?"

"Sweetheart, you've had a long and stressful day. Ruki needs to sleep. You need to get some sleep. You'll see Appa very soon."

With that he turns away and busies himself laying mattresses, sheets, and pillows on the floor, a makeshift bed for the three of us.

It's going to be a long night. I hope sleep will give me a few hours of reprieve, help blot the awful reality we're living in until I wake up and have to face it all over again.

⤪

The sharp sting of antiseptic—the smell of danger, crisis, the unpredictable—invades my nostrils. White-uniformed nurses. Gurneys. People wearing sad, defeated expressions. My mind is screaming at me to flee the hospital. Every step I take toward the ICU seems a mile long. Maya is walking beside me. I want to see Appa, make sure he's in one piece. I don't want to see Appa and what he's become. The post-accident version of him.

My sisters have tried to prepare me for this moment. There are no bruises on his skin, they've reassured me. But he doesn't look like the Appa we know, they've warned me. He looks disoriented, like he's not really here, they explain.

Try as hard as I might, I can't picture Appa in a hospital bed. This is a man who is always on the move. If he isn't hurrying through the front door, grocery bags in hand, he's rushing off to an A.A. meeting, or a twelfth-step call.

As we near the ICU I try to gather myself, the bits and pieces of information everyone has fed me jangling in the emptiness inside.

Maya intuits that I need support, takes my hand. I clutch her hand like a lifeline. We stop at a glass panel. The unit is dimly lit so I peer in, Maya's face next to mine, our noses pressed to the glass. "There, look," she says, pointing.

A figure sits slumped forward in a plastic chair. My chest constricts. It's Appa. He's wearing a coffee-brown hospital gown that falls to his knees. It is one size too large and has slipped off one shoulder. His jaw hangs slack. For a split-second I wonder if he knows we're here, but then realize the glass only allows for one-way vision. His hair, always neatly combed back with Brylcreem, is a messy nest. I notice his eyes, how his left and right pupils are unfocused. He's squinting but I don't know what he's seeing. Does he know where he is and why? The lack of synchrony gives him a strange, distracted look, his expression vacant. This is what G didn't want to describe to me.

This is not my Appa. This person looks like a madman.

I try to shake off the disloyal thought as soon as it emerges in me. My eyes close involuntarily as if the very act will erase the image I'm struggling to absorb.

When Appa walked into a room, his smile lit up the space. His smile reached his kind and twinkly eyes, his face reflected strength and intelligence. The man who I'm looking at bears little resemblance to the Appa I've admired and adored.

My face is suddenly wet. I can't hold back my tears. I cry unashamedly, charcoal streaks of mascara running down my face. Maya opens her arms to me; I sob on her shoulder. This is all wrong. I'm the older sibling. I should be the one comforting her, assuring her that Appa is going to pull through like he always does. But right this minute, my courage has fled. My body is shaking with fear, the fear of what lies ahead for Appa and for all of us. I feel as broken as the father I see before me.

Maya, wordless, rubs my back. She saw the worst of it. Appa sprawled unconscious in the middle of a crowded road in Chennai, froth pouring from his mouth. She mobilized help, rushed him to the nearest hospital. My twenty-three-year-old sister was present and able to function in the swift current of crisis. And here I am, falling apart because I can barely look at him. Shame sears me. Maya continues to remain silent. She doesn't exacerbate my shame, simply lets me feel what I need to feel in the moment. Tenderness is the most selfless act of kindness she offers me.

COMBUST

No surgical intervention necessary. The doctors' pronouncement drops like sweet honey into our waiting ears. "The hard work begins now," the neurologist reminds us, instantly pouring cold water over our relief about not having to schedule rotations and hospital visits. "He needs a lot of care. There will be a lot of confusion."

Appa is fifty-eight. The doctors choose caution over optimism. When we inquire about his memory loss, they say whatever is lost is lost and whatever returns will return. Only time will tell how much of the submerged will surface and what memories he will be able to access. We, as a family, can do nothing but live with the discomfort of not-knowing.

Over the next week Appa's condition stabilizes enough and he's discharged from the hospital a few days later.

When the ambulance carrying Appa enters the parking area in front of the apartment, a sense of hope rises within me. The hospital attendants settle him in bed, tuck the sides of his blanket and adjust his pillows. *Appa's home. We'll take it from here and make sure he heals. We've got this.*

That sense of hope is precariously balanced with the fact that I'm still having trouble accepting this version of Appa. His vibrant, intelligent face looks disoriented. His eyes, where mischief and humor once sparkled, are vacant holes.

Ruki squirms in my arms. I smile at Appa; he smiles back, but there's a beat of hesitation.

He points to Ruki. "Who? That baby?" His word bank has been tossed and shuffled. He must retrieve one word at a time.

"My baby," I whisper. "Appa, this is Ruki. Your grand-daughter."

A giant lump of grief clogs my throat. Amnesia is a sock in the gut. What I don't know in the moment is that it isn't one punch but a series of recurring blows.

Are memories of earlier, happier times all we're going to have? My mind offers up a memory of Appa walking down the length of the hallway in their home cradling two-month-old Ruki in his arms as he croons an ancient song to her.

"Your baby?!" He says now, the surprise in his voice unmistakable. "When...your marriage?"

I turn away to hide the tears pooling in my eyes. *He doesn't remember the wedding. The day he gave me away to G, one of the happiest days of his life—and mine.*

How much more has he lost, I wonder. How will our family function together if Appa can't thread together the sequence of events that make up the story of our lives?

The attendants present Amma with a folder that contains the discharge instructions. Amma asks me to pay them, and I welcome the moment of distraction. This is how we'll get through the losses that will change all our lives. Life will distract us momentarily and we will grab those distractions to steady ourselves for the strength to bear the next onslaught.

❧

It's time for G to head back to Delhi and return to work, but his heart is not in it. Cupping my face in his hands he says, "I'll be thinking of you. I wish I could stay and help."

I've decided to stay on in Chennai for another month. Amma needs me. My sisters could use some support. Ruki reaching new milestones is bound to bring levity and soften the gravity of this situation.

He kisses me and the baby over and over holding us tight, feeling like he's jumping ship during the worst of the storm. "I'm just a phone call away. Write regularly. Let me know how everything's going."

Our days are packed. There's much to be done. Appa's meals and meds require close monitoring. Plus, meals for the rest of us, the baby's schedules, grocery store runs, and a million other parts that make up the running of a household. Worn out by the day's endless to-do's, we sleep deeply at night. All except Appa whose disorientation around time cycles continues.

Amma needs her sleep. She's on her feet all day long. So, the four of us siblings maintain night vigil taking turns by the hour—at least until Appa's sense of space and time right themselves. I take the first slot from 11 P.M. to midnight so that I can get a few hours of sleep before Ruki wakes me up for her morning bottle. At midnight, I awaken one of my siblings and we rotate shifts until dawn paints the morning sky.

One night I awaken and realize the apartment's front door is wide open. I run outside to see Appa standing at the top of the stairs. I wake the others and we gently guide him back to bed, preventing a potential fall down the stairs. Another night we catch him about to pee in the kitchen sink, convinced that it's the bathroom. Each time, one of us has been gently tapped on the shoulder by some invisible force, helping us to avert the disaster just in time.

The part of Appa's brain responsible for emotional stability and inhibition control has been affected. Usually cheerful and calm, he's now overcome by unpredictable emotional outbursts that take a toll on us, especially Amma.

"I'm hungry. Give me breakfast," he demands. *Please* and *thank you* have flown right out the window.

"You ate breakfast only half an hour ago," says Amma.

"No. I'm hungry." He pouts like a three-year-old who's been denied chocolate for breakfast. And then the accusation. "You don't want to give me food."

"I served you three idlis with coconut chutney..."

"So, I'm lying?"

This is a daily drama. Over time we learn to do the dance differently. When he asks for breakfast minutes after he's finished the meal, Amma walks off into the kitchen pretending that she's getting it ready. Five minutes later, Appa has forgotten the request and a volatile situation is diffused by a carefully-chosen act of manipulation. Over the next months and years, we will become experts at improv, crafting and adapting to situations as they arise.

ॐ

December 1994. It has been six months since Appa's accident.

G, Ruki, and I have relocated to Chennai and moved into a three-bed apartment in a quiet suburb.

Three years of married life have whizzed by. I've had a taste of life in Delhi, but my soul missed Chennai, my hometown. Given the combination of G's frustrations at work and the aftermath of Appa's accident it makes complete sense for us to pack up and move to live closer to my parents.

Ruki is fourteen months old, and my family is thrilled that they now have a ringside view of her growth milestones. I enjoy having my sisters over for meals and lazy conversations, assisting with Appa's caregiving, and becoming Amma's ally. The brief period—Appa's post-sobriety and pre-accident time—of relief is over. She finds her plate heaped and spilling over once again.

On the surface, things seem to have worked out. But we don't know the deeper why's of our move. We have no way of knowing that Appa will lose his job as resident warden in the rehab facility and my parents will no longer have a home. We don't know that my sisters and my parents will move into our four-room apartment and live with us for the next eight months. We have no clue that Appa's health will be compromised over and over resulting in a series of hospitalizations and revised medication protocols. We could never have imagined that, with my brother living and working far away from home, the universe will appoint G as the custodian and caretaker of the family he married into. The years that follow will require us both to stretch ourselves in ways that will test our resilience, courage, and resources.

FLICKERS

Infarct of the frontal and parietal lobes is the diagnosis. Cold medical jargon that fails to explain Appa's deep confusion or retrieve a father-daughter's shared memory bank. Appa's memory is a complex labyrinth where words are like Scrabble tiles shaken in a bag.

He remembers his childhood home and those who peopled that home but is unable to hold on to our names or the simple details of our lives. A typical morning begins like this. "I want..." His fierce frown communicates his struggle for the right word from his dwindling vocabulary bank.

"That...that. Yes. The thing."

"You want food?" I try. I don't even say *breakfast.*

"No. The case." He looks at me, then nods, sure that he's made his request known.

"The case?" I repeat. "Which case? Your office briefcase?"

He stares at me. There's a hole where the word *briefcase* once lived in his memory files.

"You want your office bag?" I try again.

He shakes his head no. On the edge of frustration, he grits his teeth. Then he mimes finger-combing his salt-and-pepper hair. "This," he says.

"Oh, you want a *comb*."

When I hand him a comb, he offers me a thin smile. "Case," he repeats.

How on earth are we going to survive in a world of renamed objects that don't match?

Everyday words like bread, towel, and pillow now have new monikers.

He has no memory of Ruki, the granddaughter he patiently rocked when she wailed in the wee hours from a colic attack. When she caught her first cold he lit squares of camphor in a small brass holder and waved the fumes over her.

He suffers frequent seizures causing him to lose another piece of the puzzle that kept him anchored to reality. It's one more slide down the slippery slope from where he must begin the uphill climb all over again.

Even as Ruki learns to crawl, sit, stand, walk, and run, her small world expanding into larger horizons every day, Appa's life contracts with every new health challenge he battles. He is fed. His bottom is wiped for him. He is washed, diapered, shaved, and powdered. His shoulders which were round and strong are now bony, his clothes hanging off them. His sturdy fingers that once expertly shuffled a pack of cards, shake and tremble now. His ruddy face is lean and weathered, a place where shadows of pain flicker from endless needles: insulin shots, blood draws, and intravenous doses of vitamins that pump life force energy into him.

"No school today?" he asks me one morning. He has no memory that I now have a child who will soon be ready to enroll in an early Montessori school program.

"School is closed today, Appa," I reply. I wonder if I'll ever get used to this brand of improv. My heart breaks over and over to see my father reduced to this pathetic human.

"When can I go home?" he asks, lying in his own bed in his bedroom.

"This is your home, Appa," I say. I offer the truth once in a while. Maybe it will spark some recognition of the familiar. But the hope I'm holding on to is withering away.

"No, this is not my home. I want to go to...that other home. That home...where Thaathi lives."

He's asking for his mother who's been dead for more than two decades.

"That house is locked. She's gone to the store. We'll go there when she's back." I'm buying time, knowing that his demand will soon fade away into the fog of fugue. We try not to challenge his narratives. We let him live with the comforting thought that what's real to him is also real to us.

His mind has wandered back in time, slid into the unthreatening groove of his childhood. The past is more alive to him than the present, and the future doesn't exist. I wonder if this is his brain's way of protecting him.

The injustice of it all kills me some days. Here was a man who had devoted the rest of his life to supporting alcoholics and their sobriety, but the universe has knocked him off his purpose in the cruelest way possible.

With our move to Chennai, G and I have officially surrendered our personal bubble. We're in our early thirties and thrust deep into a season of caregiving.

Our attempts to take a break and go on vacation are invariably interrupted by unexpected emergencies. Appa's health takes an unexpected nosedive. Someone phones us, we cut short our trip, and head back home to support the family. Crisis management is our new normal.

Not once does G complain about any of it. He simply rolls up his sleeves and gets the job done. When the hospital needs a deposit, he writes a check. When Appa has to have a biopsy and a family member has to be present, he takes time off from work. While I stay home with our toddler, he takes turns with Maya and wordlessly endures the discomfort of sleeping on a hard plastic chair outside the Intensive Care Unit.

A specific moment at the Delhi train station comes back to me. I was returning to my parents' home after our avant garde engagement. As we were saying our goodbyes, G had no idea what he'd signed up for when he looked at me, pure love shining from his eyes, and spoke the words: "All your problems are now *my* problems."

৵৵

It has taken three years and Appa's progress is slow and steady. He has regained enough mobility and confidence to walk to the corner store for a loaf of bread or escort Ruki to the play area.

With six adults (seven, when my brother visits) and a toddler, our apartment in suburban Chennai is bursting at the seams. I cast my mind back to the luxury of the bubble G and I had created in the early years of our marriage.

A childhood memory surfaces. Six adults—my three siblings and I, two parents, and my grandma—living in a two-bedroom apartment. My parents got one bedroom. The second bedroom was overcrowded with boxes, thick tomes, metal trunks, and an assortment of odds and ends. Grandma and us kids slept on thin mattresses spread out on the living-room floor. Yet, there was never a sense of feeling crowded. Personal space was an alien concept in the ecosystem of a middle-class Indian family. We had no understanding, or expectation of it. In fact, I grew up never having had a room of my own.

There's definitely more space in our Chennai apartment, but there are also more meals to cook, more laundry loads, and more people breathing the same air.

My husband is a man who thrives on solitude. His generosity in welcoming my large family to stay with us is not something I ever take for granted. But doing the right thing doesn't always mean feeling right about it. Our bedroom becomes the cave he craves. An introvert who's mostly lived on his own, sharing space and energies is hard on him. I struggle with his quiet moods, coming as I do from a family where words stitch together our bonds of connection.

G is flipping through a sports magazine when I enter our bedroom. "What happened?" I ask.

"Hmm? Nothing." Flip, flip, flip.

"What's bothering you?"

"I just told you. Nothing."

"Why are you sitting here all by yourself?"

"What do you want me to do?" I detect an edge of irritation in his voice.

"Why can't you be with everyone? Instead of isolating yourself like this?"

My family huddles. We sit together, catch up, chat. When one of us is missing from the huddle, it's a sign they're upset and the rest of us go find them to make it right. I fear my family will misunderstand G's need to isolate. I realize how awkward it is for my parents to be staying at their son-in-law's for an extended period of time. The last thing I want to do is make them feel like they're a burden on us.

"I do a lot for everyone. I don't ask for anything from anyone. Why is it a problem if I just sit here quietly and read a magazine?"

A part of me understands; another part of me wants him to mingle, to be one of us. It's exhausting, this tightrope walk that I'm teetering on between my husband and my family of origin.

Translating one's language to the other feels frustrating, almost impossible. Navigating the borders between two spaces—our marriage and my maiden family—is tricky. The need to make my family feel at home, to me, is as important as honoring my husband's need to claim his space.

When my in-laws visit from out of town they have no choice but to stay with relatives because our overcrowded apartment cannot accommodate them. Tradition dictates that a man's home belongs to his parents first. A married son and daughter-in-law are primarily responsible for his parents' well-being. My in-laws are large-hearted enough to shrug off the inconvenience, but it leaves me feeling stuck and deeply embarrassed.

Even as I find myself tiptoeing through these disparate spaces, Ruki crosses the borders between these two worlds with childlike ease. Basking in her grandparents' and aunts' adoring attention, she embraces the 'more the merrier' idea. She cuddles with Grandma on the couch and watches her favorite TV show; crawls into her aunt's lap and demands one more story; and is so charming with her grandpa that he cannot resist walking her to the neighborhood bakery for a chocolate éclair.

It will be eight months before my parents move into a rented apartment, all of us siblings chipping in to make it work financially and physically.

Before I can exhale and draw a fresh breath, a new crisis demands our attention.

Amma phones me in a panic one afternoon. "Appa's had a seizure. An ambulance is on its way."

I call G at work.

"I'll leave work early, stop by the hospital, then come home," he says, and I know he's about to drop everything at work and morph into the angel of rescue one more time.

When he arrives home a couple of hours later, I'm in tears. "I've had enough!"

He shuts the door, then gently holds me. "Why are you upset? Things are under control at the hospital."

"That's just it. How much of our lives is going to be about my family needing you and me all the time? We don't get a break. What about *our* lives?" My anger is hot enough to steam up the room.

"It's just a difficult situation, Ums. At least I have a job that allows me to take time off and be available."

"It's not fair," I continue. "Sometimes I wish we lived in America. Then we'd be too far away. We'd have a real excuse. We wouldn't have to drop everything and run every time there's a crisis. I'm tired of being on constant-call. People who live overseas are so lucky. I'm sure they worry about their parents, but at least they get to live their lives."

I don't know it at the time, but the memory of this emotional outburst will come back and haunt me a few years later.

Over two years of a peaks-and-valleys medical journey, Appa survives the worst and emerges a battle-scarred warrior. He even

manages to find part-time employment at an accounting firm within walking distance from their apartment. His brain injury has compromised his life in many ways. Entire albums of memories return intact; others are lost forever. But what he does recover in spades is self-confidence. Waking up each morning, getting dressed and going to work—even if the job is several notches below the positions he's held—fills Appa with new purpose.

This situation, however, is short-lived. Errors begin to creep into Appa's accounting work and numbers don't lie. His benevolent boss chooses kindness over ruthless judgment, preserving Appa's dignity and self-esteem. He smooths over Appa's errors, corrects them, and saves the day. But this short-term solution cannot staunch the bleed. It becomes harder and harder to hide behind denial's seductive veil. Unable to absorb the slack anymore, the company has to make the difficult decision. Appa is let go.

Losing his job, a second time, shakes the foundations of Appa's mental well-being. The body follows the mind, and soon he's lying in bed and writhing in pain. The diagnosis: TB of the spine. The combination of defeat and despair takes a toll. Appa doesn't even want to get out of bed. Maya has moved away for her job and Vidya's marriage has taken her as far as the Middle East. Amma can no longer manage Appa's multiple needs all on her own. We interview and hire a night nurse.

ILLUMINE

When we enrolled Ruki in a Montessori school and I found myself with a few spare hours, the hunger to write started to gnaw at me. I shook the dust off a folder that contained a few of my writing samples and carried them to an editor, confident I'd walk out with a regular assignment: a weekly column to write. She asked me a few perfunctory questions, read snippets of my work, and assigned me one story.

What started out as one random interview soon morphed into a full-blown freelance career. My articles, personal essays, short stories, and features appear in newspapers and magazines and the thrill of seeing my byline never grows old. Over time, my writing is published in seven countries and my essays and short stories have won awards.

"You could tell stories from the Ramayana and the Mahabharata when you were three years old!" Amma tells me. "Imagine that! The neighbors all wanted to babysit you just to listen to the sweet way in which you told these stories." The story has now become family lore.

It was my paternal grandmother who kindled my love of story during times when books were expensive, and libraries didn't exist. She fed me a constant diet of mythological stories from the great Indian epics, the Ramayana and the Mahabharata.

Sitting on the front stoop of our home, I'd watch her gnarled fingers fly through the air and her eyes round with excitement as she launched into the story of how Hanuman, the monkey god, grew as tall as a giant and set fire to an entire kingdom with his flaming tail. I think of her voice as warm honey one moment, and tart vinegar the next, as she morphed from one character to the next. As I listened, stroking the soft wrinkled folds of her skin between my thumb and forefinger, my imagination flew me to the battlefields of Kurukshetra and into the golden chariot where Krishna whispered courage to steady Arjuna's faltering faith to fight the war.

One moment Grandma was Surpanakha, the evil sister of the demon king Ravana; the next, she was Shabari, the hunchback devotee who bit a piece off every fruit she plucked to make sure it tasted just right before she saved it for Lord Rama.

Stories became my saving grace. Books opened me to worlds I didn't know existed. Carrying the legacy forward, I bought Ruki's first books when I was five months pregnant. As she memorizes stories I repeatedly read to her, I see how the love of story is in her blood and bones too. My two-year-old has no clue of the English alphabet but is word-perfect in reading out loud and turning the page when she gets to the last word.

I loved nothing more than making up stories for her as I spooned yogurt rice into her mouth or soaped her in the bath, stories in which she was the main character. On a whim, I wrote these stories in a journal. When I was done, I had a book of short stories and poems titled *Ruki's Saturday And Other Stories.*

SIMMERING

2001. Seven years after we moved to Chennai, the American shipping line that employed G closed down its operations.

In mid-2002 G was hired by a German logistics company with worldwide offices and an impressive portfolio of business. Since the day he signed on the dotted line and returned home, a BlackBerry and company laptop in hand, a hungry beast has taken him over. I hear his keyboard clacking away into the wee hours of the morning. It's an endless marathon, trying to outrun his fast-filling email inbox.

We argue often. Every argument follows the same trajectory: his constant obsession with work. The arguments don't get us anywhere. I still go to bed alone and sleep alone, barely knowing when he comes to bed.

One night, the mournful yowling of a street dog dredges me up from a deep dream. Pale light filters in, breaking through the barrier of my closed eyelids. Did I forget to turn off the living room lights? I peek through sleep-crusted eyes, see that the spot beside me is empty. *G is still working.*

The neon green numerals on the bedside clock read 1:34 A.M. Sleep is snuffed out, like a candle flame caught in a gust. The slow burn of anger rises from my gut to my chest and pounds an incessant drumbeat. I turn on my side, draw the sheet tighter, and try to steady my wayward breath. The dog continues to howl a mournful dirge.

Deep mindful breathing—a practice I learned in morning-yoga at the nearby ashram—does nothing for me right now. On the contrary, the rapid-fire self-righteous justifications in my head speed up my breathing. *How dare he not care about me going to bed alone, night after night!*

The voices in my head are so loud I sweep the bedclothes off me and stride into the living room.

"It's well past one."

"I know," G says, not taking his eyes off the screen, his face lit by its blue light, fingers continuing to peck at the keyboard. "I have two more emails to send out."

"How long is this going to continue...these late-night sessions?"

He pauses, sighs, looks up at me. "I told you. This is a new job. There's a learning curve. And there's a lot happening right now."

"So, *this* is our life now. Me going to bed alone, and you sitting up until 2 A.M." I cross my hands over my chest.

"I'm sorry. This is the only job that opened up when the other company closed its operations. I'm doing the best I can."

"Does everyone work like this?"

"I don't know." He sighs again. "I'll shut down and come to bed. It's the only thing that'll make you happy." A few swift clicks of the mouse and he exits the email program.

"I didn't demand that you shut down right this minute. Why don't you try to understand what I'm saying?" I shut my eyes to still my racing mind. "Never mind. I should've just stayed in bed." I march off to the bedroom, my jaw tightly clenched.

All my childhood I had to compete with Appa's whiskey bottle for his attention. *Am I not enough? Am I not lovable? What do I have to do to get your attention?* All these years later I'm still competing. For my husband's attention, his phone and laptop ranged against me.

I lie in bed, my chest heaving with sorrow. Moments later, the bathroom light turns off and G slides into bed. He turns away from me, his back a brick wall that separates us. Tears slide down the corners of my eyes and seep into my pillow silently.

We're lucky Ruki's a good sleeper. I'm glad she doesn't have to witness this ugliness between her parents. She's ten already. An image of calendar pages flying fast and blurring time flashes through my mind. Where did the years go? I think back to when she was three and we were at the playground. She'd take teeny steps and edge her way to the slide, carefully place a foot on the lowest rung, then turn to me and seek courage. It took every ounce of courage she possessed for her to climb that ladder and slide down.

Those were the days when her dad returned from work when the sky above us was still blue. The moment she spotted him she'd take off with a drawn-out "Daaa...deee," and fly into his arms. He'd scoop her up and throw her into the air. I can still hear her delighted squeals fill the air.

Those were much simpler times at a simpler job. The clunky desktop computer stayed in the office and the ordinary flip-top phone was not savvy enough for global connection. Now, work is a beast that devours G at the start of the day and grudgingly releases its vicious grip on him in the early A.M. only to reclaim him a few short hours later.

༄

A few years after my writing had been widely published, one of the Mumbai magazines I write for announces a writing contest. The winning prize is a three-day all-expenses-paid trip to Goa, a lovely coastal city in western India known for its seafood, churches, beaches, and laidback lifestyle.

I win first prize. It's a big deal because I get to take the family on a fun beach trip.

We fly to Goa and arrive at Cidade de Goa, a beachside hotel in a spa-like setting. Fragrant potpourri and colorful flowers, ocean views, sunshine, soft white beach sands, and the smell of Goan fish curry wafting on the breeze. It's the perfect getaway.

But things unravel faster than I can even imagine.

The morning after we arrived, I'm sitting under a tangerine beach umbrella, my sunglasses the perfect cover for my swollen eyes. The glass that holds my ice-cold drink is sweating moisture, forgotten beside me.

Ocean surf pounds the shore. A seagull swoops down in an elegant arc. The sky is a perfect watercolor blue. Picture-perfect images that slide away from my mental grasp, trapped as I am in the crazy thought-spiral inside my head.

Ruki is sitting on the sand, lost in a book.

The beach chair next to mine is empty because my husband is putting out a work fire. More like an uncontrolled blaze, the flames flying fast and furious, devouring our idyllic getaway. What started as a phone call last evening snowballed into a flurry of emails flying across continents (the perks of working for a global conglomerate) and phone calls that escalated in urgency. G has been up all night fielding calls and pounding out emails and I'm punctured that the peaceful holiday bubble I tried to create for us is once again invaded by the unceasing demands of work.

"What do you mean you have to work?! We're on vacation," I'd said to him in utter disbelief last night.

"It's a shitstorm. Some damaged cargo has arrived in...anyway, you don't need to know the details of what went wrong. Basically, there's utter confusion and I have a customer who's screaming bloody murder. That's my life." G throws up his hands.

His neat summary does nothing to calm the fire that's building inside me.

I stand there, arms akimbo, heat rising up my cheeks. "So… there's no one who can handle this crisis when you're away? Your *family* doesn't deserve your time?"

"Sshh. You'll wake Ruki," he cautions. After a day on the beach, she's tuckered out and tucked in, fast asleep.

G continues. "Ums, I understand you're upset—and you have every right to be. But this is my work life. Screw-ups happen in the logistics industry."

"It's always the same old story. I'm sick and tired of it."

"I'm sorry. But I have to go now. Some emails need to go out ASAP. I'll get out of your hair. Work in one of the conference rooms." He grabs his phone and laptop, pauses for a moment. "Don't wait up for me."

As his long strides echo away from us, I fall into bed and drag the covers over my head. The tears come, hot and heavy. Anger and sorrow pour out of my eyes. A million thoughts race through my mind. *He never has time for me anymore. Work is everything to him. He doesn't care about me or the writing prize I was so excited to win.*

And here we are, the next morning—Ruki and I—sitting on the beach and pretend-playing a vacation. G woke up early—if he slept at all—and left the room to hold his irate customer's hand from a beautiful beach hotel.

This is not how it's supposed to be. This was a big deal to me.

I'm enraged, but I don't want to be. I want my body to feel the peace it knows when I'm doing *pranayama*. How do I go from being mad to feeling calm? For some reason Oprah pops into my mind. I stumbled upon *The Oprah Winfrey Show* quite by accident and have been watching every old rerun we get on Indian television. The episodes are dated, but the wisdom Oprah and her guests share is timeless. Love is the greatest healing force on the planet, I've heard Oprah say over and over. Right this minute I don't feel a grain of love in my hardened heart, but recalling her words evokes something in me. I can *intend* to soften. So I do, by relaxing my face. I unclench my jaw, drop my shoulders, and ease the tension around my brows. Then I force my lips to curve into a pretend smile. I can fake it till I make it.

TINDER

As a variety of magazines and newspapers continue to publish my work, the tingly feeling of seeing my words in newsprint never gets old. Now that I have a clutch of short stories, personal essays, and features to my credit, my heart opens to a more expansive dream: publishing a book.

When my editor assigns me to interview a bestselling Indian American author whose books I adore, I can barely contain my excitement. Before sitting down to respond to my questions, she's doing a photo session. As I watch her hold up her book and pose I ache with desire. *I want what she has.*

As the photographer angles his camera this way and that and clicks away, I slip out of my body, walk over to the other side, sit in the author's chair, hold up my book, and smile into the camera. Soon the room is crowded with adoring fans, eager to hear me read from my latest book. I flip through the Post-its that flag the relevant pages and arrive at the very passage I'm about to read. I clear my throat and...

"Uma...Uma..." Someone is calling my name. Is it someone from one of the back rows?

A delicately placed hand on my shoulder yanks me out of my author dream. "My work is over," says the photographer. "Please, you can go ahead." I grimace-grin as shame floods my body. I glance at the author and wonder if she knows I've been away in la-la land. She regards me with curiosity as I gather my recorder and notepad.

❧

One morning I'm rustling newspaper sheets trying to find something to read that's not a riot, rebellion, or rape when the advertisement catches my eye. It's from a London publishing house which has recently opened its India office in New Delhi.

Seeking submissions from aspiring authors. The words make me tingly all over. I read every word of the ad and commit it to memory. The only confusing caveat is the reference to a pay-to-publish arrangement. Traditional publishing houses publish books based on the merit of the author's writing skill but this new house was saying, *If we think you're good enough to be published by us, you have to pay us.*

I've dreamed of this for so long. I want this. I know in my blood and bones that I was born to write. And here's the universe dropping a publishing opportunity right into my lap. *It's a sign.* I haven't had a full-time job since I got pregnant nearly twelve years ago. I have no idea how much this will cost. Will G fund my dream? Is it even fair to ask him to? Every aspiring writer has to begin somewhere. Maybe this is my path. What if my book sells thousands of copies? I craft arguments in favor of my dream, all the reasons why I ought not to pass this up. What I'm really doing is trying to build a bank of responses to all the questions I know my husband's logical brain will produce. I must pick the right moment to bring it up, not an evening when he's stressed or distracted by work demands.

Over the coming days the fantasy of becoming a best-selling author seeps deeper into my skin. I may be starting out with a children's book, but I know there are seeds of a novel sleeping inside me. One children's book, then a novel, then many novels, and I see myself at sold-out book events, on Oprah's couch, other stages, fans holding books out for my autograph. My fantasies become a movie in my head playing on repeat.

I'm also rehearsing my opening lines to G.

Guess what I saw in the newspaper. An ad for you-won't-believe-what. (curiosity)

My dream is really close. (intrigue)

You're looking at someone who's about to be published by a UK publishing house. (confidence)

None of them sound good, so I start over again.

Every time I think to myself *this is the moment* and approach him, my courage deserts me. What if he says no? My dream will crumble into a pile of ash. Oprah's couch will forever be something I only watch on my TV screen. He's always tried to make every wish of mine come true, so why should this time be any different? He could blow holes in every single one of my arguments. He could shrug his hands and say, 'I'll find a way to make it happen,' only because I'm uber attached to the dream, not because he believes in it. That wouldn't be as satisfying as having him on board and convinced that this is absolutely the right thing to do.

Frustrated with myself for losing my nerve and terrified by the thought that I'll miss the boat (the publishing house's mailbox must be overflowing with submissions from every aspiring author in India) I decide to put an end to the dilly-dallying and have The Conversation.

I pick a Sunday, a day when work distractions are muted.

"There was this ad in the papers," I begin talking to the face hidden behind the Sunday papers.

He lowers the newspaper. "Today's paper?"

"No. I saw it a few days ago. From a UK-based publishing house. Can you believe they've opened their India office in Delhi!"

He's still listening.

"Shall I send them the collection of stories and poems I wrote when Ruki was little?"

"You should," he replies and folds the newspaper to the page he wants to read next.

I crack my knuckles. My head is furiously rearranging the words I will say next. "Oh, the only thing is... it's a pay-to-publish deal."

He looks up at me quizzically. "What does that mean?" As clarity dawns, he says, "No, that can't be right. You pay them? If you want your book published?"

"Hmm."

"How much?"

"The ad doesn't say how much. I guess that's only if they choose your manuscript."

"Yeah. Because it's harder for a writer to say no when they pick your book and say they want to publish it. Seems like a clever scheme to me."

Here we go.

"What's the harm in mailing my manuscript?" I persist.

"I'm not saying you shouldn't. Do it. See what they say. But you know my thoughts on this. No one should ask you for money to publish your book."

My body clenches. "We don't have to think about that right now. They may not even pick my manuscript."

"Send it in. Actually, give it to me when it's ready and I'll send it off from work on Monday."

For now, I can simply focus on getting my manuscript ready and mailing it in.

Once I've mailed the manuscript, I'm jittery with anticipation. Every afternoon I check our mailbox with an obsession that borders on crazy. The first week, I'm on edge. But with each passing week my adrenaline rush eases.

And then, one afternoon, a fat envelope greets me when I

open the mailbox. It's addressed to *me*, the publishing house's logo embossed on the top left corner. It's a large envelope so it's squished inside. I extricate it gently, careful not to damage it. I want to make a ceremony of opening it and savoring its contents. But my heart is beating out of my chest, so I toss ceremony out the window and let my frenzied fingers rip open the envelope.

A cover letter and a few stapled sheets. I breeze past the polite preliminaries and leap straight to the meat. *Is it a publishing contract?*

"We are pleased to inform you that your manuscript *Ruki's Saturday And Other Stories* has been selected for publication..."

The words I've longed to hear. My heart is just about ready to explode. I have to remind myself to breathe.

I don't want to read the rest. The detritus of the contract. Not just yet. I just want to savor this sweet moment.

As the initial euphoria begins to settle, I skim the contract. My eyes are immediately drawn to the number of zeroes. My gut squeezes. I feel sick.

125,000 Indian rupees.

There's no way I can afford this. I might have to request G to fund my dream. But this is an exorbitant amount of money—even for him. We don't have this kind of money stashed away to throw at vanity publishing. It feels like the worst kind of self-indulgence. But there's a part of me that has always known and believed that my creative expression is my magic. Am I sabotaging my own dream by throwing away this opportunity? I've read stories of people who had a big dream, but little money. They took out loans to give their dream wings and ended up wealthy from following their passion. Many of Oprah's guests speak of the significant financial investments they had to make to get behind their dreams. I shake off my doubts. I'll somehow have to convince G to find the money.

When G returns from work, I open the door and wave the letter at him, a big goofy grin on my face.

"Is that...?" he begins.

"Yesss," I shout, tossing the letter into the air.

"Wow. Congratulations! I want to hear all about it." He hugs me, sets his briefcase down, and tugs his tie loose.

He glances at the cover letter I hand him. "Did they send you a contract?"

I gulp. Here it is, the moment I've been dreading. I'm the dreamer. He's the doubter. The one who wants to know the plan, the numbers, the nitty-gritty. But right now, I want to gloss over that part. My publishing dream feels fragile, atoms and molecules of desire coalescing—and I don't want it to die before it has a chance to breathe.

"Why don't you go wash up, get changed? We can go over the contract after we eat," I say.

As he washes off the grit and grime of a day gathered in the corporate battlefield, my mind is busy planning its defenses, justifications, and arguments. I'm confident that turning down this opportunity would be career suicide for an aspiring author with sky-high ambitions.

After dinner we settle on the couch. I start to unfold the stapled sheets.

"So." I begin. "They're asking for a fairly large amount—but that covers everything. The edits, cover design, proof reading... and here's the best part. They're throwing a launch party to celebrate and promote all the new authors who sign up with them. Think of the media exp..."

He cuts me off. "How much is it? What do they want you to pay?"

"125k," I say in a whisper.

"ONE HUNDRED TWENTY-FIVE thousand rupees??!"

I say nothing, simply hand him the contract. For the next few minutes, the thudding of my heart is the loudest sound in my ears as my husband reads the fine print.

"You know how I feel about these fancy pay-to-publish schemes." He sets the pages down on the coffee table. "They're making all kinds of promises just to get you to sign up with them."

I stare off into the distance, the bitterness of disappointment coating my tongue.

"Ums, look at me," he says. "You're a talented writer. Any publishing house will be lucky to have you. And they should want to publish you on the merit of your book." His words haven't melted my defenses. "But I know you don't want to hear all this."

I sigh. All my arguments have dissolved in the heat of the few sentences he's spoken. I wish I could regress to toddlerhood where rationale and reason don't exist, and you can simply stomp and scream and demand what you want right this minute. *But I just want to be published!*

"Hey, what happened?" G prods me. "You haven't said one word."

"What's the point? I don't have one hundred twenty-five thousand rupees and you're convinced it's a bad scheme."

"And you're not?"

I play with my wedding ring as I formulate my response. "It's a UK-based publishing house. You really think they've set up an India office just to bait first-time authors and get rich?"

"All I'm saying is, it sounds fishy to me. I'm not an expert in how publishing works, but even I find it hard to believe that it costs so much to put out a children's book. And my question is: why should the author pay for it?"

It's past 10 P.M. and my spirits are flattened by G's unshakeable convictions. Nor do I have answers to the barrage of questions coming at me. *Call it a night and fall into bed* sounds like a good idea. I get up. "I'm going to bed."

"But I didn't think we were done talking about this."

I shrug. "You're not going to be convinced by anything I say."

"Are *you* convinced? Do you believe we should pay this company 125k to publish your book?"

"I don't know. I'm tired. I don't want to talk about it tonight."

I *do* know. It's a lot of money. I also know that I'm really, really attached to my dream. I'm not ready to let it go.

I mope around the house for the next few days and watch my

fragile dream vaporize in thin air. My mind is spewing all kinds of stories. *He just doesn't understand what it means to be a creative soul. You can't always bring logic into everything. I wish I had the money. I wouldn't have had to ask for anyone's permission or opinion then. This is what comes of deciding to be a stay-home mother. You lose your financial freedom—and no one celebrates you for having jam sandwiches, milk, and a warm hug waiting when your child returns home after a school day.*

Over the next days, G senses the dip in my mood. "Why don't you talk to your writer friends? Ask if anyone's heard about this publishing company?"

Loathe to disagree and risk another argument, I simply nod. But I will do nothing of the sort. I have no desire to entertain any more negative voices in my head. I can't bear anyone else trying to talk me out. Sadly, I can't see a way to go forward without my husband's financial support.

We're sitting on the terrace late one evening, two glasses of red between us. "You're still upset because of what I said," G says. A warm ocean breeze plays with my hair. The white light of a full moon spills all over the floor.

"It's just—I was so excited."

"Have you found out anything more about this company?"

I shake my head no.

"I know you want this. I've tried to explain my views. But that's not what you want to hear." He takes a sip of wine. "I don't have this kind of money lying around. So, give me some time. I'll figure this out. I'll find the money for you."

"No, no." As much as every fiber of my being wants a published book with my name on the cover, I don't want my husband to have to scale any impossible mountains to make it happen. "If you don't have the money, you don't."

"Leave it to me. I'll figure something out," he says, putting an end to the conversation.

"But you just said you didn't have..."

"Do you trust me?"

I nod yes.

"We'll find a way," he says, sipping the last dregs of his Merlot.

If there's anyone I trust with just about anything, it's G. He's my safety net. He won't let me fall. Ever.

⁓

A few days later.

When G returns home from work, he's smiling big. The man who usually walks in the door with a I-just-crawled-out-of-the-corporate-trench look is actually smiling. A new client win, maybe? An exciting new opportunity at work? A meeting with his team that went really well?

"Looks like someone had a really good day." I give him a welcome-home hug. He sets his briefcase down. "You'll have your check tomorrow.

"What check?"

"For the publishing house."

"But I thought we decided to..."

"I told you I'd find a way—and I did."

"How? Where did you find the money?" I search his face.

"Okay, don't freak out when I tell you."

Now I'm really freaking out.

"I sold our Zen."

Maruti Zen. Our precious four-door hatchback.

"What?! Why..."

G places a hand on my cheek. "I know how important this dream is to you. It's okay. Money, cars... that stuff comes and goes. But you'll have your published book."

I throw my arms around him, hug him tight. "I can't believe you sold our car to make this happen!"

"We'll wait a while and look for another one."

"I don't know what to say, except... thank you."

The signed contract and check are in the mail to the publishing house. The first edits of my book land in my inbox the following week. It's a slim volume, a children's book of short stories and poems, so the editorial process moves along swiftly. The day the cover art is finalized it all begins to feel real. I stare at the book cover mockup, the title lettered in navy blue and a sprinkle of happy images: a bouquet of flowers, a cute dog, and a dark-haired child with sparkly eyes.

When the proofs arrive in the mail a week later, I am alternately speechless and shrill, my excitement swelling and filling the entire apartment. My hands tremble as I hold the proof copy. The bigness of the moment as special as the day I laid eyes on Ruki for the first time. Minus the agonizing birth pain.

"Here it is," I hand the copy to G. What I read on his face is, *I'm happy you're happy—and I'd have done anything to see this happiness shine from your face.*

As promised, there's going to be a book launch party in Delhi. I read the email invite every few minutes and pinch myself. Soon, our tickets to Delhi are booked and I feel just a little taller and walk a little straighter.

I stand in front of my closet, my head humming with excitement. Which outfit to wear? When G walks up to me and whispers an idea, I nod and smile. My new beginning as an author calls for a brand-new outfit.

❧

We're in the taxi—G, Ruki, and I—driving to the venue of the book launch party. I've been on a jittery high all evening, the dream I've held in my heart now close enough to touch. In just a few minutes I will be among a clutch of first-time authors toasted for our maiden publishing success. Silently rehearsing possible questions from the journalists, I even pretend-fake the blink as a camera flash catches me by surprise.

We leave the hotel with plenty of time to spare. As the taxi navigates the crowded roads of Delhi and eventually nears our destination, I look outside the window. *This looks like a regular residential neighborhood.* No cars parked in chaotic clusters, or people milling about. No signs that it is the venue of a book launch event.

I push a button and the window slides down. "Is this the right place?"

The cabbie is searching for the correct door number.

G pulls out the scrap of paper on which he scribbled the address.

"Here, *saab*?" The cabbie enquires. "I stop here?"

"One minute." G glances alternately between the paper in his hand and the door numbers we're driving by.

A tall white concrete building stands alone shrouded in darkness. The number on the building is 37; the building next to it is 38. But 36 is what we're looking for.

G opens the taxi door, steps out.

"Stay here, Ruki," I say, following him.

"Where's 36? I don't see it." My mouth feels dry. The first hints of foreboding tug at me.

G is walking up and down the street, counting off the door numbers. "30, 32, 34, 39...What the hell. Only 36 is missing."

We walk up to 37 and ring the doorbell. Maybe 36 is on the other side. Perhaps we need to drive around to approach it. It's probably just a silly construction thing.

No one comes to the door. Nothing happens.

I pull the publishing contract from my purse, check the phone number, and begin to dial. The phone rings and rings and rings. I turn to G. "No one's answering at the company either."

"Let's go. Nothing's happening here."

"Wait. Why don't we drive around to the other side? Maybe 36 is on the other side," I hang on, desperate, a last-ditch effort.

G sighs in frustration. "Okay, let's give it a try. But I doubt we'll find anything there."

"What happened, Mama?" Ruki asks, when we return to the cab.

"We can't find the address, sweetie."

G instructs the cabbie to try the parallel road.

The cabbie drives slowly as we scan door number after door number, but 36 is nowhere to be seen.

"Show me the printout of the email they sent you with the event details."

"Here." I hand G the sheet of paper. "We have the correct address. The street name is right, but there's no 36. And 36 is the number on the address they sent me."

"Well, there's nothing more we can do," he says.

Swirling in a sea of shame I slump in my seat as we head back to the hotel. *G was right all along. This is a scam.*

My husband is unusually quiet on the ride. Glittering malls and brightly lit high-rises fly past our taxi window, but everything is a blur because the voices in my head have complete dominion over me.

Why didn't you listen to him when he shared his suspicions about the pay-to-publish scam? You made him sell the family car to fund your dream.

What's the price of a dream? How far did I have to force him to stretch because I wanted it? Why did I miss all the red flags—the vague responses to my email queries about the event, the fake fluffy words that covered over the real truth of what was going on.

Back in the hotel, G is sitting on the sofa, his legs outstretched, eyes on his cell phone. My stomach churns with regrets. There are no words to make this right, but somehow I have to try.

I sit beside him. "I should've listened to you." I knead my fingers so hard they hurt. "I feel stupid even saying I'm sorry. I mean...I feel just—awful right now."

"It was an expensive way to learn the truth. But you know I don't enjoy saying *I told you so.* You're disappointed—and I'm sorry."

Grateful as I am for his forgiveness, a red flare of vengeful anger sizzles inside me. "We should go to their office tomorrow. I want to expose them, demand my money back."

"Not worth it. They'll say you have your published book. They'll say they delivered what they promised."

"But they didn't! What about the launch event? We spent all this money to fly here and..."

"Ums, these companies have fancy lawyers. This is their game. We're just ordinary people. How are we going to fight them? You really want to go down that road?"

He's right. Again. This time, I will listen.

"Let it go. It was a mistake, a costly one. Let's put it behind us."

A part of me wants revenge, wants the fight and fantasy of taking the publishing company down. But the wiser part of me prevails. I don't want to invest any more time or energy in a company that is morally bankrupt.

SOUL KINDLING

As Ruki begins seventh grade, her life brimming with school projects and friend outings and mid-term tests, vistas of time open up for me. I feel the teacher in me stirring awake and stretching toward a new horizon. After some research I land on a Business English course offered by the British Council. I take the course, write the exam, and receive a certificate from Cambridge University, which puts me on the Council's list of trainers.

As a part-time trainer the Council sends me to IT companies where I train technically skilled software engineers who struggle with sub-par English language skills. With shrinking global borders and growing international business, Indian companies need to keep up with the rest of the world. My job is to improve the Indian professional's language skills: write better emails, make quality presentations, and handle business conversations with confidence. It's a fun gig that pays handsomely. Working three half days a week and being home in time for Ruki's school bus is the perfect arrangement.

In managing my freelance writing assignments with corporate training, life starts to feel meaningful in a whole new way. Not too many people make a good living doing what they love. Maybe I *am* living my purpose.

Purpose. Many of my favorite Oprah show guests—Carolyn Myss, Gary Zukav, Marianne Williamson, Cheryl Richardson—speak eloquently about purpose. We're here for a purpose, our lives have meaning, and our divine destiny is coded into our cells. These words create a holy hum inside my body.

The idea of an intentional soul mission feels exciting. *What did I come here to do? How do I find my path and purpose?* The questions are tiny seeds that drop into the soil of my consciousness. Before they can take root, however, they're pushed aside by a more pressing concern or obligation. Ruki needs me to sign a field trip form. Amma calls to ask if we'd like to go over for Sunday lunch. An editor sends me on an urgent assignment. My soul retreats, goes into hiding in the face of all these distractions. Until next time.

It's so thrilling to watch Oprah's audience members clapping and stomping that I wish I were sitting in a chair in Harpo Studios watching Oprah walk onto her stage. I rise to my feet with all the women around me and welcome her, my voice hoarse with cheering, tears of joy and disbelief streaming down my face.

Other times my fantasy involves Oprah holding up her latest Book Club pick. *My* book. I watch myself sashay onto the most coveted stage in the world, hair and make-up professionally done as a thunderous applause erupts from the audience.

Right that moment, an electric drill starts up in my neighbor's apartment and drops me down from the clouds with a discombobulating thud and into the mugginess of a hundred-degree Chennai day.

My dream dissolves instantly. It's an impossible dream anyway. From where I sit, Chicago seems as unattainable as the moon.

Our lives in Southern India feel settled and secure. We live in a 2700 square foot home, a ten-minute walk from the ocean. G's work makes him a regular globe-trotter. He is thriving in a busy season of his career. I continue to maintain that his hours are crazy and unsustainable, and often feel crowded out by the multiple demands on his time. He reminds me that it is all the hard work and his devotion to excellence that make our life possible—overseas vacations, perks, and pleasures. I pout but have to grudgingly agree.

I stay present to Ruki's blossoming life, the mother who never misses a school play or sports day, the one who attends every school exhibition and fair.

It is this cozy life groove that the universe jolts us out of. Change arrives, the kind of change we could never have imagined. It will require us not just to give up our snug groove; it will demand that we uproot ourselves, grow new wings, and fly in skies of a completely different shade of blue.

GLOW

"Dad and I want to talk to you about something important," I say to Ruki. The three of us are sitting on our outdoor terrace. It's late, a muggy August evening in 2007. Not a leaf stirs. My skin feels warm and sticky. A watery moon spills white light over the patio tiles before she glides behind a thin cloud-cover.

Ruki, just shy of fourteen, regards me with open curiosity.

Her dad takes the lead. "We have an opportunity to move to the U.S."

I'm watching Ruki, her face like a sunflower opening to the first rays of the morning.

"Mama and I have been talking about it," G continues. "But you're also a big part of this decision. You're doing so well in school.

All your friends are here. So, before we move any further, we want to know how *you* feel about it."

"The U. S.?" Ruki whispers in awe.

I'm curious about her reaction.

"Also, we have a pretty comfortable life here," I add. "Is it worth the trouble, starting over in a new country? I don't know. But then it's also an opportunity for you to study there. Go to university."

Ruki is listening. The words are moving inside her, seeking a place to land, to roost.

"Sweetie, we want to know what you think. You seem excited. But it's a big move. And we know how important friends are at your age."

"Let's go," Ruki cuts to the chase. "Can we live someplace where it snows?"

I'd expected teen apprehension, but it looks like her excitement exceeds any misgivings at this stage. After all, she's only fourteen. Fourteen-year-olds change their minds. She may wake up tomorrow and declare that she doesn't want to leave the school she's been going to since first grade and friends she's known all her life.

Ruki was a newborn when her aunt, a U.S. citizen, applied for us to immigrate. Our interest was alive at the time, the dream of moving to what many called the promised land. But as time went by and there was radio silence from U.S. Immigration, our faith withered, then died. It's fourteen years later now and the U.S. government has begun to process our paperwork.

The question of *Do we stay, or do we go?* has been front and center in our recent conversations. G and I come at it from different perspectives, weigh the pros and cons, take turns at playing devil's advocate to each other's positions, and continue to grapple with the question because there's no tidy answer.

My parents live with Maya. Appa's health isn't as wobbly as it used to be and Amma's world is a model of devotion to his care and well-being. I live only a couple of kilometers away which is a relief given Maya's frequent travels for her job.

It's almost impossible to imagine living a continent away from my family. But then we've put our lives on hold all these years to tend to their needs. If G is keen on going on this adventure—traveling to a new country and making a life for us there—I'll support his choice.

Having sampled American life only through the pages of novels I've read and movies and shows I've watched, I wonder what the real thing will feel like. At forty-three, I'm equal parts curious and trepidatious. I've never lived anywhere except India. But Ruki's life can be a wide-open doorway to a world of new experiences and adventures: studying in an American university, drinking deep from a distinctly different cultural cup, and the invitation to think independently, a far cry from the family-centric collective culture G and I were raised in.

Our first trip to the U.S. happened soon after Ruki's third birthday. G was invited to a conference in New Orleans, so I flew with him. We spent three glorious weeks traveling from New Orleans to Memphis, Knoxville, and New York. My memory locks in on the taste of sugar-dusted beignets. Jazz trailing us every street we walked. Women in sequined bras leaning over wrought-iron balconies who whistled to prospects walking down Bourbon Street. A bus trip down Baton Rouge to visit Oak Alley plantation, evoking one of my all-time favorite books *Roots* which I read as a teenager. Statue of Liberty. An obedient row of ducks that stepped out of the elevator and marched single file on a red carpet at The Peabody.

The sprawling green acres everywhere we went captivated my soul, my reality being a country of nearly a billion humans who lived and worked and jostled each other for space. Families of six and seven lived crowded, claustrophobic lives in tiny, airless apartments while gigantic American homes contained so few people.

When my sister-in-law and family visited from the Midwest, I'd be awed by the content of their open suitcases, enchanted by the dreamy scents of soaps and lotions, bars of chocolates in every imaginable flavor, even tiny jars of baby food.

We're so close in the application process now that I can almost touch and taste the experience.

But this I know. Vacationing in a country is vastly different from living there. Friends and family have underscored all the reasons why it would be a mistake to uproot our lives and move to an unknown country and culture.

Do you know people there carry guns?

Teenagers kiss in the school hallways.

Ruki's at such an impressionable age. You think it's a good idea to expose her to a culture where sex, drugs, and alcohol are a way of life?

She'll forget her roots, our tradition and culture.

A truckload of ifs and buts are dumped on our ambivalent brains. G and I talk every night and the pendulum continues to swing. All the reasons why this would be a perfect move; then all the way over to the other side, wondering why we should trade our well-ensconced and comfortable lives for uncertainty.

"The company *will* find you a position, right?" I ask one night as we're rehashing pros and cons for the seven-hundredth time.

"Yes," says G. "That's nothing to worry about. It's one of the advantages of working for a global company."

"Do we know which part of the U.S. the company will move you to?"

"Chicago, most likely, is what I'm hearing."

I squeal with delight. "Ooh! That's where Oprah lives!"

"Right. And we're going to be her neighbors!" he teases.

"Sometimes I wonder if it'll be too much of a culture shock for Ruk. I mean, she's only fourteen."

"Of course. And not just Ruki. It's going to be very different for you and me as well. But she seems very excited. I haven't heard one negative argument from her."

"What if she finds it hard to make friends? Those kids, they seem so different."

"That's part of the challenge. We'll just have to trust that it all works out."

"What if we don't like it there?" I pause. "We may...but there's an equal chance we might not, right?"

"We'll rent our home here. Just in case things don't work out and we need to parachute back. I think the company will rehire me here."

I nod, unconvinced. It seems like a lot of work, tugging free the deep roots of our lives here to flirt with a six-month American experience. But we both know that opportunities don't arrive with iron-clad guarantees. Most of all, what we both agree on is that a bigger force holds the threads of these changes and decisions. We're united in our belief that we must choose faith over fear.

"If this is our time and we're meant to go, everything will line up," says G. "You and I both know that God is in charge here. We must trust that whatever will be will be."

A long exhale, and I touch the place inside me that knows. The place that knew G was the man for me. I know I can trust that place. Again.

෯

A few days later, a thick manila envelope arrives from the U.S. Consulate. Numerous forms to fill out. Health checks to schedule. Affidavits and notary signatures.

We mail the documents back and almost instantly they mail us a fresh set to review and action. Our dining room table is a sea of documents: marriage certificate, affidavits, letter from the employer, employment contracts, and ID's.

One September morning our interview letters arrive. There's a slight problem, though. G is in Spain on a business trip and won't be back in time for our interview. I remind myself of how we've been holding this opportunity lightly. Is this a test from the universe? Does this mean we're not meant to go—if he's unable to make the interview?

"Give them a call," says G. "If they can move our appointment to a different date, fine. If not, well then, I guess this is it. We don't go to America."

When I call, the consulate efficiently reschedules our appointment.

God is still calling the shots here.

The interview is a breeze. We're told to return to the Consulate in a couple of hours to pick up our provisional green cards.

"See what I mean?" says G. "Every step so far has been effortless. It feels as if this is meant to be."

Three hours later, our visas are stamped. It is real. We're about to cross an ocean to begin life in a new country in our mid-forties.

PART 3

Burning

EXPLOSION

I've had a love-hate relationship with telephones—landlines and cellphones—since January 27, 2009.

The day Amma died.

It was the ringing of a beige desk phone that announced the death of my mother, the voice of my brother breaking the news to me.

It was my husband's mobile phone—going straight to voice-mail—that cut off my oxygen supply in that moment of grief-stricken terror.

A friend's smart phone pings and flashes and interrupts intimate storytelling when I'm recounting a fond Amma memory.

The curious text-don't-talk culture we live in forces me to

condense a sorrowful ramble into bite-sized coherence.

Each word delivered through my brother's broken voice on this chilly January morning, a pile of stones crushing my chest. "Uma, I...I have some sad news." A pregnant pause, a portent of pain. "Amma passed away."

Everything in my body slows way down. Amma's breast cancer was diagnosed in May 2008 and she's pa... in January 2009?! My brain won't even let that word take form.

I convinced myself she'd be part of the survivor statistic. Now she will, forever, be a part of the cancer mortality statistic.

She can't have passed away. That can't be true. I spoke to her just two days ago.

"What?! How?"

"I don't know the details... it was very sudden. Maya and Guru are handling everything. But... I'm flying to Chennai. If you'd like to go..."

"How can I...? What about Ruki?"

My daughter is a sophomore in the nascent months of her American high school experience. How can I get on a plane and fly halfway across the world? She needs me. But then Amma needs me too. Or does she? She's not here to need me anymore. My baby sister—Maya—needs me. My husband needs me.

That's too many needy people. I can't take care of everyone.

My head is spinning. I don't know what to think, where to go, whether to go. Mahesh senses my utter inability to make sense, says *take care,* and hangs up. How do I do that?

Who will take care of me now that Amma is gone?

My overloaded brain suggests one solitary action: Call G. I grab my cell phone, my shaky thumb scrolls through and lands on my husband's name.

Sorry I'm unable to take your call. Please leave me your name, number, and a brief message and I'll call you back as soon as possible.

Someone please tell me the voicemail etiquette when you must inform your husband that your mother just died. I don't know. So I hang up.

My body can no longer hold me up on trembling legs. I slump onto the oatmeal-colored carpet, a deep primal wail rising up from the depths of my belly. *Amma, Amma, Amma.* I can't stop calling out to her. Where are you? How could you leave me? How do you expect me to go on? I can't. I just can't. I don't know how to live without you.

Endless labored lamenting. And out of nowhere, the sobs die down and a fury roars out of me. It has the power of a blaze that needs to burn something down. I rush to the family altar and rage at God. How could you do this? Oh, I trusted you. I prayed. But you let me down. You took her away. How could you?

Eight months. That's all the time she had from the time they caught the cancer. Not enough to even grow a baby.

A cancer diagnosis was the furthest thing from my mind that beautiful spring day in May when life was lush everywhere I looked. Three-week-old immigrants in Chicago, we'd spent the entire morning spring-drunk on the magical flora and fauna of the Botanical

Gardens.

A few hours later, I'd opened my laptop to find Maya's email that tilted my world forever. *Amma has cancer.*

And still later that same day, G had driven me to the nearest Barnes & Noble. "Let's get you a journal," he'd suggested. "You make sense of things when you write."

I curl up on the carpet and whimper, a broken child unable to fathom a world without her mother in it.

Every part of me wants to be in India. To weave myself into the known and comforting tapestry of family. To let this bottomless pain cut into me alongside the people who are living this nightmare: Appa, Maya, Vidya, my grandmother, aunts, uncles, and cousins.

Appa. I've been drowning so deep in my despair that I haven't spared a thought for him. Does he even understand the finality of this ending? The man who shared a bed with Amma for forty-seven years, silently watched her long dark hair fall out in clumps and barely questioned her changing appearance because his child-like brain didn't even understand the word "cancer." My already-shattered heart can barely stand it. Each shard is a fresh cut as I ponder Appa's abandoned self.

My ringing cell phone pierces the deathly silence of the wintry morning. I glance at the name, raise the phone to my ear, and manage to croak out, "It's Amma. She… she…" Speaking the words will make it real.

G's voice is calm, measured. "I'm so sorry, sweetheart. I'm

driving home right now. I'll be with you as soon as I can."

Driving from Indianapolis, it will be a couple of hours before he gets home. What do I do with myself? How do I hold my crumbling self until I feel his arms around me, gathering all of me?

Minutes later, my phone rings again. G has set up a three-way call. My brother and I are patched in. Fifteen minutes later, he's arranged air tickets for me and my brother's family to fly to Chennai for Amma's last rites.

When G walks in the front door and puts his arms around me, I fall apart all over again. He rubs my back and lets me cry. When my heaves and gulps finally subside he pulls out a giant handkerchief, wipes my face, and says, "Let's pack your suitcase, then we'll go pick up Ruki."

Incapable of formulating a coherent thought, let alone make decisions, I simply follow him into the bedroom. I stand in front of my closet and stare at clothes. Jeans. Tops. Skirts. Shirts. What does one pack for last rites? How many clothes? My body is vertical, but feels lifeless.

I feel G's hands on my shoulders, leading me away from my closet. He sits me down on the bed, then turns to the closet and starts to pull clothes off the hangers. As he's folding skirts and blouses, he fills me in. "You're flying on Lufthansa. Late-evening flight. Ruki and I will follow as soon as I've organized our tickets."

Ruki. Her grandmother was a constant and beloved presence in her life until we moved to Chicago. Amma is an entire universe of love to Ruki. Images flash across my mind. A colicky Ruki finding safety only in Amma's arms. Their cozy cuddle, watching Ruki's favorite show *Small Wonder*. Reading picture books. Playing board games. Amma always saved an extra bowl of spinach-in-coconut-gravy, Ruki's favorite dish. Ruki stayed with my parents when G and I took couples trips to the U.S. and Thailand.

How will my precious girl deal with the loss of an entire universe, one that sustained her from the day she was born?

Gigantic snowdrifts packed against the curb. Icicle-sculptures frozen on slanted roofs in mid-drip. The whoosh-whoosh of winter slush that car tires kick up. The tight fist of anxiety twisting in my belly.

An old man shovels his driveway, red-faced with exhaustion. A young woman stares at her phone while her dog is taking a pee. The unceasing motion of everyday life continues while mine has crashed to an abrupt halt. Tears roll down my cheeks, an endless outpouring. My husband drives silently, his one hand curled around mine.

We rush into the school lobby and request the front desk staff to alert Ruki. *Family emergency.* The PA system crackles to life, the starting point of an avalanche of chaos in her simple school day. Within minutes, Ruki's walking down the corridor, her urgent strides bridging the distance between us, her face clouded with worry.

My tongue refuses to speak the words that I can never, ever take back, the words that will forever alter the landscape of her life.

Her father steps up. "Ruki, sweetheart. There's no easy way for me to say this." One beat. *"Paati* passed away."

"Oh," is all Ruki says. She blinks swiftly, then swallows. There's no room for any embarrassing displays of emotion in a high school hallway.

"We need to get home," G continues. "Mama is leaving for Chennai on the evening flight."

She gives me a hug. "I'll go get my stuff," she says, marching off toward her classroom.

Seated in the backseat of our Honda Acura, safe from the awkward stares of her peers, Ruki allows her tears to flow. I reach for her hand, squeeze it. There are no words, just the shared intimacy of a loss that has stolen all our words away.

Back in our apartment, I wander from room to room like I'm exploring the void of After. My life, our lives have all morphed into strange unrecognizable shapes I can't relate to.

An hour later, my brother walks in the front door with his wife and toddler in tow.

Someone puts plates, cutlery, and food on the table. Was it me? Someone gathers my bags, tucks my ticket in my purse, and reminds me of it. Someone loads the dishwasher. Was it me? I'm walking through a wall of water, feeling my way, trying to keep my head up so I can breathe.

☙

Chicago to Frankfurt. Frankfurt to Mumbai. Mumbai to Chennai. Three airplanes, twenty-two hours. Time dissolves, fluid and mutable, as we fly through countries, continents, and time zones.

When the airplane finally spits us out, every limb in my body hurts. We gather our bags and clamber into a waiting taxi. The taxi ride from the airport is an exquisitely painful slow strangle. Finally, we're at my parents' apartment building. We stumble out, disheveled and weary.

Someone says, "They're here." I plod past a blur of faces, familiar and foreign. Friends, uncles, cousins, Amma's neighbors, the flower-seller, the woman who irons clothes, the watchman...

Maya is cutting a swift path through the throng to reach us. She collects us in a huddle and whispers, "Appa is in the hospital. He had a seizure. A team of doctors will bring him here in time for Amma's last rites."

Dear God. Is there a God? What kind of God piles on one burden on top of another without a chance to catch our breath?!

I walk in the front door of Amma's living room. It feels like wading through a river of sorrow. Tear-stained faces look at me. Someone squeezes my hand. An arm drapes over my shoulder. A palm strokes my cheek.

My eyes squirrel the room, searching for the one person I want to see. My ninety-one-year-old grandmother. Amma's mother. I find her in one of the bedrooms and thread my way toward her. Her arms flung open and empty, she sobs through the words, "She's left us...gone." I gather her soft, old hands in mine. We cry together, a daughterless mother and a motherless daughter.

"Go take a bath. It's getting late," someone hurries me. There are rituals to perform, auspicious timelines to honor. Did I remember to pack a sari? I have no idea what's in my suitcase. Maya hands me one of Amma's silk saris with a blouse to match and saves the moment.

I made every effort to avert my eyes from Amma's embalmed body in the glass box sitting in her living room. *Amma's body.* Those two words married together were my first earth-home. Her womb, where I started life. Amma's body has been a temple of devotion in service to her family. A refuge, a sanctuary, a place we all turned to for renewal.

Twenty minutes later. Bathed and dressed, I must now face the moment I've dreaded since the phone rang in our Chicago apartment. I must will my feet to walk up to the glass box that holds my mother's mortal remains and give her a grateful send-off, a final act of love.

⚜

I reenter the living room, this time searching for my aunt. Aunt Chandra—Amma's sister—and I have shared a special bond since I was a kindergartner screaming to let go of her when I had to step into the classroom. I cling to her; she holds me tight, our tears drenching each other's shoulder. Next she cups my face in her palms, looks at me directly and delivers strength into my eyes, then turns me around to face my mother's lifeless form.

This is not Amma, is my first thought. Her bluish skin, her distended belly, her expressionless face forever frozen.

A moment of sharp relief follows. *Ruki won't have to carry the burden of this image.*

My fingers claw at the coffin. Maybe if I just rescue her from this glass cage, she will come to life, blink her eyes open, sit up and smile at all her favorite people around her.

But my mother remains stiff and mute and gray as my tears fall and fall and fall, unable to gather me in her arms and comfort me as she used to. I bury my face in my aunt's shoulder, unable to watch as two men lift her body out of the box and place it on the floor in preparation for the last rites.

Relatives and friends try to staunch my tears, fix my sorrow with utter inanities like, "She suffered so much; at least it's over" or "Appa needs you all now. You must be strong for him."

Soon, the priest pronounces the auspicious hour and requests my sisters and me to step forward. The honor of bathing Amma's body and preparing her for her final journey falls to her three daughters. It's a fitting parting gift to the mother who cared for us all her life. The priest places brass pots of holy water in our waiting palms in readiness for the purification ritual. *Walk three circles around her and pour the holy water on her body.* As the water hits her face, her nostrils, Amma doesn't flinch. But I do. It's a punch in the gut.

The mother I adore is not in this body anymore. Her vibrant joyful essence has escaped, the body now an empty shell, a pile of tissue that has served its earthly purpose.

Next, we rub freshly ground turmeric paste on her forehead, cheeks, and feet. I apply a dot of vermilion *kumkum* powder in the center of her forehead. We lay jasmine and marigold on her head, place a rose garland upon her, then drape her cold body in the warm tones of a gorgeous mango-yellow silk sari.

What happens next is a moment I will return to innumerable times. It is *the moment* my Soul expands out of my physical body, taps me on the shoulder and whispers "It's time."

The startling clarity of this moment will stay with me for days and weeks and I will call it my *moment of awakening.* It is a moment I will mark as a turning point in my life.

It is the moment I died and was reborn.

"The hospital van is here," someone says, alerting us to Appa's arrival.

I look up. My father stands in the doorway hunched over his walker, his face grief wracked. Two attendants guide him to a chair next to Amma's body. He eases into it, shadows of pain and confusion playing out on the landscape of his features. "Why did you leave me? How will I manage without you?" His voice cracks, the emotion too heavy to carry.

Wordlessly the four of us close ranks around him, a physical protection of progeny we believe will shield him from the tsunami of heartbreak. "We'll take care of you, Appa," I say, rubbing his clammy hand to remind him that we're still here. He sobs silently as the priest continues his rhythmic chants. The four of us bear witness, unable to buffer him from the horror of losing the person who shared a life with him for forty-seven years.

The priest alerts us. *The last sequence of rites will be conducted in the courtyard.* The attendants signal that it's time for Appa to head back before his circuits suffer emotional overload. A swell of emotion rises within me as I watch Appa's retreating back. I need my father. But my father needs me more. He's as bereft as a child who has lost a beloved mother, the events that led up to this moment a frightening puzzle he cannot make sense of.

The pall bearers take their positions, place Amma's body on a bamboo bier, and carry her outside. What was, so far, a private expression of grief now moves into the public arena. We circle Amma's body seven times throwing rice grains in her mouth, a symbolic act of feeding her soul that must traverse a long journey before it attains *moksha* and merges with the One.

The courtyard crowd grows bigger. Drivers, maids, and random onlookers want one last glimpse. The flower-seller who brought flowers for Amma's deities and the woman who ironed her clothes dab the corners of their eyes with the soft ends of their cotton saris. They touch her feet and seek her blessings. Amma has transcended the realm of mortals. She is now a soul, her divinity restored.

The pallbearers carry the bier, slide it into the back of the van. Amma's silk-draped body is ready to take its last journey to the crematorium. The silk sari that shrouds her body, the sole possession that Amma takes with her on her final journey. I'm still staring at her lifeless body imagining that it might come to life when a sliver of golden light pierces the gray fog around my brain and deposits a thought.

It doesn't come to me in the moment. I fail to register the

significance of this idea and the power with which it will turn my life upside down. What I don't yet know is this: buried in these words is a powerful summons from my soul.

We come into this world with nothing. We leave with nothing. Why, then, do we spend our entire lives acquiring, accumulating, and chasing after stuff?

My brother and uncle climb inside the van. Mahesh will collect her ashes a few hours from now and immerse them in the ocean, the chanting of shlokas and churning surf carrying Amma's mortal remains deep into the ocean's watery womb.

❧

Inside the apartment, we wash the floors, cleanse the space, light a single oil lamp to place in the spot where we washed and bathed Amma's body. We will wake through the night, taking turns to tend to the flame, for it must burn for three days and three nights straight.

Walking through the rooms of my parents' apartment, I touch the things Amma touched just days ago. The bifocals with the badly scratched lenses she reached for soon after she woke up in the morning. The small jar of Vicco Turmeric cream she smoothed into her face after a bath, the smells of sandalwood and turmeric mingling in the air. A small stack of *Ananda Vikatan,* her favorite magazine to savor before her afternoon snooze. Her faded and frayed home slippers. The items that signaled moments of transition in her day.

Later in the day I toss her nightgown into the washing machine. All her stuff is still here, but it's as if *she* never was. An entire human's sixty-plus years of existence has been erased. How does a person go from living a full, embodied life to vanishing in one quick instant, the last breath canceling out everything?

The 160-pound body that took up space, had needs and desires, and a context for the humans in her orbit is now an invisible essence floating in the ethers. She is now memories in photo albums. The albums that will fade over time, memories morphing as the brain sifts, sieves, and shifts on its journey through time and space.

Where did she go? It's a question that will haunt me for a long time, the exploration of which will open a sacred portal into death and dying. For now, all that is present and real is the ache in every bone that carries the weight of grief.

✿

G and Ruki arrive in Chennai a few days after the last rites, their transatlantic journey long and arduous because of winter weather delays.

"Samira called," G says. "She'd like to have you over for a meal." Samira is a friend I seldom decline.

I shake my head no.

"It'll do you good to get out of the house," he tries.

"I don't *want* to go."

"She's just being nice."

"Then maybe *you* should go."

"I'm only trying to help you feel better..."

"No!" The strength of my vehemence surprises me.

My husband's *I-want-to-fix-your-pain* attitude feels like skin being ripped off an open wound. *This is my pain. I'll damn well wallow in it.* I swallow the words I want to hurl at him.

I want to sit right here—in the living room—where Amma breathed and moved and lived. It's where I feel closest to her. The vicious grip of pain is my last link to her. I don't want to go any-where. I don't want to do anything. I just want to sit next to Maya who has been on this eight-month cancer trajectory with Amma and bombard her with questions: what did Amma say, what did she eat, and how did she look leading up to the last moments of her life. I'm so tired I want to sleep. No, I don't, because when I wake up I'll lose Amma all over again.

The world outside Amma's front door is suddenly wild, teem-ing with irrational dangers. A world without her in it untethers me. Amma never worked outside the home a single day of her life. She was ridden by anxiety if she had to travel alone and rarely made decisions without consulting the entire family. How did she come to represent safety and security in my life such that I am terrified to face the world now?

SCORCHED

Two weeks after Amma's death, Ruki and I are back in suburban Chicago. G is still in India, finishing up work-related travel. My high school sophomore is instantly sucked into a stream of schoolwork and theater rehearsals.

My new job at the retirement community—teaching basic computer skills to the seniors—is waiting for me. Three weeks into the job I'd flown to India for Amma's last rites. The very thought of wearing my work clothes and work face is exhausting. All I want to do is curl up in bed with a fluffy blanket around my shivering body and stew in my sadness.

That's a great option if you want to lose the only job you found.

Monday morning, I drag myself under the shower, pull on my

black pants and cobalt blue shirt, and slide behind the wheel of my Toyota Corolla. I'm forty-five years old but I've been driving less than three months. My fingers wrap around the cold leather of the steering wheel and my stomach muscles clench. The wintry white landscape adds an extra dimension of terror to the experience.

The seniors at the retirement community greet me like I've never been away. Today I'm grateful for minds that have forgotten, rheumy eyes that don't register my sadness, and slow-moving humans who must focus all their energy and attention on pushing their walkers forward.

In the evening, I pick up Ruki after her play rehearsal and plod around the kitchen making heavy weather of getting a meal together while she disappears into her room to do homework. G has stacked the freezer with an array of nuke-friendly veggie meals. We will, over time, become zealous label-readers. But for now, the ease of an instant meal is a lovely novelty, coming as we do from a culture where every meal is a production that spans the spectrum from chopping to final garnish.

I stare at the boxes, spoiled for choice. My stomach feels queasy at the sight of all this food. My body has forgotten how to be hungry. I crave Amma's simple, home-made *rasam*—a fragrant lentil-and-tomato broth she'd season with a teaspoon of ghee, drizzling chopped fresh green cilantro as a final touch.

I envy my teenager's appetite as she wolfs down rice pilaf and curry and helps herself to seconds. A half hour later, the kitchen counters are wiped, the dishes are drying on the rack, and I kiss

Ruki goodnight.

Now it's just me and my ever-present companion, Sister Grief.

We come into this world with nothing. We leave with nothing.

Sitting by the warm pool of lamplight in the living room the tears I've held in all day begin to fall. In the breath that catches in my chest is the longing for my sisters, my family in India. Suburban Chicago feels like a lonely planet where I'm cut off from everything that means comfort and compassion.

I think of my sisters. Nothing matches, not our roles, realities, or time zones. Maya is in the middle of her workday as my day is ending, and Vidya's day is just beginning. Appa is Maya's main focus; my five-year-old nephew is Vidya's; and here I am, tending to the elderly whose worlds I barely know.

I don't have a single friend in this country. No one whose hand I can hold, or shoulder to weep on. My mother is invisible here. Nobody knows her. There are stories, but no one to share them with. What sense does it make to tell someone about a character in a book they haven't read? Amma doesn't exist in this new life of mine; and she dies all over again, buried in lonely anonymity.

I miss my husband. I miss his arms, my safe space where I know I'll be held. He calls often, tries to tune into my mood through the sound of my voice. But something in our dynamic feels different now. Maybe it's because I have nothing to give. It's hard to stretch a conversation that starts with him asking, "How are you feeling?" and me saying, "I'm sad all the time." He alternates between awkward silence and trying to fix my sadness. It feels inadequate, hurtful. The harder I cry, the harder he tries. He feels responsible for my happiness. He wants me to be happy. What he doesn't know is that I can't allow myself to be *happy*, that happiness will cut me off from the last thing that ties me to Amma. My grief is the final cord of attachment that connects us. I hear the frustration in his sighs. We say bye and hang up.

Outside the window, snow falls from a heavy sky. Frost carves patterns on windows and frozen icicles hang from sloping roofs. It's my first winter, the first time I've scooped snow in my gloved palm. But I'm not available to its magic. Frozen in my endless pain I wonder when, if ever, I will thaw.

Sunday morning. Ruki and I are at Dominick's, our local grocery store. I stand in front of the fruit bin and stare at apples and oranges. It appears that I've lost the simple ability to buy fruit. Pick up apple. Smell it. Feel it. Toss it into cart. But I stand there, the simple sequence lost to me, unsure what to do next. Thankfully, my fifteen-year-old rescues the situation. She slides the grocery list from my limp fingers, grabs apples and oranges, then purposefully wheels the cart around the aisles grabbing low-fat yogurt, frozen waffles, milk, and dishwasher detergent. I follow her, grateful to be relieved from the superhuman task of making decisions about brands and bargains.

One evening I'm sitting in the living room lost in thought—my current default setting—when Ruki walks up to me.

"Ma," she begins. "I really don't like that you're home alone so much."

I work at the senior living community, The Palms, from 10 A.M. to 1 P.M. Ruki doesn't get home until seven, now that the opening night of her school play is close and rehearsals are in high gear. Her dad is still in India on work, so she knows I have a good half-a-dozen hours to waste or weep before she's back home with me.

"I can drop out of the play," she says. "It's not like I'm *in* the play. I'm just the Stud Ass. Miss Smith will find someone else."

I smile at her reference to Stud Ass, the theater crowd's lingo for Student Assistant. "No way," I protest. "This is your dream, Ruk, and I can see how much fun you're having."

"Yeah, but as we go into tech week I'll be home even later."

"That's okay. Dad will be back by then."

"But you know he'll travel again."

"Sweetheart, I love how much you care, but you don't have to do this."

"Mama, I don't know. I just feel—"

Ruki's been paying attention. All my usual distractions—reading, Oprah shows, writing—have lost their charm. Bogged down alternately by the intensity and lethargy of grief, most days my energy tank is at zero. But *my* grief is *my* job. It's not something my fifteen-year-old must feel responsible for. I pat the empty spot on the couch beside me.

"Come, sit," I say. Ruki settles down, tucking her legs beneath her. "It's really sweet of you to worry about me. I want to be honest with you. I'm not going to be fine. Not for a while. But I'll be okay. It's only been three weeks since..." I pause, the words sticking in my craw. "But I don't want you to quit the play to stay home with me. You have to trust that I'm going to be okay."

I put my arms around her, and we cry together. "It's okay to cry," I say. "We love *Paati,* and we miss her. And I'm not going to hide every time I cry. When we cry together, we're here for each other. There are good times and bad. And we share it all. That's what being family means."

G returns home two weeks later and our lives fall into a familiar groove. When you have a high school sophomore with a 6 A.M. schedule, you just get up and get going. We clean. We cook. We shop. We do laundry. We arrange our lives around Ruki's school schedules.

Somehow I believe that showing up for life and willing time to move will make my grief recede further and further, that my heavy heart will lighten with every new calendar day. Yet everything feels stuck—and different.

Grief is a whole new country, I'm discovering. I have no map and often find myself stumbling through swift weather changes. As quickly as I try to grab onto a ray of light that pokes through pewter skies, the skies dissolve into a torrential downpour. And I stand there, drenched and in despair.

The bottomless river of tears that pours out of me baffles my husband. Not only has my pre-loss default setting been happiness; I manufacture and bottle it for the rest of my family. Now my singular setting has become 'unpredictable.' G doesn't know how to rescue me from the white waters I helplessly flounder in. He has used up the few words of comfort in his 'consolation' vocabulary. Every time he looks at me the question I see looming large in his eyes is: What's happening to you?

His loss seems as real as mine.

"Haven't you cried enough?" he asks.

The frustration embedded in his question renders me speechless.

How could he! My mother just died.

"You're going to make yourself ill."

Again, not very helpful. Stop talking.

"I don't care," I snap.

"I say this *because* I care."

He calls this caring?!

"Don't tell me how..." I leave my sentence unfinished because I'm loath to defend my emotional state or explain when my setting will return to 'happy' again.

Shoulders hunched, he walks away retreating into a sullen silence, his attempts at 'caring' rebuffed. I feel abandoned and alone, the salt of his words stinging my open wound. The chasm that yawns between us is real. His childhood wound of *not good enough* and my wound of *you don't matter* move into positions on opposite sides, ready for battle.

You're too sensitive. You cry too easily. You need to be stronger.

Words that have been uttered to me over and over again.

The same words torment me one morning when a wave of grief knocks me over and crushes me while I'm at work. Overcome by shame I escape to the nearest empty stairwell and have an ugly cry. When I return to my desk with swollen eyes my co-worker and dear friend Andy gives me a hug.

Then he looks at my sad face and asks, "Hey. Listen. Have you thought about therapy?"

I've never been to therapy. I have no clue how to find a therapist. In India, my family, and friends of the family were my therapy. But here I am, trying to navigate these unfamiliar choppy waters all on my own. My husband, stunned by the enormity of my grief, wears a bewildered look these days. The only thing that feels real these days is my grief; yet I don't know how to do it alone.

I shake my head no. I sense I'm holding inside me a river of tears I have to cry. Sitting in a therapist's office and talking about my feelings isn't going to make it all better. What my soul craves is a gentle guide who can walk beside my grieving self—a spiritual Sherpa—and open me to the deeper mysteries of death and dying.

We come into this world with nothing. We leave with nothing.

This singular truth, the one that triggered my awakening, keeps me up in the wee hours. More questions are pushing their way to the surface. The need for a mentor who can help me open to them feels urgent. *What happens when we die? Where do we go? Do we come back? Is this a one-way ticket or a return-trip?*

Andy cuts into my thoughts. "Why don't you meet Randy?"

"Who's Randy?"

"He's my housemate."

"Is *that* what they call it these days?" Andy is the only person who can get me to crack a joke in the middle of a death-and-dying conversation.

He laughs, shakes his head. "No. It's not what you're thinking. We're just buddies."

"Okay, go on," I say, my tongue pushing my cheek out.

"I'm *serious!*"

"Okay, I'm kidding. Tell me more."

"Randy spends most of his time mentoring young Christians."

He's Christian. I'm Hindu. I know nothing about the Bible. And I'm not crazy about being bait for religious conversion.

"I don't know anything about the Bible," I say. "And I don't know if that's what I'm looking for."

"Oh, Rand doesn't force stuff on anyone. He's really cool. Why don't you guys meet? See if you vibe."

And that's how Randy, a white Christian man, opens the doors of his beautiful heart to my questioning Hindu self. Randy will mentor me for the next two-and-a-half years, holding space for my soul inquiry with books, discussions, and reflections.

"God can, and will, use your pain," he says often. Something in his words strikes a chord. My mind flashes back to Sister Valerie, the nun who taught me Psychology in college, the only human who was privy to my suffering. "I see how much you're suffering because of your father's drinking," I hear her soft, gentle voice. "But God is carving a statue out of you, child. It hurts when He chisels and sculpts, but when He's finished with you, what will emerge is a beautiful statue that will bring joy and beauty to the world."

What I hear in their combined wisdom is *There's a purpose to all this suffering.*

My ninety-minute monthly sessions with Randy are a safe harbor in the midst of my furious storm. All pretenses and defenses melt away during these sessions and my messy self shows up full on. I weep. I rail. I rant.

Our sessions being pro bono, Randy can only fit me in for a single monthly session. I need more. As we discuss possible options, Randy moots the idea of a grief support group at a neighborhood church.

"What's a grief support group?" I ask, as he hands me a copy of *Life of the Beloved.* We're getting ready to work through the spiritual themes in Henry Nouwen's book.

"It's a group where people who are grieving come together, talk, share, and generally offer support. I think it'll be useful," he says, jotting down the name of the church on a slip of paper.

In the absence of my Indian village, and a husband who's confounded by my grief, a group of fellow grievers sounds like the closest thing I'll have to a family here.

My heart won't stop hammering. My mouth is so dry I could choke on my tongue. My feet want to flee. I'm standing in the atrium of a megachurch, a monolithic steel-and-glass structure, the home of Jesus who started life in a humble manger. I gawk at the café, impressive rows of decadent desserts lined up in a display cabinet. All around me are potted plants and cool curtains of gurgling water. Scripture verses make up wall posters. Elegant computer stations are neatly tucked away in discreet corners.

The Indian churches I've occasionally visited with my Christian friends rarely contained anything more than a wooden cross and a bleeding Jesus, functional pews, a Bible, incense, and a small bunch of flowers.

This church seems more five-star spa, less a place of worship. All my assumptions are upended. My insecurities rush to the surface. Everywhere I look, white people wearing officious looks scurry around. I rub my forearm, hyper aware of my brown skin.

Making my way to the auditorium, I stand at the doorway and peek inside. It's as vast as a sports field in there. Round tables with placards announce the type of grief support offered: *Loss of Spouse. Loss of Sibling. Loss of Child. Loss of Parent.* I pick my way through a crowd of grievers, all scanning the room to locate their table.

I find my group and a chair, then glance at the people in my circle. Tamara. I learn that she's our group leader from her name badge. Her warm smile helps slow down my heartbeat.

Once everyone is seated, Tamara bows her head to lead us in prayer. We take her cue. Then, she invites each of us to share whatever's on our hearts. Everyone looks around the table, waiting for someone to begin.

Grief has its unique timbre. The thought of giving voice to your pain is scary. Before you've spoken three words, your throat floods with tears, trembles, and cracks. Your pain is now spilling all over the place, a glass of red wine that seeps into, and stains everything it touches.

Some brave person finds a shred of courage and begins. She chokes, stumbles over her words. The person sitting next to her reaches out a hand, steadies her. We pause, share the weight of the moment. We stitch our words together to help each other. Our Indian, Swedish, Italian, Polish, and Latina skins fall away. Pain has no color, ethnicity, or specific geography. We're all survivors who have chanced upon a shore, a space where we can cry without being judged 'overemotional,' vent our fury without shame, and speak the unspeakable: what we failed to say, do, and give, the enormous regrets that weigh us down.

When the circle ends, I leave with the comfort that grief is a universal thread in the tapestry of humanity. I'm not a crazy person; I'm a human who feels things deeply. I will return to this group week after week for nine whole weeks—to our little tribe that must learn to survive the storm that battered our lives.

LUMINOUS

In the turbulence of grief is a tiny island of peace: my work at the retirement community. Tending to humans at the sunset of their lives, somehow, feels meaningful. The community has created an online portal for them. My 'job' is to teach them how to send emails and stay connected to far-flung family. I also help them upload their yellowing photos—of streetcars, one-room schoolhouses, gramophones, and juke boxes—so their grandchildren can peek into a world that once existed. It doesn't take me long to figure out that old folks with arthritic fingers and macular degeneration aren't exactly enthusiastic toward a digital keyboard and mouse. What they're much more open to is easy companionship and a listening ear. I'm invited to tea when they open thick photo albums and introduce me to another era and tell me long rambling tales about streetcar dates and dancing the foxtrot.

When this was the only part-time position that had opened up for me back in early 2009, I'd seriously questioned the wisdom of the universe. I took it because the economy was in freefall and jobs scarce. But what did I—an immigrant from South Asia—know about the ways and worlds of American seniors?! It was all utterly foreign to me, their food, music, movies, and religious persuasion.

Never question the wisdom of the universe, is what I learned.

As I settle down with Doris, Mary, or Jeanette, it dawns on me. I may have no clue who Dean Martin is or the lyrics of "Dancing in the Rain," but I do know empathy. My heart hurts for the losses these elders have survived. They've had to say goodbye to an entire era of living: homes and neighborhoods where they brought their babies home, raised them, and sent them out in the world. They've traded in their cars, their independence, their fifty-year friendships. In turn, they offer me the gift of understanding as they validate how confusing it must be for me to be uprooted from my country and culture when I'm mourning my mother.

The grief of dislocation becomes the bridge that connects our hearts.

Every day I have the blessing of companioning someone whose emotional baggage weighs them down. An adult daughter fighting cancer. A stepson who is let go from his job. A grandson struggling with drug addiction. The death of a best friend, the terrible loss of connection in a sixty-year marriage when a spouse is diagnosed with Alzheimer's.

As I hold their wrinkled hands, zip my heart wide open, and allow their pain to enter me, something amazing happens. My pain mingles with theirs and we're both carried on the soft current of compassion.

The days when I open my eyes and the morning light reminds me of my loss all over again, these seniors pull me up and out of my self-centered agenda. They imbue my life with fresh purpose. Every time I listen to someone, normalize their tears, or hold their hand, my own load is lighter. I set down my sorrow for a while, pull a deep breath into my lungs, and am present to life again. It's true, what they say. The line between healing yourself and others is faint, often invisible.

❧

Winter chill burrows into my bones. I can't seem to get warm, no matter how many layers I wear. Grief messes with my inner thermostat. I lie awake late at night curled inside my cozy comforter, my toes freezing inside fuzzy socks. That singular question—why we spend all our lives acquiring, accumulating, and chasing after stuff—is the ticker tape running inside my head. It triggers multiple questions.

Who am I? Who did I come here to be?

Why am I here? What did I come here to do?

How am I meant to live my life?

We arrive in a tiny human body. We grow and grow and grow some more. We go to school. We get degrees. We get jobs. We get married. We get the bigger job, the bigger salary, the fancier house. We retire. If we're among the fortunate we limp into old age with nothing more threatening than the typical aches and niggles. And when our time is up, we leave. Vanish without a trace.

My soul tells me that I'm missing a few key pieces of the puzzle. *There's got to be a point to all of this.*

I have no idea what that point is, but the question pounds at my skull. *Who am I? Who am I? Who am I?* I know I'm a soul, but my identity has been anchored in my roles. Daughter. Sister. Wife. Mother. Writer. Trainer/Coach. So, I tuck the questions into some far corner, a mental nook, and attend to life.

When I was in Chennai for Amma's last rites, a friend handed me a copy of *The Tibetan Book of Living and Dying* by Sogyal Rinpoche. I pick up the book and begin to turn the pages. The words gently nudge awake a part of me that's been blissfully asleep. The book rouses me from the trance of the life I've been living and opens my eyes to the inevitability of death and dying. *Everything that is born must die.* The pettiness of holding onto grudges and grouses in the scheme of the finite nature of this life we've been given seems like an awful waste of time. Being laser-focused on what I'm here to create while I'm still here takes on a new urgency. Amma had sixty-eight years, then she vanished like a wisp of smoke, leaving behind her lingering soul fragrance.

My mind travels back in time to the flower-seller at Amma's death rites. What she remembered about Amma. *Amma always asked about my son who is not mentally well. She always saved a box of sweets for me during the festivals.*

Like morning light rinsing the darkness of the night sky, it dawns on me. Life is never about what we take with us. It's always about what we leave behind. Love is what Amma left behind. She lives on in the warm memories of the people whose lives she touched while she was here. Love was her most precious offering to the world. Our only job is to leave our heart print as we move through our world. That's what lives on long after we're dead.

The need to cleanse my moral slate powers me with fresh resolve. I begin to make a list of people I've wronged, fallen out of favor with, cut out of my life, held a grudge against—and commit to making it right. Over the next days and weeks, I write emails and letters. I call. I seek forgiveness. I offer apologies and take ownership for my part in the estrangement/conflict. What's different this time is that I'm no longer attached to their reaction to my apology. Some won't forgive me. Some will continue to be angry with me. My sole agenda is to clean up my side of things. When I'm done, I feel as if I've shed karmic pounds.

Being mindful that we're not promised tomorrow seems a kinder way to live today.

Wheelchair-bound seniors are energized to push their wheels a little faster when they see me, 'the computer lady' approaching. The ones with walkers pick up the pace when they spot me in the distance. As much as they love me, I represent the Computer Lab, their least favorite destination. Their dislike of digital education is a real problem, but I know my job is to encourage them to try.

I don't enjoy alienating the seniors. If anything, I want them to feel more connected with me, their peers, and themselves—not less.

That thought is the seed for a Life Story group in the community, an opportunity for the seniors to sit in a circle and share stories from their lives. Buoyed by the support of the management, I gather the seniors every Monday afternoon with a list of questions I generate on a specific theme. *Favorite Travel Memories. Songs of the Thirties. Best Friends. Holiday Celebrations.*

Occasionally, I sneak in a questionnaire on a sticky topic. *Forgiveness. Legacy. Regrets.* As the seniors warm up to me and to each other, they open their hearts. The thaw is gradual but over the weeks and months, the crust around their hearts—hardened by tough living during wars and the Depression era—begins to soften.

The stories of healing are heartwarming. One woman calls her adult son after years of estrangement. Another seeks forgiveness from a friend she cut ties with because of a silly misunderstanding, the details of which neither can recall. One of the ladies who attends my group starts to chronicle her stories, a legacy of love for her family.

It is humbling to watch them set down years of hard and heavy emotional baggage and embrace peace and reparations as a way to live out the final chapters of their lives. Many of them struggle to have conversations about death and dying with their adult children and families. They feel safer to venture into that scary territory in our little safe space. It's a sacred witnessing I'm grateful for.

May 2009. Nearly four months after Amma died, G and I feel the need for more elbowroom and thus begins the search for a town-home. Our realtor drives us around potential properties, we go to open houses, and pore over blueprints. Now that I have a steady paycheck coming in, the dream feels closer. The perfect home presents itself by the end of June and we become first-time immigrant homeowners.

As I empty out closets, sort through stuff, and pack boxes, grief is my constant companion. It pulls me under when I least expect it and reminds me that nothing in my current life is more important than being present to the emotions that rise up. A part of me feels shame for still crying, still having bad days, still not getting it together. As if I'm doing grief wrong. It's because I'm the only one who's crying. Shared grief is so much easier to hold. I also don't have the ability to condense this primeval outpouring of emotion into tidy sentences anyone can understand—least of all, my husband.

I've noticed that frustration, anger, and impatience are regulars, recognized acquaintances in G's life. They drop by unannounced and leave in due course. Grief, however, is a stranger, a suspicious character who is unwelcome. A threat to the deeply held values of fortitude, control, and presenting a brave face to the world.

He is helpless in the face of my messy grief. He doesn't know how to fix my pain or make it go away. Nor does he know when I'll be 'okay.' 'Okay' in my life has gone on a long walk with no return date on the horizon.

With no one to share the weight of this sorrow, I carry it alone.

Back in Chennai, Maya has her own struggles—a full-time job, travel, and tending to Appa's needs. Hired nurse-assistants come and leave, threatened by Appa shaking his cane at them and his utter lack of cooperation. Locking himself up in the bathroom and refusing to open the door, Appa has managed to rile the most resilient of those nurses. It pains me to hear that Maya has had to rush home to rescue the situation, interrupted by an urgent call in the middle of a work meeting.

Given this situation, complaining to her about the emotional loneliness in my marriage seems downright churlish. I try not to take up space on our transatlantic phone conversations and choose to focus on Appa instead. I allow her the space and time to vent, happy to do this small thing and contribute to her mental wellbeing.

Locked inside my private hell, my grief experience alienates me from anyone who's uncomfortable with it. Especially the person who held my hand and shepherded me to the safest shelter in every storm we've lived through. This storm, it's become clear to me, is mine to navigate alone. It's an awfully lonely place to be. We're stranded on opposite sides of an engorged river, the only bridge between us rickety, unsafe.

What is sometimes even more painful than grief is the slow erasure of the loving moniker *Amma* from our family vocabulary. Shorn of its deep tones of affection it has become a landmine word, one that could trigger the ground beneath our feet to explode when we least expect it, cause floods of tears, and an indeterminate descent into depression. Maybe G feels the need to protect me (himself?) from the possibility of an explosion.

I'm not ready to let go. I wonder if I'll ever be.

SNUFFED OUT

As much as I'm enjoying my work at The Palms it's increasingly clear that things aren't exactly rosy at the partner company that hired me. People are let go. Budget cuts are a reality. By the spring of 2010, my hours have been slashed to five a week, and I'm mostly dealing with boring admin tasks. I find myself straining at a leash that gets shorter and shorter by the day.

Reflecting on the work I've been doing for a year reminds me of how easeful it used to be. It was the days before the computer lab was set up. My job was to get to know the community residents. I'd walk the long hallways each morning, a prayer on my lips. *Use me, God, wherever my presence is needed.* My feet would mysteriously stop outside a random apartment door. Somehow, the senior who opened the door to me was invariably in need of comfort: a hug, a story to share, tears to be witnessed. Thirty minutes later, they'd thank me for showing up as if the Lord had heard their prayer. It happened over and over, deepening my trust in the Divine. *I'm a messenger on a mission.*

Every interaction with the residents of the community brings back fond memories of my paternal grandma, an indelible part of my childhood who shaped the storyteller in me. She died of old age in her bed at home, surrounded by family. Both my maternal grandparents lived with my uncle and aunt until the end of their lives.

Something in my heart breaks every morning when I enter this community. The seniors here live in fancy apartments but lead lonely, isolated lives and get to see their family only on the weekend or during a community event like Mother's Day.

Conceding to the seniors' resistance to stepping into the computer lab, I try to serve them in ways that are meaningful to them. But with my dwindling hours, the company begins to question my approach. I cannot bill the hours I spend 'chatting' with residents. They'd like me to use my time to convince the seniors of the need to become digitally proficient. The leash is now beginning to strangle me.

I want to offer them what they need. And what they need is companionship.

In a world where bottom lines and profit margins rule, my opinions are simply white noise. My frustration reaches boiling point and one day I decide to quit my so-few-hours-and-so-much-heartache job. I'm down to earning nickels and dimes anyway—and I'm bored to tears every minute of the five hours I spend logging data into the system.

There is one problem, though. I've grown attached to many of the seniors. The thought of walking through my day without their weathered faces marking its passage brings up some sorrow. The Life Story group I started is thriving and the grief of bailing on that circle is real. I wrestle with myself day and night. The situation is ridiculous: force the seniors to do something they have zero interest in (learn how to email) and take away the social connection they truly crave (sit around the table and share stories). I have little control over any of it, but the sheer injustice of putting profits over people angers me. Every day the idea of quitting sounds more and more attractive.

Next morning, I'm organizing files at my desk when the intercom buzzes. It's the Activities Director.

"Hi Dina," I say, wondering if she's calling about a scheduling change. The start time of my Life Story group gets pushed back occasionally when a community shindig is on the calendar.

"Hi Uma. Would you mind stopping by my office before you leave today?" Dina asks.

"Sure. A calendar change?"

"Well," she pauses a moment to consider. "No, it's fine. I'll just tell you when I see you," and Dina hangs up on me. As puzzled as I am by our cryptic exchange, my attention is soon diverted by a flurry of emails that land in my inbox.

When I stop by Dina's office which is in the lower level of the building, she's on the phone. I pop into the Art & Craft room next door to say hello to the seniors whose heads are bent over their artistic creations. One of them is painting a watery blue sky while another is coloring spring flowers into her garden.

"Come on over, Uma. I'm done talking," Dina hollers.

Dina's desk is a holy mess. Files and loose sheets of paper are stacked tall, a precarious pile. Dina has a new granddaughter whose baby photo is pinned to the board above her desk.

"What's up?" I ask.

"Well, a little bird told me some big news." Dina raises her eyebrows and shoots me an enquiring look.

The news of my leaving isn't official yet. But I've shared it with a couple of seniors, the ones I'm closest to, hating the thought of springing a surprise on them. They pinky-swore confidentiality but may have let it slip.

"Oh, you heard," I say, making a sad face.

"That's what I want to chat with you about. And I wanted to catch you before you made your decision public and told everyone."

I wait for her to say more, not sure what she's getting at.

"Are you taking up another job?" Dina asks.

"I don't have one lined up, if that's what you're asking."

"Then, we'd like you to keep coming here and running the Life Story group."

My jaw drops. "Really??!!"

"The seniors *love* your group. It's one of the most popular ones on my Activities Calendar. So, if you'd like to keep coming back, we'd love to have you."

"Keep coming back?! God, Dina. I've spent sleepless nights wondering if there was some way to keep coming back—even if I'm quitting the partner company. You know I adore these seniors. You have no idea—" and then the tears come, happy tears because I get to keep doing the work I love. As the realization sinks in, I bounce on my feet unable to contain the joy of this invitation to stay.

Dina starts to laugh. "Look at you!"

"Can I give you the biggest hug?"

Dina gets up from her chair and I scoop her up, swaying from side to side in pure elation. Then I wave goodbye and float right out of the room on a cloud of euphoria. The universe knew how to slice this cake just right, I think. Keep all the delicious creamy frosting and the red cherry, let the rest go.

I will run that Life Story group for the next decade.

I quit my computer lab position at The Palms in mid-April, then fly to India in July to spend some time with Appa. While I'm in Chennai a series of health fluctuations lands Appa in the hospital, his condition deteriorates, and he passes away in early August. Exactly eighteen months and twelve days after Amma died. As much as we mourn him, the overarching feeling is one of relief that his soul has fled the compromised body-cage ending his seventeen-year-long struggle.

G arrives in Chennai one day before Appa passes.

My siblings and I are with Appa in the hours before he takes his last breath. We rub his feet, tell him how much we love him, sing his favorite songs, and let him know he's free to go. We promise to look out for each other.

G encourages me to extend my stay in Chennai. He knows it will help soften the grief Maya will meet within herself given the care and devotion she has invested in managing Appa. "You had to rush back to Chicago when Amma died. Stay longer this time if you want to. I'll put travel on hold so I can be home with Ruki," he says.

I don't have a job in Chicago to rush back to. I'll fly back home a couple of weeks after Ruki starts senior year. So, I extend my stay in Chennai by another month. Maya and I sort through Appa's stuff and decide what to donate, toss, and keep. We grieve. We laugh. We tell stories. We heal.

"You'll miss Appa. He's lived with you all this time," I say to Maya.

She looks wistful, smiles. "He'd become my child. But he was such a sweet one. Yeah, I'll miss him. Especially when I come home from work. His face would light up with a happy smile."

"What you've done for our parents... I mean, I don't even have words. Sometimes it's hard for me to shake off the guilt that I left you to deal with so much all by yourself. I wasn't here when you needed me the most."

"Don't be silly. It's not your fault, Ums. You couldn't look into the future and predict how all this would turn out."

I hug Maya, grateful that we were able to tag-team as long as we did. Somehow it all turned out okay.

On the thirteenth day after Appa's passing, we celebrate the release of his soul by sponsoring lunch for the residents of an elder-care community. We arrive early, serve the meal, and receive their blessings.

It's the end of an era called Caregiving for Our Parents.

SOUL MAKING

When I return to Chicago in the fall of 2010 I'm immediately struck by the changed pace of our lives. Ruki's days are consumed by insane amounts of homework, school projects, plays, and a new chapter looming on the horizon: college. We're swimming in the deep waters of grants, scholarships, letters of admission, and college choices.

G is fueled by twin passions: proving himself at his new role and the quintessential immigrant dream—sending our daughter to an American university.

In complete contrast to my family's focused forward path, I'm steeped in a thick soup of inertia. I think back to my twenty-six-year-old self who started her first job in advertising right out of college. I'd forged ahead, made more money, enjoyed more success and validation than I imagined possible. The upward trajectory continued when I started my freelance career as a writer while staying home with my child. That self has wandered away into the wilderness, lost in the mists of another time.

My shock of gray hair, dark eyes, brown skin, and 5 foot 5 ½ inch body looks the same on the outside but all my interior furniture has been rearranged without my knowledge or consent. I'm constantly bumping into things and tripping over stuff, lost in the layout of my new life.

Grief has shaken my foundations hard and crumbled me, until I stand in the rubble of my earlier life, the earlier me. It feels like walking through life without skin. I scrape and bruise, no matter where I turn. Although I've created my own family, Amma's death feels as if a tornado ripped the roof above my head. Naked and shivering, I don't know where home is anymore.

My new self, birthed from Amma's ashes, has no drive, ambition, or desire to prove anything. I have zero motivation to find a j-o-b. The thought of getting dressed and doing a daily commute feels like wince-walking in a tight pair of shoes with no permission to take them off. Adrift from society's prescriptive framework for adulting, I am a lonely misfit.

Souls, they say, whisper. Mine screams at me. *Serve. Make a difference. Make every day count.* I have no choice but to obey. Even if it makes no sense. Even if I can't place a pretty frame around it and explain why. Even if it means I'll be staring at a bank balance that will constantly shame me.

Even if Dina, the Activities Director, saved my gig at The Palms, facilitating a weekly Life Stories group pays almost nothing. Yet I look forward to Monday afternoons because the opportunity fuels me with purpose.

I don't know it yet, but I will come to call this period the apprenticeship of my soul. The rhythms of the soul are slow. Quick-fixes, speed, formulae, and planning—the stuff I used to navigate my other life by—have evaporated. I'm called to submit to the pace at which the divine works. Waiting, trust, faith, and surrender are non-linear; yet they lead me to where I need to go next.

Almost serendipitously books find me and help me navigate my new path. The *Tao* teaches me that all doing emanates from non-doing. The Buddhist texts explain that *Dukka* or suffering is caused by attachment. My beloved teacher Wayne Dyer says that all we can do with this life we've been given is to give it away. *Don't let money be the reason why you don't serve,* he cautions. His words worm their way into the cells of my being and rearrange my programming. The reality of federal loans and college tuition have no place in this newly configured version of me.

My crisis has become my crucible. I find myself sitting in the fire of this crucible, letting it burn away what cannot follow me into the second half of life where my soul's new theme is *meaning* over *ambition.*

Death, dying, and the sacred work of shaping a legacy take up all the space in my head. I don't want my decisions to be dictated by the stress of survival; I want love and service to lead the way. How can I leave my heart imprint on the world before I die, is the question that's central to my life now.

We come into this world with nothing. We leave with nothing. What we do leave behind is the love we create while we're here—and that's what I need to focus on.

࿐

Three months since Appa died, and I returned from Chennai. My days are spent facilitating the Life Stories group which is one hour on Monday afternoons, volunteering with the elderly in nursing homes and senior living communities. Whatever they need, whether it's a back massage, someone to listen to long-ago stories, or wipe their tears. I sing to those who are so far gone that music remains the only bridge to their hearts.

As the sands of time slip through the hourglass, I show no signs of applying for a job. I know it's only a matter of time before G asks me questions I have no answers to. How can I explain myself? I rehearse different scenarios. I try out scripts in my head, pray, meditate. But, really, what am I going to say?

My soul wants me to serve.

The only thing we leave behind is love—and that's what I plan to do.

My purpose is calling.

None of this is going to cut it for my Type A guy whose brain is wired for logic, specifics, rationale. In moments of sheer desperation I cry out to God, to Amma, to whoever is listening on The Other Side. *Help me! Give me the words. Tell me what to say.*

My usually fiery Leo energy has gone into hiding, but my husband's Aries energy head-butts us right into the conversation. "So, have you looked at any job opportunities?"

Twist wedding ring and stare at floor is my response. Except for the Life Stories group which pays me the princely sum of one hundred dollars a month, I've been unemployed for eight months at this point.

"Ums?"

There's no easy/right/correct/gentle way to say it so I decide to come right out, spill the words, and deal with the mess. "I...I don't want...I'm not sure that I...want to find a job."

Silence sizzles between us. "I don't understand," he says. "Most of the world works. There are bills to pay. Ruki's getting ready to go to college, we've bought this place, the car payments...Anyway, I don't need to explain all this. You *know* this." He strokes his beard, then looks away. "I know you've had a hard time losing Amma and Appa. It hasn't been easy, but we... we have to continue to live here."

He just gave the mean girl in my head more ammunition. *You're so selfish. How can you not care about your family? What kind of wife and mother puts her needs first? And you call this God's work?*

I'm sinking in a sea of guilt. My three India trips in two years have been a financial drain but not for a moment did G let that be a consideration in whether I traveled or not. We definitely took into account my income when we bought the townhome. Now a corpulent college bill is moving closer and closer toward us.

In twenty years of marriage this is perhaps the first time I look into my husband's eyes and see disappointment there. It pierces me. He's never questioned my choices; he has always supported my decisions. But in this moment he's being forced to confront a truth that's so at odds with everything he was raised to believe. I—his wife—am placing my mystical purpose above mundane practicality.

All these years we've been true partners in every sense of the word, moving hand in hand toward our goals: Ruki's education, investing in a home, a vacation stash, salting money away for retirement.

How could I have known that Amma's death would present the fork in the road, the moment where I'm choosing to disengage my hand from his to follow the path less traveled? Leaving him alone and bewildered?

A furious sparring rages inside me. My ego says: *You're foolish. You're destroying everything you both built together.* My soul whispers: *All is being taken care of. Move forward confidently.*

In the meantime, he's waiting for me to speak.

"I...I don't know what to say," I begin.

A measly statement, but it's all I have to offer. As I'm searching for the next words, a new energy from within takes over. My husband deserves better than this—and I'm going to give him the truth as I know it even if it sounds utterly ridiculous and self-centered.

I clear my throat. "Ever since Amma died, something has changed inside me. I didn't ask for it to happen—but it's happened. And I can't seem to go back to the person I used to be. It feels as if God is moving me in a new direction. I don't know what it is. I don't

know where it's leading, except that I feel a powerful urge to serve."

G stares at me for a moment, then sniggers. Wrapped up in that snigger is anger, pain, confusion, and disappointment. "So, God doesn't want you to serve your family." The acid in his voice stings.

"No, that's not what..."

"We have two mortgages. One in Chennai and one here. You know all this. I don't know why I'm standing here explaining it to you!"

I can't argue with anything he says. My gut twists in pain. I'm angry with Amma for dying and with God for dragging me down this crazy cosmic path.

What I want to say to my husband is: *You think this is easy for me? I didn't plan on any of it when we moved. You think I'm doing this because I enjoy being selfish and inconsiderate? My world has turned upside down. I don't even know who I am anymore. So, no. I don't have neat little answers to your questions. Don't ask me. Ask God.*

But I don't. I swallow the words, bury them behind my ribcage.

"We all have dreams," G continues. "And we all want to follow our dreams. But that's not how life works. You get up each morning, get dressed and go to work because your family has to eat and live in a decent home."

Every word takes a bite out of me.

"What happens if I wake up tomorrow morning and decide I've had enough? That I don't want to go to work? Is that even an option for me?" he asks.

"I didn't choose this. It...it chose me," The words come out strangled and strange. I follow it up with a feeble excuse. "If that even makes sense."

His shoulders drop. He walks away, leaving me to steep in my own shame.

Every fight we have in the next few months follows a similar trajectory. The same old arguments. Tired questions. Words, shards of glass that lodge in my throat. And my husband lists all the questions that I don't want to, and cannot, hear. *What happens if I lose my job? What happens if we can't afford Ruki's college tuition? What happens if I drop dead?*

We hit walls and dead ends where words dry up. Deep down, I know this. G is a good husband, a good father, and someone who lives by the rules of the real world. He's doing the best he can to keep our family on solid ground. It's not his fault that he cannot understand what gives me life now.

What gives me life is the moment I enter the nursing home. Where the flow of love given and received is all the grace I need. Every tear I mop up, every wrinkled hand I hold, every long, disjointed ramble I offer my loving attention to, makes me grateful for the real estate I take up on this land, this earth.

DYING EMBERS

Hospice. A familiar word to most, it's foreign to me. But it's in the air in senior living, always whispered in somber tones. I'd never heard the word in India. Maybe it has something to do with a hospital. A specific service? A department? A wing?

It shows up every now and again in a library flyer, a billboard, a form. When something pops up in my world repeatedly I know it's a sign. But just as the word shimmers on the edges of my attention and teases, life interrupts, distracts, diverts. I have to drive to Ruki's school. We're out of milk and I need to stop by the store. My phone rings. The word evaporates, only to return later and tug at my attention in a different form.

A chance invitation from a friend to go see a play turns out to be the 'sledgehammer from the universe' moment. The protagonists in the play: a mother who's dying from cancer and her caregiver daughter. What's more, the play is sponsored by a hospice organization. I check their website later and learn about an upcoming volunteer training program. I do the only thing I can. I sign up.

When I show up for my first volunteer shift, someone at the nurse's station requests me to stock the linen closet. For the next thirty minutes, I put away pillowcases, bed sheets, comforters, towels, and patient gowns where they belong. I drive home profoundly weary and call my volunteer coordinator.

"Hi, Jen," I begin, not knowing how she will receive what I'm about to say, but knowing I have to say it. "Today was my first shift."

"How'd it go?" Jen asks in her raspy voice.

"It went okay. But that's also why I'm calling."

"Was there a problem?"

"No, no. Nothing like that. They had me stock the linen closets today. I don't know if it's okay to ask...but I, you know, really want to spend time with the dying. That's why I went through the training. To sit with people who are at the end of their lives. And I'd love to support the grieving as well."

I exhale and wait, hoping Jen will understand.

"Oh my gosh, Uma. Of course. And let me tell ya, this is not a common request I get. Most volunteers want to do filing, or stock the closets or make the coffee, get involved in fundraising. But I can see you're different. Next time you stop by, we'll have you set up."

On my next visit, a nurse says, "The lady in 216, her name is Sue, would like a visitor." Jen has made good on her promise. The staff has been alerted that I want to visit with the dying.

Sue is surprisingly young, her body tired from failed cancer treatments. She's buried under thick blankets. Only her face is visible. Sharp ocean-blue eyes, cracked lips, and a beautiful set of teeth.

I introduce myself and ask if there's anything I can do to make her more comfortable.

"I'm scared," Sue whispers, tears filling her blue eyes.

I wait, sensing there's more.

"I haven't told my daughter that..." She closes her eyes, pulls up the energy she needs to speak her next words, "...that I'm dying. She's only fifteen."

I take her hand in mine. My eyes land on the red puncture marks on her forearm from the IV's and blood draws. "I understand how hard that can be."

"How do you tell your child?" Sue wonders aloud.

"How much does she know?"

"She thinks I'm getting treatment for cancer. In a hospital."

"Well, it's not an easy decision."

Sue nods. "I don't wanna leave without saying goodbye."

"You get to tell her in a way that's right for you. She might appreciate you being vulnerable when you tell her you were scared to lay this on her. It won't be easy on her—or you. But then all the time you have from then on becomes really precious. You get to make the most of your time with each other—knowing what's coming."

Sue looks deeply into my eyes. "Are you a therapist here?"

I laugh. "No, I'm a trained volunteer. I'll be working with the bereavement department soon."

"They should make you one. You're *good*."

I smile at her. "Maybe you'll appreciate a visit from our chaplain too. He can help you go over the specifics of how to share this with your daughter. Would you like me to mention it to him?"

"That would be wonderful. Thank you so much."

Next, I stop by Room 301 to see John. John never married, has no kids, no family. He lies there all alone, a vase of fading yellow flowers on the bedside table for company. His eyes flutter every once in a while. The music system plays soothing spa tunes, one track changing to the next as life leaks out of John's body. A frail figure on a white-sheeted bed dragging in all the breaths his body is allotted before his soul is set free.

Dying, I realize, is hard work. I call his name, but he doesn't respond. Some part of him must hear me, I think. I speak to him as if he *can* hear me, remind him that he's loved, that whatever's on the other side is safe and beautiful and free. Not that I *know* that. I've never had a near-death experience. But that special place inside me which knew G was the right man for me knows this too—and I trust it.

Spending time with a human who has days or weeks to live feels like a transcendent experience. Some folks are just plain mad they've been robbed of time. Some are so tired of coping with, managing, and enduring the pain they're ready to call it quits. Some, having spent their entire life unconcerned with the question of what's beyond this life, are in real fear about letting go so they cling to life by a fraying thread. But almost all of them have dropped the masks they've worn most of their lives, their hearts finally open to telling the real truth about the lives they've lived. These are precious moments of the purest connection—and I can hardly believe I get to be the confessional, helping them set their baggage down and travel lightly into the light.

When I get home, however, G thinks my awakening has reached a new level of crazy. "You're grieving your mother. You should be with happy people. Why do you want to be around people who are dying??! I don't get it."

What I want to say: It's like going to the university of life. I'm learning so much from the dying about the lives they didn't get to live. Their regrets, lost dreams, and opportunities. These people are so real because they have nothing to lose. The thing they feared the most is happening—and there's no turning back. Don't you see how rich this is for me?

What I say: "I don't know how to explain it. But when I leave that hospice facility, I feel lit up. I don't feel burdened by their pain or sadness. So please don't worry that I'll be sadder than I already am."

My time with the dying is measured in moments. Some days I meet someone for the first—and perhaps—the last time. One precious final encounter, and a blessed meeting of two souls. More than ever, I realize how much of our time is wasted in meaningless pursuits: money, promotions, cars and houses, fancy titles, and treasures.

We're walking each other home, says spiritual teacher Ram Dass. I'm shepherding the dying home. As the finite grains of sand drop through the hourglass of their lives, I rub lotion into their papery hands, sing Indian hymns, channel white light and trust it will melt some of their pain, and pray their crossing is gentle and safe.

LIGHTWORKER

Eyes closed, I sit in lotus pose and try to focus on my breath. Thirty minutes every morning is what I'm going for.

When I feel lost I pull angel cards for guidance and direction.

My choice of literature these days is books on past life regression, reincarnation, deep soul writing, and near-death experiences.

I spend my days with people who are walking the final miles of their lives, and folks who are staring down the barrel wondering when the trigger will be pulled.

My husband's world consists of corporate profits, bills, worrying about the economy, mortgage and melting icecaps.

We live in parallel universes governed by entirely different sets of laws.

Silence rises, thick and strong, an invisible wall between us. I have much to say but nothing that he wants to hear. Spiritual teachings extol silence as an elevated experience, a blissful state. What often goes unaddressed is silence's shadow side, a side that feels punishing to the recipient. Silence can shut people out. Silence can gag. Silence can withhold all that feels like connection and closeness. For me, a lover of words and conversations, it feels as if all the oxygen is sucked out of a space, leaving me light-headed and confused.

In an effort to stir the still, deep river that is my husband I drop pebbles in, sharing tidbits about my interactions with the seniors.

"I ran into Howard today," I throw out the conversational bait.

Ninety years old and wheelchair-bound, Howard serenades me with love songs. He is relentless in persuading me to run away with him to Hawaii where he promises to show me the good time.

"Oh, your boyfriend," says G. "Where does he want to romance you next?"

"This week it's Hawaii," I laugh. "And then he asked me what car I drive. Told him I drive a Toyota Corolla. He says: You're not a Toyota kinda gal; you're a Cadillac kinda gal!"

I share how I helped Frank complete a crossword puzzle and read to Nancy who fell asleep halfway through the first page. These shared stories create a few simple moments of connection. They become the conversational crumbs that sustain us for one more evening. Later we fall into bed, exhausted and alone, unable to find solace in each other's skin. Spooning and snuggling belong in our past.

The overwhelming weight of grief has moved in and taken up space in my tissues and bones, and chased bodily pleasures into some unknown realm. I'm constantly lugging around the crushing weight of a backpack of bad feelings. Pleasure has become an alien. Intuiting this, G leaves me alone. Soul versus soma, I've handed over my allegiance to the former.

More and more I feel trapped in a cosmic cage of my own creation. I no longer fit into the other Uma's body or intellect. This body I've moved into still feels unfamiliar. I'm slowly getting to know its topography, discovering all the hidden rooms that exist in this space, and finding my way through them.

Ruki is in the final stretches of her research, filling out applications, crafting well-thought-out essays, and doing a million things in preparation for college. Father and daughter discuss parent loans, federal loans, and grants. I sit on the periphery of the circle, feeling unwelcome. What's probably more accurate is that I opted out of the circle. It's hard not to feel like the outsider, though. I'm hyper aware of the choices I've made. I'm not contributing to my daughter's future. Guilt and grief perch on my shoulders and poke at my sanity all day long.

How I hear my soul's whispers through the tumultuous storm raging inside my mind is a mystery. But I do. *All is well,* She says. *All is being taken care of,* She reassures. There is an indefinable quality to these mystical messages that softens my shoulders and calms my scrambled internal monologue. Something in me knows all will be well.

The most authentic connections I share are with the elderly and the dying whose pretenses have fallen away. They let me wander inside their broken hearts and peek into the secret nooks where guilt, shame, and grief live.

It wouldn't be an exaggeration to say that The Palms feels more like home than my own does.

Nothing makes us more aware of the urgency of living life than being in the presence of the dying. When I say goodbye to Debra in 109 I never know if I'll see her again. In my life, goodbye isn't a casual wave anymore. Goodbye is heavy with the knowing that it could possibly be our final encounter on the earth plane.

When I walk into 211 the following week, Sue's bed is empty. On the clean white sheets is a new human, Mark, surrounded by friends and family walking him on the last leg of his life.

Next I stop by Ellen's room. Last week she and I giggled together as she shared with me the story of how she burned her first dinner as a new bride. Today, her eyes are closed, and she struggles to pull in breath, the gurgle of mucus evidence of her extreme labor. It makes me pause, slows me down enough to take a deep in-breath, gratitude rushing in on the oxygen.

My next visit is with Brenda who is chatty today. As I settle down, she begins to give voice to a litany of regrets she's carrying. "I wish I'd attended my son's baseball games instead of obsessing over my quarterly sales report. If I could have a do-over I'd read more, watch more sunsets, and hold my husband's hand when we walked." Brenda reminds me to hold all that is dear to me close to my heart. It's impossible to regret-proof a human life. We can, however, call in tools like intentionality and mindfulness to course-correct.

If I can live life in such a way that I will look back in contentment when my own death arrives, I know I'll go in peace.

I think about my life, G's life, our lives.

G is preparing to take on a new international role at work, one that will require him to travel more. It's more of everything. More meetings. More phone calls. More emails. His constant need to aspire to a standard of excellence and prove himself at work has been at the center of most of our marital friction. Life in Chicago has been busier than ever. The preoccupation around what needs to get done always takes precedence over being present for each other.

Time is slipping away, I want to shake him and enunciate the words. Neither of us is going to be around forever. Let's sit on the couch. Hold hands. Talk about things that matter. Share our love. Lean into long hugs. *This* is what matters. *This* is what we'll miss and regret not having made time for. Not the email that wasn't sent. Or the client call that went to voicemail. *Put your phone down. Come, sit next to me. Let me hold your hand and tell you who I'm becoming and why.*

Courage deserts me. Longing tugs at me, yet I cannot speak the words. My husband bears the burden of our lives, flying solo because I refused to step up. Every part of him, I fear, will rise up in defense—and I will be the perp, not the victim. What's more, I know most of the world will take his side, see his point of view on this and question my choices, alienating me even more. My loneliness is so real I can touch it.

SPOOKY

I chance upon the show on near-death experiences quite by accident, but I'm instantly hooked. Each episode features two to
three stories of regular, everyday folks and their after-death adventures. Mike died in a car crash. Glenda coded during heart surgery.
Melanie took her own life. In each case, their soul crossed over to
The Other Realm and had to make a choice: do I stay or return to
earth to complete what's unfinished? The ones that chose to return
to their loved ones did so because they had a purpose to live for:
young children, a mentally unwell parent, or the desire to teach
what they'd learned when they died.

Where did Amma go? is an ever-present inquiry in my life. The
universe leads me to people and books and shows that offer me not

just clues and possible answers, but a great deal of comfort and peace.

Books about NDE's remind me that I'm a once-in-a-lifetime cosmic event. And now, this show. It captures people leading perfectly normal lives when a freak tornado or lightning strike turns into unthinkable tragedy. They die and are instantly bathed in the white light of unconditional love. Mystical encounters with angelic beings, deceased loved ones, or Jesus change their perspective of life and death.

Did Amma meet a Being of Light?

Did Thaathi show up to receive her on the other side?

I envision Amma wrapped in a radiant sun of love beams, every trace of her physical pain melting away. I visualize my grandfather opening his arms to her with a smile. Maybe her cousin who died early showed up and surprised her. My endless imaginings abound with wonderment.

Something in my bones feels the truth in these messages. Remembrance of a divine realm stirs within me, a place I belong to and will, one day, return to.

That Amma simply got off the train at an earlier station and will be there to greet me when my time arrives is the sweetest promise. My skin breaks out in chills, a warmth suffuses my heart.

Death doesn't have to be scary, it reminds me. *We get to go home, a home where nothing but Love exists.*

In the episode I'm watching, a young woman is rushed to the ER following a massive stroke. Every moment that follows is critical.

My eyes are riveted to the screen when G walks into the living room. "What're you watching?" he asks.

"Ssshh," I caution, not wanting to miss a split-second of the action.

"Oh, wow," he says as the screen fills with images of a slack-jawed woman on a gurney, a bevy of white-coated doctors, and the pained faces of family members, Code Red blaring over the PA system.

Suddenly a soft white ball of energy whooshes out of the woman's body. All the machines she's hooked up to bleep to a stop. As this white energy, this spirit, travels into star-studded skies, a second ball of white light suffuses the clouds and opens to reveal a young man, the dead woman's partner, we learn. He's the first to show up on her afterlife reunion team.

"Wait, what's happening?" G peers at the screen.

I hit the pause button and bring him up to speed. "She just died. That cloud of energy," I point the remote at the TV "that's her soul leaving her body, crossing over to the other side. And that's the guy she was married to. He must've died before her, that's why he's now showing up to receive her on the other side." I turn to him. "Come, watch with me. This stuff is fascinating."

He shudders. "Creepy."

"Why? We're all going to die someday."

"Yeah, but that doesn't mean I have to watch people dying and… all the rest of it."

I restart the show. The woman then has an encounter with her guardian angel who asks if she wants to stay or leave. She decides to return to her kids and does so with a richer appreciation for her life and the conviction that death is not something to be feared.

Turning off the TV I sit in silence. Every time I reach out to G eager to share an aspect of my new life, I meet a distinct lack of interest. It feels like a rejection of my reborn self. As seductive as this brand of spirituality is to me, one that constantly lures me to learn more, a part of me dearly wishes I could crawl back into the skin I shed, the identity that was less complicated, the one my husband knew and understood—but I don't know how, or where to find her.

EMPTY NEST

For months, I've been hard at work on a secret project to ritualize Ruki's rite of passage.

I reveal it at dinner a couple of nights before we drive Ruki to a small private liberal arts college in Rock Island, IL where she will begin the next phase of her life. Ruki chose the 150-year-old institution, and they in turn welcomed her with a healthy scholarship sloughing off a chunk of what her dad will have to pay. Even so, he'll pay a hefty amount.

Once the waitress departs with our dinner order, I pull the gift out of my bag and hold it out to Ruki.

"What's this?" She asks with rounded eyes.

"Open it," I say, taking in G's raised eyebrows.

Impatient fingers tug at the pink bow and wrapper, and out comes a navy journal. As Ruki flips through the pages, I watch her face gently crumple. Her eyes fill with tears. The journal is a series of letters I've written to her. Little bits of wisdom on falling in love, homesickness, and mindful living. In the pages are recipes of her favorite foods, anecdotes from her childhood, stories about her grandparents, insights, and life lessons I've gleaned from my forty-seven-year journey as a human.

G and Ruki shake their heads in amazement and declare it a hard-to-outdo gift.

Two days later, we're in a wooded college campus decked out in summer's lush green. We say hello to Ruki's dorm mates and their parents, help unpack and set up her stuff, then find our seats in the auditorium to listen to the college president welcome the incoming freshmen.

My heart bursts with pride and brims over with sadness. Eighteen years ago, I committed to giving the best parts of me to my child and this feels like a moment of culmination. *This is it.* She's flown the nest we lovingly feathered with safety, comfort, and nurturance.

"Good afternoon students and parents..."

The college president's booming voice reels me back to reality. As he drones on about ethics and expectations, my mind struggles to focus. Every ticking minute reminds me we're getting closer to The Goodbye. Ruki and I made a promise to each other that we won't cry. "Ma, if you start, I won't be able to stop," she cautioned me. The last thing I want to do is embarrass her in the presence of peers who will soon become her surrogate family.

When the time arrives, I lean in and linger over our hug. I pull away and look at her. My baby, my child, my toddler, my tween, now my precious teen perched on the cusp of adulthood. A swell of emotions rises within me, but I hold it together, kiss her on the cheek, whisper a hasty goodbye and rush out the door, G behind me.

We're officially empty nesters.

In the safety of the car speeding down I-80, hot tears drench my face. G looks at me in surprise and asks, "Why are you crying? What happened?"

Irritation flares inside me. *Our daughter just left home after eighteen years with us. Do you really have to ask that question?!*

The one person who understands my tears and knows how to be with me when I cry is now getting further and further away from me. My heart squeezes so tight it hurts.

G waits for me to respond.

"Do I have to explain why? We just dropped Ruki off." Now my tears are turning into hiccupping sobs.

"It's been such a nice day so far. Everything went well. Do you really have to ruin it all by crying?"

Someone could have slapped me on the face and it would have hurt less. That he cannot come up with one kind thing to say devastates me. This feels like the worst kind of beginning to our empty nesting.

He could've held my hand and that would've been enough.

He could've said, "I understand." Two simple life-giving words.

He could've been inclusive. "I'll miss her too."

Anything but this. Anything but words that dump a load of guilt in my lap for ruining a perfectly lovely day.

Is this how we're going to live the rest of our lives, me having to cry in the privacy of my bathroom to manage my husband's discomfort with emotions?

SACRED SORROW

Working closely with the counselors in the hospice organization to support the dying and the bereaved, conversations around the emptiness of loss, death, and dying are now intimate territory for me. Most of the world shies away from having these conversations.

The irony as I reflect is how easy it is to speak with the dying than with the living. We dialogue about regrets, forgiveness, and the purpose of pain; not vacation destinations, buying a home, and the fluctuating graph of the U.S. economy.

I'm often called in to support patients who need an extra dose of sensitive hand holding. When a patient dies, I hold space for family members who wish to unburden themselves. I'm now much more aware of a person's energy field. Cleansing my aura has become a go-to spiritual practice. I take a few moments to breathe and center—leaving behind the energetic remnants of my day that may well include frustration, anger, or grief—before I enter the space of the dying.

When I return home, my peace frequency has taken a hike to God-knows-where. A heaviness wraps around me. Much as I long to share some of these stories with G my neck tightens at the thought of his discomfort around conversations that involve dying people and grief. So, I eat my words, stuff them deep down, and say nothing.

Over time I start to share my experiences on social media, and grieving women approach me for support with the loss of a beloved, an empty nest, the end of a long friendship, betrayal, a parent's Alzheimer's diagnosis, or a loss of identity. Knowing from personal experience how hard it is for most people to sit with you as you slow-burn in pain and how lonely journeying through grief can be, I decide to take the heat. My soul wants to serve the broken-hearted, the ones who feel untethered, hopeless, and unable to believe in a better tomorrow. *Let me hold that belief for you until you can hold it yourself*, I say to them. As we sit together with Sister Sorrow I help them breathe through their painful emotions. I catch their feelings as stories spill out of them. We are each other's teacher.

The grieving mother of a 17-year-old who died in a car crash teaches me a valuable lesson, one that I will never forget. She makes her way into my Zoom room shredded by grief. Her insomnia is insane, she's desperately trying to drown in work so she can anesthetize her pain, and she's pissed at all the mothers whose children are alive and well.

And then, the tears come. Tears that she must keep locked up all week because the world doesn't want to see them. I stay afloat in the waters of her grief, but I often feel like a pitiful pail as the ocean of her sorrow comes roaring at me.

Over our many sessions, I invite her to share stories about her precious boy moving through the stages of a newborn, baby, toddler, young child, tween, teen, and the person he grew into as a young adult unaware that he would always stay seventeen. I catch the sparkle of fond reminiscences in her wet eyes. The love embedded in that shared experience is a sunbeam piercing a dark cloud.

Every time we close out a session, I find myself wondering if our time together has offered even a smidgen of value to help heal her broken heart. At the end of six months, the testimonial she writes makes me weep with gratitude.

"You have no idea how much you've done to heal me. Sitting with you, I could let go, be myself, and cry my heart out. Every tear that I shed has been a healing release. I'll never stop grieving my son, but you taught me to love my broken self. I'm not a basket case. I'm a mother who loved fiercely."

It is a moment of compelling clarity. Tools and techniques have their place but what the grieving need most of all is a safe, non-judgmental space to wail.

DISTANCE

Why does my husband hate my tears?

The weight of his judgment—'out of control'—presses down on me. My tears rarely elicit compassion or comfort. Instead, they trigger his anger, especially if my sobbing was caused by the friction between us.

I've always been a crier. Spectacular sunsets make me cry. Weddings cause me to well up. So do fond remembrances at memorial services. I cry when a newborn is placed in my arms, the freshness of life and possibility and new beginnings. Each time I watch the final episode of *Friends* I cry—and I've watched it half-a-dozen times.

The pain of Amma's death is a constant agony, and my tears

won't stop. Being shunned for crying when I'm already hurting is another layer of wounding. Broken me just can't seem to get it together. G has no idea how to comfort me, what to say, or how to get me to be the Uma I used to be: fun, happy, his forever sunbeam.

"He doesn't know how to fix you anymore, Ma," old-soul Ruki's incisive remark during one of her visits home is on point. Our daughter has had a ringside view of my transformation and the shifting marital dynamics between her dad and me.

I no longer want to be 'fixed,' or 'made happy.' Being rushed to get over my feelings frustrates me. What I'd like is for him to sit beside me, take my hand, and let me grieve. But the look of defeat that comes over his face when I cry makes me a) feel bad about my tears and b) want to manage his discomfort.

The old me was easily appeased. A surprise gift, an impromptu ice-cream, or a coffee date would do it. G loves shopping and is a fantastic gift-giver. Everywhere he travels, he brings me something. A bottle of perfume. A scarf. A bag. Chocolates. Books by my favorite authors.

My shifting self-truths have changed my tastes. Perfumes and purses I once squealed over now leave me cold. These days I read spiritual literature and NDE memoirs, so he no longer knows what books to buy. I spend money on scented candles, crystals, books by Ram Dass and Eckhart Tolle, and tarot decks. One birthday season I handed G a wish list of book titles he could buy me—and he was seriously offended. The secrecy surrounding my surprise birthday gifts used to be a delicious thrill. Now, my changed desires have left him lost and confused.

Occasionally I read about a couple who meet randomly and the instant soul recognition they experience during that first meeting. Somehow they both know their incarnation is about unfinished karma from a prior lifetime. When I come across such a story, I tuck it away to share with G. Same with a spontaneous healing someone experienced upon waking up from a dream encounter with a healing angel; or when a toddler pointed to the bridge the mom was driving by and told her he had died there 'before;' or when a medical intuitive gazed at an aura and knew exactly how her patient's physical body was compromised. The stuff about how we're so much more than our body and mind excites me, and I want nothing more than to exclaim over these findings with my husband.

Among the many mythological stories my paternal grandmother shared with me, the story of the hunchback devotee Shabari has stayed with me. When Shabari learns that Lord Rama will be passing by the trail near her cottage, she starts to pluck a variety of fruit from the forest trees. "She would bite each one," Thaathi would mimic Shabari taking a bite, pucker her lips or crumple her face in distaste if the fruit tasted sour or bitter. "If it was sour or bitter, she would throw it away. Shabari only saved the sweetest, most luscious fruit for her beloved Rama." Shabari's is a story of sweetness and love and devotion.

Shabari-like, I gather snippets of story to share with G. My mind insists he won't be interested or he'll just think I'm weird. When I do pluck up the courage and pull a story out, G nods in a distracted way. I can tell he's waiting for me to get to the finish line so he can turn back to his phone screen which holds more promise.

My mind casts back to the early khus-scented days of our marriage, a time when we were fresh, young, and bursting with desire to know every detail of the other's body and mind. Music has always been G's big passion. Acutely aware of my complete ignorance about western music, I'd sit with his book of lyrics open in my lap, Clapton's raspy voice on the stereo, and try to learn the songs. The longing to share his passion was so compelling. Yet G has little interest in the world that contains magic and meaning for me now.

You chose this, my mind reminds me. Most of the world would agree. But I know differently. My path chose me. My calling called out to me. My soul literally shoved me down the road less traveled.

❧

A few months before Ruki began freshman year in college, G took on a new role in the company which requires him to travel overseas for two to three weeks a month.

No matter where he travels to, he calls home to check on me. He even cooks a few dishes and stocks the refrigerator before he leaves home. "You think I'll starve if you don't cook before you leave?" I pose the question playfully.

"No. But I feel good doing it. You're going to be all by yourself for so long."

My husband cooks and cleans and shops and makes sure my Mini Cooper's gas tank is topped up. He has never, ever forgotten my birthday or our anniversary. In fact, he always plans something special which includes flowers, gifts, cards, and a nice dinner.

My forty-seventh birthday, the first after both my parents had passed, was one I dreaded. But when it was time to bring out the surprise cake, I was undone. G had ordered a cake with two pretty plastic butterflies perched on the frosting.

His love language is acts of service. My love language is quality time.

When he talks I like to sit beside him and listen. I'm curious, interested. I ask questions.

But my acts-of-service guy finds it hard to stay on the couch for too long. An errand, a task, a phone call beckons. There's always something to be attended to, something to be *done*.

The quality-time gal is left sitting alone on the couch wondering why he can't gaze into her eyes, ask questions, listen, tell her that the path she's walking matters, *she* matters.

Equally the acts-of-service guy is disappointed that the gleaming kitchen counters, well-stocked refrigerator, and unloaded dishwasher are invisible to her.

TRUST

As a hospice volunteer I'm assigned to visit with Rose who lives in Walden Nursing Home. I hear a commotion as I turn the corner to her room. It's a balmy afternoon when I arrive for my volunteer visit.

Rose's usually soft voice is high-pitched, an undercurrent of agitation signaling that something is amiss.

"No, go away," sitting in her wheelchair, she waves a gnarled arm at one of the nursing aides. "I *said* I won't take it!" The bottle of pills and glass of water in the aide's hands tell a whole story.

"Hi Rose," I lean down and look into her eyes. She's dressed in a pale-yellow cardigan blemished with coffee stains, her fearful eyes darting between me and the aide.

"She's trying to..." and then Rose beckons me to get closer and whispers in my ear, "*poison* me!"

"I can't wait here all day. I've got to get to the other residents," says the aide whose name tag reads Shirley.

"What's going on?" I ask, trying to get a handle on the situation.

"She won't take her anxiety meds. So, of course, her anxiety is sky-high." Shirley finishes with an eye roll.

"She wants to kill me!" Rose hisses out the words.

"Okay, I heard that and I'm not trying to..."

"Oh yes, you *are*."

"*Whaat*?! I'm just trying to do my job here." Shirley's injured pride is apparent to me.

I take Shirley aside. "Shirley, I can see you're just trying to do your job here. And thank you for showing up every day and doing what you do." I drop my voice to a whisper, glancing quickly at Rose who's now distracted by an unraveling thread of wool in her cardigan. I continue. "Rose doesn't mean what she says. It's not *you*. It's her anxiety."

Shirley sighs, shifting her weight from one foot to the other.

"Do you mind if I try?" I ask, wondering if she will see this as an attempt to upstage her.

Fortunately, Shirley nods. I walk over to Rose. "It's time for you to take your pills."

Rose shakes her head from side to side. "She wants me gone. I don't trust her."

I hold her hand. "Can I give them to you?"

She looks at me for a brief moment, then nods yes.

Shirley shakes out a couple of pills into my palm and hands me the glass of water. I place the pills in Rose's palm and watch as she washes down the meds with a sip of water.

"Thank you," says Shirley.

"No, thank *you*, for not taking this personally."

In a healthcare system that's tremendously short-staffed and training needs often go unmet, my empathy is clearly divided between Rose and Shirley.

Driving home an hour later, I think back to how I'd started the day with a *Use me* prayer, as I often do. In helping mediate a peaceful outcome between Rose and Shirley I feel 'used' in a deeply nourishing way.

Humming as I prepare dinner, I hear the garage door. Minutes later, G steps through the door. "Hi love!" I say in a joyful singsong voice. One look at his thundercloud face and all the joy bubbling through my being evaporates. I swallow the story about Rose that I'd been planning to serve up at the dinner table. *How dare I be happy when he's feeling so crappy.*

"Rough day at work?" I tread gently.

"What's new? Another day, same old shit." He sighs, the air around us sinking with desperation.

"If you want to talk, I'm happy to listen."

"No. It's fine," he says.

We pick up our plates and plop down on the couch, the television's surrogate chatter a comfortable cover for our awkward silence. CNN with its daily litany of depressive news accelerates my descent into the doldrums.

When the silence becomes oppressive, I turn to G again. "What's bothering you?"

"It's nothing you can help me with."

I don't contribute to the family kitty but does my entire value in this marriage hinge on that? As I'm grappling with the guilt deeply embedded in my you-don't-bring-home-a-paycheck narrative, G's next words cause my gut to clench.

"I'm going to sell my car."

"What...why?!"

"The EMI is too high. It'll help release some extra cash for college tuition. I'll lease a car for the next year or so."

I don't know what to say.

He stretches and yawns. "I'm going to bed. It's been a long day."

"Do you have to...I mean, isn't there any other...?"

"Do you have a better idea?"

I shake my head no. I make a few hundred dollars a month. My credibility is a big fat zero.

Watching his back as he starts to climb the stairs to our bedroom, a fog of exhaustion drops over me. *Dear God, what have I got us into? Am I making all this spiritual shit up? Where is this leading? Is it even leading anywhere?*

The voices in my head are screaming. *You're a selfish loser. You get to have what you want, but your husband has to pay the price.*

Ouch, ouch, ouch.

My scaredy-self mind starts to spew out a bunch of solutions.

Maybe I can find a job at Starbucks.

Maybe I can ask the hospice facility to hire me—but I don't have the right degrees.

Maybe I can ask G to sell *my* car—he'll never do it.

Maybe, maybe, maybe...

A fresh wave of grief surfaces. I no longer know who I am. I've always held jobs that paid well. I was confident at negotiating pay raises. Even as a freelancer I challenged the narrative that writers should be happy someone is willing to publish their work, and often declined assignments that didn't pay well.

Who have I become? Everything that mattered to me then no longer does. Everything that matters to me now was not even a blip on my cozy, comfortable life back then. The foundations of my being have been shaken loose. The sacred work of recreating my new self is long, lonely, and arduous. Most importantly, it requires me to throw the rule book out and simply trust. None of this makes sense to the world. Or my husband. But something in all of this makes sense to me. I don't know why. I don't know how. It just does.

The curtain of peace that came over Rose when I looked into her wild, anxiety-ridden eyes and calmed her down is a moment I cannot put a price on. Is it selfish to serve complete strangers and not serve my own loved ones? Are they less important? Why should they be any less important? Isn't wanting to secure my loved ones' lives alone an act of selfishness when so many are struggling out there?

I swirl in the familiar vortex of confusion, but my soul finds me once again and pulls me back to my center. She whispers again. *All is well. Trust. All is taken care of.*

APOLOGY

It's 8 A.M. The gaudy fuchsia pink Post-it stuck to the kitchen counter makes my eyes hurt. *I'm sorry I screwed up. Again.*

My husband's message is a tad confusing.

A thick cloud cover blankets the sky on this winter morning.

I stayed in bed until the garage doors slid close, and I was sure that he was off to work. It's easier to hide when you don't know what to say and your head is full of everything that's wrong with your husband.

I read the note again. Is he owning up for his part in the argument we had last night? Or is this his way of dumping an apology on me so that we can move beyond it and get on with our lives? The perfect conflict-avoidance strategy. Almost immediately I feel bad for entertaining this thought. I mean, *To own up is divine* and all that stuff. But a moment later, the strength of my fury reasserts itself.

It's been a few days since he dropped the bomb about selling his car.

My mind travels back to the previous night. It's late evening and a blast of winter chill blows through the mudroom door when G walks in, end-of-workday weariness all over his face. I bridge the distance between us, ready for his it's-good-to-be-home-honey kiss.

"Wait, wait," he shrugs off his black Eddie Bauer winter jacket. "Let me get out of these layers." He proceeds to unfurl the scarf from his neck, unlaces his shoes, and patiently peels off one sock, then the other.

Just then, his cell phone rings. Someone from India, Australia, China... several countries are waking up as we in North America are winding down our day. I can tell by the look on his face that a logistics crisis is brewing somewhere.

Turning away I walk back into the kitchen, then carry the dinner dishes to the dining room table. Continuing to talk on his phone, he goes upstairs, changes, comes back downstairs and we start to eat.

Dinner is a silent affair. The only sounds are chewing and the angry emotions that only we can hear. He looks a million miles away and I hate myself for feeling like an abandoned child. Tears tighten my throat. I swallow them with the mustard-speckled yellow dal and rice.

Why do I always have to come last? After every urgent shipment or missed shipment or delayed shipment? All I ask for is a welcome-home kiss. Why is that so hard?

I am a woman and I have a woman's mind, but I hate that I have it. Ever so efficiently, my mind pulls up the folder titled, "All the Times I Came Last."

When we were on vacation in a remote location in Ooty and a crisis had him standing up on the roof of our resort, waving his cell phone over his head, searching for a signal.

All the nights I sat alone at the dinner table and swallowed a meal because he was saving a client's shipment.

All the nights I went to bed alone while he cleaned up his email so he could wake up to a lighter inbox.

"A shipment was delayed." His voice brings me back to the here and now. "And the customer is going nuts," he says, helping himself to a bowl of yogurt.

What's new I feel like saying, but don't.

"Bloody idiots! I told them this might happen. Why the hell don't people listen?" he rants. I tune out.

Not hearing a response from me, not even a uh-huh of validation, he looks up. I continue to eat, head bent over my plate. I'm miffed at being sidelined and don't give a damn about a shipment that went wrong.

"You're upset," he pronounces. "What did I say *now*?" I hear exasperation in his voice. "I wanted to get out of my winter jacket and before I knew it this idiot from China called."

"It's okay. I'm okay," I lie. I'm a terrible liar, especially when it comes to my emotional state. My face screams *Feeling Abandoned.*

I'm so not okay. I deserve a smile and a kiss when my husband walks in the door after a twelve-hour workday. But no. That's like asking for the moon.

The rest of the evening is a blur: clearing up the kitchen, WGN news, and three pages of a book I barely absorb. Sullen silence hangs between us, a giant chasm in our bed.

And now, it's a new morning and here I am holding a pink note in my hand and wondering what he meant. I don't know what to think. I know what I feel and it's a feeling I want to hold on to. *I'm right. You're wrong. You owe me.*

As I lay in bed until he left for work this morning, my mind ran the treadmill of everything that's missing from our marriage. We don't have conversations. We don't do stuff together. We don't make love. Why are we even together, living like cozy housemates? To prove something to the world? Or to his parents who are living a half-century-old marriage? Or my parents who had forty-eight years together before my mother died? To cleave to tradition, culture, where we come from, who we are? Where the C-word is worshipped. It's everything. Commitment.

I'd slept so poorly I'd heard his alarm go off and all the usual morning sounds that followed. Unloading the dishwasher, making tea, the shower, the tinkle of a spoon against his bowl of oatmeal, the opening and closing of garage doors.

Now, I stare at his written apology and wonder if he'll ever get it. Will my husband understand what I seek from our relationship? Tears pool in my eyes and spill onto the kitchen counter.

A part of me feels stupid for having a big emotional reaction to a seemingly random event. Husband walked in from work. Needed to peel off winter clothes. Phone rang. Kiss was delayed because shipment was delayed. End of story. Period.

But the story that plays out in my head has complicated plot twists and sinister motives. It becomes all about priorities and missed moments and end-of-life regrets. Wiping my eyes, I grab a mug and start to make tea.

Feeling entitled and self-righteous in this moment, I completely fail to see how I'm placing my personal happiness on a platter, handing it to my husband, and saying: *This is your job. Take care of it.*

SOUL VOWS

Who are you becoming?

It's the unspoken question I see in my husband's eyes as he asks me if we need to put lentils on the grocery list. Or when he hands me a mug of tea. Or asks me if I want to watch an action movie to which my answer is mostly no.

On the eve of an official dinner we must attend he asks, "So, how should I introduce you?"

"Your w-i-f-e?!" I enunciate the letters slowly for dramatic effect.

"No, that's not what I meant. What should I say when people ask what you do?"

While we lived in India my all-consuming dream was to get a

Master of Fine Arts degree in creative writing. No Indian university offered such a degree, but I fantasized about somehow enrolling in an American university to make it happen. When Amma died and my old self died with her, the MFA dream died too.

My husband doesn't get that that dream has run out of steam. Every opportunity he finds, he reminds me of it and encourages me to pursue it. These days my soul dreams of guiding, teaching, advising. *Purpose* is the fire that ignites my being. No matter how many times I try to explain this, G's denial of it seems to stem from his grief over my lost dream. To someone who took a lot of pride in my writerly success, the most obvious next step for me is to go to school, earn a degree in writing and publish books. How can I expect him to hold on to intangibles like purpose and meaning and legacy?

Anger rumbles within me. "Tell them I spend my time with dying people. And that I also help people who are grieving because someone they love died."

The silence in the room is heavy. The part of me that wants to ease his discomfort steps in and rescues the moment. "You could say I'm a writer. That's true too."

He nods, relief softening his features.

Here I am, stepping out of all the boxes, stripping away every label. Wife. Mother. Sister. Daughter. Writer. Grief Coach. Volunteer.

Unbecoming, I realize, is a long, slow, sacred unfurling of all the guises I've taken on. Peeling off these veils one by one will get me to the core of my naked truth. The truth of *I Am*.

My husband, like most of the world, hates the uncertainty of the unknown. The secure pinning of an identity feels solid to him. I, on the other hand, am floating in nameless waters, willing the current to carry me to my unique shore.

In the life Before Amma Died, I existed in a state where I'd forgotten. Now I remember. I know something deeper, and I can't unknow it. Forgetting and remembering. It's a constant dance between the two states, stumbling over my feet as they negotiate new terrain. In the before-Amma's-death version of me I walked through life wrapped in a seductive silken veil. I'd forgotten my origin story and why I'd come here. The after-Amma's-death version of me has awakened from the trance. She remembers. The pulsing, throbbing urgency of purpose, the sacred devotion to service, and the simplicity of letting my soul lead the way.

I had to remember in order to 'wake up.' Just as I had to forget in order to 'be asleep' in the five-sensory world, believing in what I thought was the real world and choosing to operate within its rules.

It's impossible for me to go back to sleep now that I'm awake. I can't pretend or deny what I know for sure. I can't fake forgetting.

The world of quick fixes is at odds with the rhythms of the soul. I can't stick my transformation in a microwave and thirty seconds later... voila, I have a new identity, a neat box I can step into. Peeling away an old identity is painful. It hurts to grow. It takes time. Soul growth is about surrendering to patient unfolding.

I'm waiting, moving at the gentle pace my soul dictates. Unbecoming, then becoming. I'm getting to know this person I'm becoming. She's still not fully formed or familiar. It's like trying to slip into a costume that I know is right for me, but the newness of it feels distinctly foreign and the fabric sometimes chafes at my skin.

What I know now, I can never unknow. That I'm a soul in a temporary bodysuit, here for the purpose of living my highest life which includes service, satori, and sensual pleasure in equal measure.

Still, there are days when my monkey mind slips into a brief fantasy about returning to the forgetting state which might be easier. The innocence of fitting in, belonging to a world where the majority share a common agenda. Where I can wander in the addictive trance of materiality and the restrictive experiences of a 3-D life of success, advancement, money, and possibly an unglorified death.

But I know this. As easy as it would have been on my marriage, I don't belong in that life anymore. Nor do I harbor a desire to return to that life. I'm beginning to like my new skin, letting the old one fall away, crumble, and merge with the dust of the earth.

My soul vows hold as much meaning now as my wedding vows do.

BUDDHA'S WIFE

A friend, a loving witness to the depth of my grief and the disconnection in my marriage, recommends a somatic energy healer.

The moment I step into Lyla's healing center, everything in me untangles. I take in her space, breathe it in. The soft glow of votive candles. Fragrant curls of smoke from twin incense sticks. Rose quartz, amethyst, and moonstone gleaming in the gold of candlelight. Fresh flowers. Goddess art on the walls.

As I lay on Lyla's massage table and let her skilled fingertips intuit and unlock spaces in my body and release my pain, tears slide down the corners of my eyes. Lyla kneads and I cry. She stretches a limb and I surrender. She touches a tender spot and my pain trickles out. Her fingers stir memories, awaken buried pain, and unearth parts of me I didn't know how to hold.

She is silent and patient, letting me cry as my body slowly lets go of the wound-weight it's been carrying.

After what seems like a long time she whispers the words. "Talk to me. What have you been carrying?" Her kind words, like gentle raindrops, crack open the heat of unspoken words and truths.

"I don't even know where to begin," I offer.

"Begin somewhere, anywhere. It doesn't have to make sense." Lyla presses a warm compress on my lower back.

"My mother died, and my life fell apart," I begin. Out of the depths of my bones rises the painful story of my boundless grief, the emotional distance in my marriage, and confusion around the purpose of my awakening, my ferocious desire to serve, and the dilemma of walking the path of the mystic while living on the material plane. Everything gushes out of me, the story I haven't been able to give voice to. Lyla listens with the patience of an ancient oak tree, her hands on my skin medicine for my insides.

Thirty minutes later, I'm dressed and ready to leave. I say goodbye and turn the door handle when Lyla's voice stops me. "Uma, wait."

I look over my shoulder and see Lyla running a finger along the spines of a row of books on her shelf. She stops when she gets to the one she's looking for.

She walks up and hands me a hardbound copy of *The Buddha's Wife*. "I don't know why, but something tells me you need this book."

I don't understand it either, but I accept it, smile, and step out.

Over the next few days, I open the book and read the story of Yasodhara, Siddhartha's wife, who woke up one morning to discover her husband gone, leaving her and their six-year-old son Rahula. Siddhartha, the mystic, in pursuit of enlightenment to ease the suffering of the world. Devastated by the abandonment, Yasodhara rides the waves of grief, anger, denial, and betrayal.

The book chronicles her evolution as a wife, mother, and woman who eventually finds her strength and purpose in bringing together a sisterhood, a *sangha* of women. It's the soul medicine Yasodhara needs to move towards forgiveness. Yasodhara opens her heart and embraces her purpose: the responsibility to guide the circle of women to honor their inner wisdom when their outside world crumbles.

My story has me in the middle of the circle, the struggling victim and my husband, the one who has abandoned me emotionally. I berate Siddhartha for leaving and identify with Yasodhara's suffering.

Unlike Yasodhara, I'm still searching for my tribe, my *sangha*. My suffering human self recognizes the need for connection in community, and the need to commit to the path that is calling to me.

INNER FIRE

Days after we moved to suburban Chicago in 2008, I'd joined a local writer's group. The group was an assortment of wannabe writers and published authors working on a range that straddled everything from sci-fi to memoir. Oblivious to the tectonic shift that was headed my way—my mother's death—I'd started to write a novel about two mothers who lose their children under different circumstances and find healing in the friendship that blossoms between them. I'd finished the novel, tried shopping it around without success, and left it to gather digital dust on my hard drive.

One Saturday morning I was in the shower when the knowing flooded me that my next book was going to be about Amma's death and my transformation. When I walked into Barnes & Noble for our

weekly meeting, one of the writers was passing around fresh jour-
nals for everyone. A sign, if ever there was one. *Here's your journal,*
the universe was saying. *Start writing.*

Becoming a Hay House author was a long-cherished dream of
mine that refused to fade, even with all the rhetoric that the company only published authors with an impressive platform, a gazillion social media followers, and tons of visibility.

It took me two years to write my loss memoir *Losing Amma,
Finding Home.* A mystical experience set the stage for my Hay House
dream to come true. I was in India visiting my sister Maya in April
2013, four years after Amma's passing. One morning I was in a
bubble of post-meditation bliss as I picked up a Hay House book
I'd been reading and flipped to the back cover. The address of Hay
House India glowed as if it were lit in neon. Something inside me
whispered. *Call Hay House and tell them about your manuscript.*

Confused about this guidance yet trusting that divine summons was not to be ignored, I picked up my phone and tentatively
punched the numbers listed on the back cover. My mouth was dry,
and my tongue twisted itself into knots when I heard a female voice
say, "Hay House Publishing."

"Please may I speak with someone in the Editorial department?" I didn't know how I said that, but it felt as if someone was
speaking through me, supplying me with the right words.

Moments later I was speaking to an editor, explaining the
premise of my memoir. I told him I had a finished manuscript. All
I remembered from that conversation was him asking me to email

him the first three chapters of my book.

A month later, Hay House wanted to read the entire manuscript. A few more weeks passed before I received an email from a senior editor: *"I have started reading your manuscript. I should hopefully get back to you by mid-June."*

Something in my being knew that the decision would become known to me on June 18, Amma's birthday. In the week leading up to that date, I kept the hotline to heaven really busy.

"Amma, you know how long I've dreamed of being a Hay House author. I'm really close to having this dream. You can make this happen for me from where you are. You know how hard losing you has been. I didn't ask for my life to be upended this way. Let my transformation not be in vain. May our story serve the world."

I showed up at my home office and opened my email on the morning of June 18, a swarm of butterflies swirling in my belly.

There was an email from the senior editor. *"I have read the entire manuscript and we would love to publish it!"*

Tears pouring down my face, I fell to my knees in utter gratitude and thanked Amma. Fingers trembling with emotion I grabbed my phone and called G who was driving. My blubbering sobbing confused him enough, causing him to panic and pull over to the shoulder of a Houston freeway.

He emailed me later. *"Fantastic news and truly amazing that it should come on Amma's birthday. Your book deserves to be published and read and your journey shared."*

A box full of my printed books arrived a year later. I held one to my heart and wept. For me, for Amma, for G, and for everyone who would be touched and transformed by my words, my story, my purpose. A holy moment, it had the feel of bells ringing and angels singing.

SILVER WEDDING

G is riding the wave of a deeply energizing season of work, his travels taking him to Istanbul, Melbourne, Bangkok, Shanghai, Köln, London, Barcelona, and Vienna. New business wins prime him to pump even harder. I find myself sitting on the sidelines of his life, watching and waiting, for crumbs of attention.

It's hard to believe that Amma has been gone for seven long years, but what's real is the grief of disconnection between G and me gradually hardening into a rock of resentment. The very sight of his work phone and laptop—digital mistresses—burn me up.

We're coming up on our twenty-fifth wedding anniversary. Unbeknownst to me G has been planning a grand surprise: a two-week trip to Italy. Terrible at keeping secrets, he blurts out our holiday destination to me one week before we're due to fly. As much as I love a good surprise I'm okay that he spilled the beans. It's fun to plan what to pack.

After a three-day stopover in Rome where we take in the sights—the Vatican, Pantheon, Colosseum—we travel through Naples and the lush green coastal beauty of Capri before arriving in Calabria. A region of rugged mountains, old-fashioned villages, and a dramatic coastline, the drive to Calabria takes my breath away. We arrive at the secluded beach house where we're staying in Pizzo. A sprawling beach is only a ten-minute walk away.

We unpack, shower, and settle in.

G turns on his iPad to access his music collection. Loud jazz fills the space. "Isn't that too *raucous*?" I ask, hoping he'll turn down the volume.

Instead, he's ticked off. He (mis)understands my question, believes it signals my resentment that he's listening to music. I try to convince him that that's not true. Soon our exchange degenerates into a pointless argument and we go to bed, both nursing a giant sulk. Next morning, I wake up and remember my awful behavior. I apologize for being insensitive to his need to play music at whatever volume he chooses, and G returns the apology owning that my question triggered him.

When I come downstairs after a shower the next morning G is staring at his iPad, absorbed in a game of basketball. The noisy game and commentary drown the delightful birdsong in our tucked-away beach house, so I head off to the front porch.

"Why did you go outside?" G asks, a few moments later.

"Because it's too noisy inside."

He snaps his iPad shut.

"You don't have to do that," I say. "I wanted silence, so I stepped outside."

"It was only a sixty-second clip. This was an upset win and I wanted to check the scores," he justifies.

Once again, our words tangle in frustration and anger. Clearly, we're not on the same wavelength. I fail to understand why he's distracted by his devices and doing his own thing when we're on our 'milestone' vacation. The rest of the day we communicate in grunts and monosyllables, then go to bed upset with each other. Again.

When I wake up the next morning the combined weight of despair and guilt presses down on me. This is supposed to be our special anniversary vacation, but our wires have crossed ever since we arrived in Calabria. Our marital milestone seems to be jinxed.

G holds out a steaming mug of tea as I arrive downstairs. "I think we need to talk."

"I'd like that," I say, always happy to use words to bridge a broken connection.

We each own our triggers. His trigger: I "walked out" on him because he was watching a game; my trigger: his digital distraction.

I want to hang out on the beach for a couple of hours. G has developed a monster cold, and the wind has picked up, so he'd rather stay indoors. But he asks me several times if that would be okay—he wants to make sure I don't mind going alone.

I walk to the beach and sit down on a piece of driftwood to watch the ocean. Waves pound the shore and surf curls like pretty white lace, only to rush back and be embraced by another wave. I see two figures in the distance walking toward me. As they get closer I can tell it's a man and a woman. They're holding hands and talking, their steps a hypnotic rhythm of togetherness. He leans down and whispers something to her. She giggles. Then he drapes an arm on her shoulder and nuzzles the side of her neck. Watching this scene of tender intimacy I tear up, thankful for sunglasses that hide my crying eyes.

Why is it so hard for me and G to have this? Why do we argue so much? Why doesn't he ever want to hold my hand? Am I not desirable anymore?

Of the few people on the beach today some are walking, lying on beach towels, reading, snoozing. Everyone seems to have someone to share sun, sand, and surf with. Except me. A wave of self-pity drenches me.

The words I often share with clients come back to haunt me. *You're looking at someone's current chapter and basing their whole life story on this chapter.* Why is it so hard for me to apply this wisdom to my life right now?

Even as I wish nothing but happiness for the beach walker couple, I realize that I'm writing a story for them that may bear little resemblance to the one they're actually living.

Maybe she has cancer, and this beach holiday is her last hurrah.

Maybe they're both cheating on their spouses.

Maybe he will dump her later tonight.

Who knows what anyone else is living through, thinking about, or motivated by?

I run a mental tally of my husband's positives and there are plenty. Wonderful cook. Devoted husband. Caring father. He honors my freedom every way he can. He always buys me gifts, never denies me anything I want. Why isn't that enough for me? Why am I intent on qualifying his goodness with "yeah, buts?" My man is a solid Atticus Finch. Why do I yearn for a Nicholas Sparks hero?

❧

"Happy 25th!" G wakes me up with a sleepy kiss. We cuddle in bed for a while, then shower and get dressed.

"Why don't you say a prayer for us?" I ask G.

"Me?!"

I'm the prayer-sayer in our family, but he accepts the challenge and shapes a beautiful prayer for our special day. After lunch we drive to a sea cave, the Chiesa di Piedigrotta, situated on a fisherman's beach. Legend has it that in 1665 a ship from Naples ran into a fierce storm and was about to crash against the rocky cliffs below Pizzo. The captain prayed to a picture of the Madonna on board the ship and begged her to save him and the crew. The ship was battered to pieces, but every man was saved. As an act of thankfulness, the captain installed the Madonna's picture inside a cave carved out of rock exactly at the spot where they miraculously reached the shore.

At the town square we stroll past tiny shops selling trinkets and tee shirts, spices and chocolates, posters and prints. Later we order dinner, pizza for me, and shrimp drenched in a bright yellow curry sauce for G. Time melts away as we relax over the delicious meal and people-gaze.

When G pulls out his cell phone and starts to scroll, all my triggers rush to the surface. I leave the table and wander over to a ledge overlooking the bay wondering why I'm never enough, not even on our silver wedding anniversary day. G senses my mood and his own darkens.

On the drive back to the beach house, I try to explain.

"I don't know why you have to check your phone when we're having a nice meal on our twenty-fifth wedding anniversary at a beautiful location in Italy."

"I don't know," G says. "I can't just switch off. I think about work all the time, I have ideas." He sweeps a hand across a stunning sunset to our left. "It's my work that makes all this possible."

His justification is gasoline to my fire. We argue some more and when we pull up to the house, we're both reduced to tears at the futility of our efforts to be nice to each other and falling short, again and again.

"Please. I'm sorry," I say. "Forgive me. I don't know why this bothers me so much. I'll try to be more understanding."

We go to bed, books in hand, emotionally exhausted. We barely last a few pages.

"Sorry for screwing up your day," says G.

"Can you say something positive before we close out the day?" I ask.

"I love you."

We hold each other and fall asleep.

SILENT SCREAM

Some days I feel I'm living inside a silent scream. Screaming out loud is not allowed. No one will understand it. *What's wrong with her? She wants to scream? Just look at her life. Where's the gratitude?*

Desire is a squeamish word in our vocabulary. Immodest, shocking, bold. When I view my longings through the lens of *desire* I convince myself it's wrong to want what I want. But then again I wonder. Why is it petty and selfish for me to want deep, heartfelt connection with the man I married?

The world tells me that if my husband is committed, cooks, cleans, shops, pays the bills, buys me gifts, and never, ever forgets my birthday, I must smile and feel deeply contented. I have no right to ask for anything more. Such a man is a prize catch. I *know* this. So, the fault for *wanting more* is all mine. Something is wrong with *me*. I'm the selfish, ungrateful bitch, the one that demands something he doesn't know how to give.

My heart won't be silenced. It wants what it wants and I'm not sure I need to make it wrong. Believe me, I spent many years dancing between the difficult questions of *why can't I just be happy with what I have?* and *why do I make my longings illegitimate?*

The long silences in our relationship feel punishing.

Long silences become sacred pauses when they're inserted into meaningful conversations. For a time, I tried to hide from the truth that long silences meant we had nothing to say to each other. There's no bridge on the planet that connects conversations about the NBA, geopolitics, and the logistics industry with ones on purpose, legacy, and the urgency to lead a meaningful life. These are the very different realms G and I occupy.

There is a key distinction, though. It hardly matters to him whether I understand or engage with his interests. He doesn't expect me to enjoy an NBA game. He simply enjoys my presence in the room and sometimes wishes I wouldn't leave the room when I get bored, but he won't press charges. A noble perspective.

In sharp contrast, it matters to me that he listens to a podcast that set my heart on fire, or parts of a book that made me cry. I've spent the last decade making myself wrong for what I want and trying to deny what I desire.

When I chance upon the work of Belgian psychotherapist Esther Perel, her words stir awake long-buried compassion. "Even a good marriage leaves people with longings for certain things their marriage will never be," she says. "So, do they accept that, make compromises, and say, 'You can't have everything in life,' which is what we always did? Or do they say, 'I deserve more. I want to experience that thing and, you know, I have fifty more years to live than I used to.' It's not necessarily that we have more desires today, but we do feel more entitled to pursue them. We live in this 'right to happiness' culture, and yes, we do live half a century longer than we used to."

Perel speaks to the truth of my heart when she says, "Today, we turn to one person to provide what an entire village once did: a sense of grounding, meaning, and continuity. At the same time, we expect our committed relationships to be romantic as well as emotionally and sexually fulfilling. Is it any wonder that so many relationships crumble under the weight of it all?"

I grieve that what G and I once shared can no longer exist, even as we're navigating a new landscape and our place in it, both as individuals and as a couple. Whereas the initial shock of finding ourselves on our individual paths has worn off, I continue to swing from one tree limb of emotion to another in wild, chaotic arcs. From grief to anger and bargaining to denial before I circle back to grief again. Acceptance is an invisible target in the foggy distance. Will I ever get there?

PANDEMIC PANIC

We're in San Francisco when the pandemic hits.

When G quit his job in Chicago in the fall of 2019 and accepted a new position at a logistics start-up in San Francisco, Marin County became the place we called home.

That move happened only eight months ago, but G is already frustrated with his new job. Conversely, I'm utterly enchanted by our life here, the endless ocean, redwoods, and our hillside apartment where deer visit.

A series of synchronistic events reopen the door to his old job, but there's a twist. The position requires us to relocate to Germany. Quitting the west coast job with another in hand is a huge relief, but I'm crushed that we have to pack up and move again within six months.

G's last workday in San Francisco unleashes a flood of emotions in me. Immense relief that I no longer have to open the door every evening and watch my man walk through the door looking utterly defeated. Deep sadness that this new west coast life we've barely begun is already coming to an end. The tug of resistance to packing and moving and starting over. Anger because I like it here, in the Bay Area. *I don't want to move.*

The pandemic shutdown stalls our relocation plans. We cannot travel. The German company FedExes my husband a phone and laptop to get him set up for remote work starting April 1, 2020.

Now that G's work is on the European time zone, the West Coast is the worst place to live. By the time he's scanned through his morning emails, the East Coast is eating lunch, Europe is ready to call it a day, and Asia is getting ready for bed. He has 6 A.M. and 9 P.M. calls, erasing all boundaries between work and personal space.

I've always worked from a home office. I had a Zoom account way before it became the new trend, and the entire world switched to it. I love my space. I don't want to share my queendom. When I'm working, I'm working. G misses watercooler conversations. I never had them. He pops into our spare bedroom—now my office— for a random coffee break or chinwag. I'm not pleasant when I'm interrupted.

We're both home and eating in so we run out of food more quickly. More grocery lists. More shopping and cooking and clean-ing. Domestic trivia intrudes into my quiet space and sacred work time. Everything about this new normal feels fundamentally abnormal to me.

All day, CNN continues to keep the collective amygdala activated with constant updates on the rising Covid death toll, and shortages in masks, gloves, and ventilators. Store aisles are empty as people race around grabbing every last roll of toilet paper they can find. This is no longer the stuff of reality television.

Our toilet roll supply is fast dwindling, but every trip to Safeway has us leaving empty-handed. We're down to our last two rolls when I throw up my hands, look heavenward and say, "Okay, we've tried everything we can. Now it's up to you."

Finally, Uma, God seems to say. *It took you all this time.*

Within twenty-four hours, we have a miracle. When I open our front door one morning, I almost weep at the sight of a carton of toilet paper rolls sitting on the doormat. A fuchsia pink Post-it stuck on top bears a simple heart sign and our neighbor's signature.

Certainly, a first in my life, weeping at the gift of toilet paper rolls. But such are the times we live in.

One tiny act of kindness. One giant act of love.

We must have mentioned the toilet paper roll shortage with our lovely neighbors over a fence chat. That they tucked the info away carefully and bought us a carton when they found one means everything to me.

I could just run out and hug them, but I won't. Because I care about them—and the best return act of love I can offer them in these times is to stay away. Six feet away.

❧

Most times when I walk into a room I find G otherwise occupied. Bose headphones perched on his head and immersed in a basketball game, comedy show, or travel video on his iPad. When the headphones come off, his head is still crowded with retirement planning, 401K, and healthcare options for a future when we retire in the U.S. and Medicare kicks in.

There's little room in there for me.

Both of us are really good at the adulting stuff. We're responsible partners in running a home. We're good about reminding each other when eggs need to go on the grocery list, a doctor's appointment has to be scheduled, or dry cleaning has to be picked up.

Matters of the soul and spirit, the things that open my heart, have no place in our combined lives. I know he cannot be my entire village. The reality is it's April 2020 and the village has vanished in the wake of a pandemic that's shut the whole world down.

I'm out walking one afternoon when I spot three women outside Peet's Coffee. Sitting on the front stoop six-ish feet away from each other they're sipping coffee, masks dangling under their chin. A sharp pang of envy pierces me. I miss my friends in Chicago, their warm hugs. I miss sitting across from them, plates of green goodness between us, leaning in and sharing whispered confidences without the paranoia of a deadly virus threatening our closeness.

I stop. I can't pass these women without saying something. "I love how you're practicing social distancing... have fun!"

They smile and wave back before turning to each other.

Even as we all maintain a safe distance from one another, I see how primal our need for connection is. Every walker I pass on the street makes eye contact, waves, offers a greeting. Even the bikers huffing their way up steep slopes raise a hand when they pass a hiker. It's a simple gesture that says *I see you. We're all in this together.*

I'm sitting on the back patio, my nose in Glennon Doyle's just-released book *Untamed.* It's a delicious sun-drenched afternoon, bird music in the air, trees rich with tender green foliage. This is about as perfect as a pandemic day gets.

I'm feeling all the feels as I get to the part where Glennon tells her husband that she's in love with a woman and wants out of the marriage. My heart aches for their three children—even as it swells with womanly pride for a sister-soul brave enough to claim what she knows is right for her.

Every bold life-changing decision involves a degree of heart-break. Someone finds a relationship that makes them come alive— and someone is staring at the ashes of a relationship that just burned to the ground.

These feelings churn inside me and crumble my carefully constructed pandemic-era emotional edifice. I walk into the living room, drop into an armchair, and feel something give inside me. Rivers of tears mark a salty path down my cheeks.

G is in the kitchen making tea.

When he steps into the living room, steaming mugs in hand, he sees my tear-stained face.

"What happened?" he asks, setting the mugs down on coasters.

"I'm just sick and tired of this pandemic," I blubber through my tears. "I've had it."

He opens his mouth. I sense the words that are about to tumble out and knock me down the slippery slope I'm already on. Taking swift preventive action, I say, "Please. Don't. Don't ask me to be grateful for everything we have."

His fix-it resolve dissolves.

I sob noisily. "I *am* grateful for everything we have. Our apartment, our health, work, food... all of it. Really. I am. But I also miss browsing in a bookstore and hugging friends. Sitting in a café and eating a salad... I hate having to wear a stupid mask every time I step out. I miss... life."

G remains silent. His logical brain needs a moment to recalibrate and respond to right-brained me.

"Well," he begins. "You feel things, so... well, you feel them."

The breath I've been holding rushes out of me. Permission is the sweetest thing. Often, the words he offers me right after my teary confessions decide the course of the rest of our evening. This one has been salvaged.

"Most of the time I'm trying to stay positive and strong and doing my thing." I pause, blow my nose. "But I also get to be human and messy some of the time."

I know how important it is to own my longings. As selfish as it feels to speak these words when nurses and doctors wake up each morning, don their protective gear and walk into their arena, it feels important to voice my needs. As an empath and a sensitive, I feel others' pain as if it were my own and can very quickly abandon my body and migrate over to theirs to take some of their discomfort away.

In this moment I'm thinking of every woman who struggles with shame and avoids speaking up. Every woman who turns away from the truest desires of her heart, things she thinks but won't allow herself to say out loud.

I just wish I could get my nails done.

I miss sitting in my hair salon and having my roots touched up.

If only I could get on a plane and take that trip I've been dreaming of.

We spend so much of our lives berating and judging ourselves, shaming ourselves for not having attained some gold standard where such longings will cease to exist.

What if the invitation is not to stretch for that seemingly unattainable goal? What if it is to simply grow into a larger container, one that can hold all the parts of who we are—the mean, the messy, and the mystic?

❧

I have big dreams for my life. To write more books, speak in front of audiences, inspire and empower. In my innocent days I made a habit of spilling my dreams. My naïve belief was that sharing my dreams with my friends and peers would amplify the excitement. Sadly, that hasn't been my experience.

Heart on fire, I'd place my tender, fragile dream in the hands of someone who found it too heavy to carry and would drop it. I'd watch in absolute horror as my dream lay in shards of shattered possibility.

Some teachers encourage you to be loud about your dreams. How can people help you realize your dream if they don't know about it, they ask. But I've come to realize an important truth. A dream is like a delicate silken cobweb. You only invite those people who can stand near it and watch in awe, marveling at the magic that's coming to life. You can't trust the cobweb to those who will tear at it, destroy it before it's even had a chance to unfurl. Sometimes we don't choose those people with care. Just because someone is your spouse or cousin doesn't mean they earn the privilege of being invited to the unfolding of this magic-in-the-mind.

It's a Sunday morning in May. We're almost two months into the pandemic that has put the entire world on hold. G and I are in the kitchen. In his left hand is a saltshaker. His right hand is stirring cooked white rice tossed with burnt garlic, red pepper flakes, and an assortment of vegetables. His hands are full. And yet, I choose this moment to place into them a secret longing of mine.

"You're an initiator," I begin the conversation. "All that Aries energy of leading and being in charge. Me, I'm a typical Leo. I just want to show up and stand in the spotlight. I have no interest in organizing and managing and marketing. I'm happy to let someone else who's good at that stuff handle those details."

Now he's crisscrossing the kitchen, opening cupboards, pulling out spice bottles, setting them down to chop cilantro.

"I just want to show up and wow my audience," I finish.

When he hears the last sentence he pauses, smirks.

"Why are you smirking?" I ask, feeling the tightness of defense creeping into my body.

"What?! I'm just smiling."

"Well, smirking... smiling—but why?"

"We're just... cut from different cloths."

"What's that supposed to mean?"

"Well, I'm a worker bee. I can't expect other people to take care of stuff and just want to... show up."

My stomach clenches. A wave of shame drenches me.

You shouldn't have said that. He's tearing into your delicate cobweb.

I rush in to explain. "I mean, what I'm trying to say is, organizing is not my strength. I do best when I'm speaking, sharing my message..." I trail off. Every cell in my body recognizes that I'm contracting, shrinking to contain myself into a box he can hold.

Shame is a timely trigger. G simply pushed a button that's still red-hot inside me. Tears rush into my eyes as soon as this realization dawns. Wordlessly, I walk up the stairs and slip into the shower. I need the privacy to let my tears flow without having to explain why I'm crying, why it's not an over-the-top reaction, and why crying those tears always makes me feel better. In the cleansing waters of a hot shower, my mind and my heart begin to speak to each other and connect the dots for me.

Shame. It's around the label of *lazy* I've carried since childhood. I didn't know it was still in there, hiding in the dark, thriving unseen.

I've been called lazy by my maternal grandmother who prided

herself on her productivity. My grandparents' home was subjected to such a high standard of elegance that every corner shone and sparkled. Her culinary creations are part of family lore. The mouth-watering meals that magically emerged did so from a kitchen that had no time-saving appliances like mixers, choppers, and grinders. She sweated and toiled over a stove in the hundred-plus-degree heat of Chennai summers to cook three meals a day for her family.

My mother and aunt were raised with the value 'the more time you spend stirring something on the stove, the more worthy you are.' My aunt passed on this value to her daughter but my mother who was more a live-and-let-live kind of person did not impose it on me and my sisters.

Somehow, my sister Vidya inhaled the value through osmosis— and became best friends with the family duster. My youngest sister Maya also found her way into, and around, the kitchen. I must have missed the gene in the cosmic factory because cooking and cleaning slid way down to the bottom of my list.

My sisters rolled their eyes at me. I didn't have the talent for domesticity, a much-coveted attribute in Indian brides in the eighties. I daresay the expectation hasn't died even though we live in an age where women excel in arenas as varied as sports, medicine, and tech.

I whip up a reasonably good South Indian meal and keep a clean home—but you won't ever find me Googling recipes or getting the dirt out from behind the dryer. I do it because I have to eat and like to live in a clean home; not because it makes me feel productive or worthy.

I think back to my mother's real concern that my husband would starve, and me countering that concern with the conviction that I'd find a man who knew his way around the kitchen.

I did manifest that miracle man who loves brooms, mops, and ladles, almost as much as he loves me.

Unexpectedly, gratitude wells up. Gratitude to G for unearthing the deeply buried wound of *lazy*. *Thank you,* I whisper. *Thank you for letting it rise so that I can feel it, thank it, bless, and release it.*

I've always had a knowing my destiny lives beyond domesticity, but this belief doesn't come from misplaced arrogance. I know it as surely as I know my skin is brown and my eyes are black. I feel it in my bones. Back then I didn't have the language or experience to flesh it out, but the blueprint was in place. My life wasn't going to be about the traditional roles a woman was expected to conform to. I've always colored outside the lines. Heck, I didn't even know there were lines.

So, I tucked my knowing away in a secret corner of my heart. I couldn't bear the thought of this wingless bird being bruised by those who had no access to my inner vision.

Being called lazy hurt my sensitive soul. And now, all these years later, my red-hot button was pushed again. What I didn't know back then and know now is this: if I don't fully, unashamedly own my belief that it is possible to find my place in the spotlight without striving and struggling, I may never experience it.

If G hadn't awakened the slumbering giant within me, I

wouldn't have known the trigger was well and alive, derailing my dream. Hard as it is, the hurt must rise to the light, be released and healed.

I'm standing in front of my bedroom mirror outlining my lips in lavender. Kohl in my eyes. Mascara on my lashes. I tame my unruly bangs with a pair of barrettes.

I'm dressing up for what feels like an event: my 1.5-mile walk to Rite-Aid to refill a prescription.

The pharmacy is almost empty when I walk in. The few employees all wear masks but seem comfortable speaking through it. My mask chafes. My breath is trapped in gauze.

My prescription refilled, I stroll through the shopping arcade. The usually bustling space is deserted, a standard notice taped to the doors of most businesses: restaurants, juice bars, gift shops, furniture stores, and children's clothing. *Closed until further notice due to Covid-19. We apologize for the inconvenience.*

Sadness wells up inside me. All these business owners face an uncertain future. How long will the virus continue to wreak havoc on the economy? Will businesses ever reopen, or is this the beginning of the end? I miss the busyness of life here: shoppers laden with bags, kids bargaining for one more toy from the display window, teenagers licking pink ice-cream cones.

G has a well-paying job. We have food and shelter, electricity, hot water, and television with more entertainment channels than we know what to do with. Why do I complain about the hours he works? Why am I blind to the bounty of the universe?

G wakes up before me.

He makes his morning tea.

I make the bed and my lemon water.

He cuts an apple into thin slices, arranges them on a quarter plate, sets the butter dish on the table. I toast a couple of slices of bread. We eat breakfast together.

I make two mugs of coffee.

We both work for a few hours. He's downstairs; I'm upstairs in my home office.

We meet for lunch between 12:30 and 1:00 P.M.

We return to our respective workstations. Meet for tea and biscuits at 4:00 P.M.

We take a two-mile walk, get home, catch Chris Cuomo on CNN with the latest Covid-19 updates, eat dinner, and put the day to bed.

G wakes up before I do.

He makes his morning tea.

I make the bed and my lemon water.

It's Day 56 of lockdown and these are the well-worn steps in our pandemic dance.

It's Day 70 of lockdown and I've hit a wall.

G and I marked a milestone, 29 years together. In celebrating this day, we're nowhere near the stunning views of the Amalfi coast, but it is a quiet, peaceful day. The most exciting thing that we're dealing with is Trump's grand announcement that he has been taking an anti-malarial drug hydroxychloroquine for a week-and-a-half as preventative treatment against Covid-19.

Stepping into year thirty, some days are lonelier than ever. Coronavirus, the killjoy beast, has a big role to play in it.

"Disasters are relationship accelerators," says an expert Oprah is interviewing on a Zoom broadcast. The cracks in relationships are being exposed in these times of intimate, yet distance living.

The apartment walls seem to be closing in on me. They are also thin enough for us to hear our neighbors' constant bickering which, as the evening progresses, ramps up to beer-fueled angry yelling. Inside our apartment the air is stuffy, the space is thick with unspoken feelings and words. The two people who live here are a continent away from each other.

It's nobody's fault.

I consciously commit to every longing in my heart. My love of verbal volleys. My deep comfort with physical affection. My gift of befriending complete strangers who spill their darkest secrets to me. My talent for listening, being a receptacle for others' tears and terrors. This is my superpower. It can't be the source of my shame. I won't allow it. In that moment, I make room for all of me.

A friend introduces me to the term *Coronacoaster* to describe the yo-yo states we're living in during the pandemic. Riding the Coronacoaster is exhausting because you never know where you're going to find yourself, often one hour to the next.

Anne Lamott, one of my favorite authors, likens it to being on a spinning Lazy Susan. One spin and I find myself parked at Anger. Anger at how the government is mismanaging the pandemic, how states are thinking of opening without adequate precautions in place. Spin again and I land in Grief. Here we are in spectacular Marin County filled with hiking trails, beaches, and forests within driving distance, but everything is closed.

My grief also relates to a specific timeline. It's June 2020. In two months, we will pack our possessions and move to Düsseldorf where G will begin the next season of his career. Three months into the pandemic and we've been cleared to fly.

Another spin and I find my hands on my heart, deep in Gratitude. Blessings abound even in the midst of all this baloney. Good health, a roof over our heads, comforts big and small.

A couple of hours later furious tides sweep away all sanity and I find myself wondering when and if the world will return to some semblance of normalcy. The uncertainty of it has me standing, palms open to the sky in total surrender. Take this over, dear God. Show us the way, I whisper.

My husband copes by doing. He makes lentil soup. He brings me hot tea. He drives me to Whole Foods. And we get through another day, wondering what tomorrow will bring.

A paragraph of spoken words is a warm-up for me. It's the end of a grueling marathon to G.

This is a real problem.

I enjoy word duels, philosophical explorations, meandering in the woods of story. I can spin words into an elaborate tapestry of arguments, probabilities, hypotheses, and speculations. I come alive in living, breathing words.

The mistake I repeatedly make is in trying to draw G into my dueling arenas. He takes the bait, but within moments feels like a fly trapped in a silken word-web. Feeling cornered he exits the game, leaving me, the spider, starving.

Over time I learn to make my peace with it. Instead of taking my words to my husband, I take them to the page. The page is patient, forgiving. Yet, there are moments when the words bubble up in my throat and I'm unable to stem the flow. I toss them out like gorgeous confetti, only to be met with monosyllabic responses or bored grunts. Sometimes I'm graceful about retreating. Other times I demand a dialogue which rarely ends well.

Living with each other in close proximity during the pandemic has dissolved the illusion that we're a couple who have things to say to each other. It is an unsettling reality.

I think back to our pre-pandemic life.

Each morning I'd kiss my husband goodbye, send him off to work, shut the front door and enter my world of one. My days were a happy collage of client-mentoring, blog posts, creating teaching content, and lunch break with a Netflix show. When G arrived home at half-past six, it was a punctuation mark of sorts. It signaled the end of our individual day and the intersection of our lives together. He'd bring me news of office politics, water cooler conversations, an interesting encounter on the ferry ride home. Sometimes, he brought me a treat from one of the Ferry Building shops. Embedded in our interactions was an element of surprise.

Now he's home. I'm home. This is our entire world—where we eat, work, watch TV, sleep. Boundaries and intersections have melted away. There's a grayness to our days, no technicolor bursts of surprise.

. I think back to something a well-known author shared in an interview. Her publisher had canceled the physical book tour planned for her third book. But because the said author had won awards for two successful books, she had an eager audience. All her events were moved online.

As fun as it was to do them, she shared how she missed the in-person interaction, book signing and chitchat with buyers who asked questions and shared bits of their lives. But what she said next stayed with me. After her Webex book event, she'd have to go downstairs and tackle a sink full of dirty dishes, deal with her kids who'd been bribed to stay quiet, and give her hubby a break from child-minding. She wasn't fully able to savor the sweetness of her book event.

I imagine her pre-Covid book event. She must have picked out a nice outfit and sexy heels, faced her audience questions with aplomb, smiled, shaken several hands, and posed with loyal fans for a gazillion selfies.

All she needed for an online event was a blouse that would look suitably elegant on her Zoom screen. She sat alone in her study or library or home office. And when the event was done, she must have traipsed downstairs to her messy kitchen and clingy kids.

LONGINGS

How do I still the longings of my heart? How do I silence the wellspring of desire? Is it wrong to want? Does it make me ungrateful?

The questions jostle in my head as I prep a salad for dinner. Cucumber half-moons and shreds of arugula slide down the cutting board and into the salad bowl, followed by long slivers of yellow and red peppers. I drizzle the veggies with olive oil and lemon juice and let it sit.

Outside the window, a charcoal-gray weeping sky.

G lights two candles and pours two glasses of Chardonnay. As we take our places at the dining table, a familiar sorrow wells up within me. It's one of those evenings when the river is in spate. We hold hands and say the Serenity Prayer as we do before our evening meal and begin to eat in silence.

I no longer know how to have ordinary conversations: about the latest Covid-19 stats, how the Indian cricket team is faring in the test series in Australia, or what the latest travel and quarantine rules are.

My soul aches for the kind of conversations my husband and I don't know how to have.

"I long for deep conversations." I verbally barf an unmet need.

"What is a deep conversation?" my husband asks, slathering hummus on a piece of bread. "I don't know how to have one."

Admitting this personal truth, perhaps, triggers vulnerability because I hear defensiveness creep into his next words. "Where's the time? Tell me what I'm not doing. What else can I possibly do during the week?"

Silently I push cucumber slices around my plate.

"What are deep conversations?" He continues. "And am I supposed to initiate them?"

"It's not an agenda," I begin. "It's not like we have to pick a set of topics and then decide that we're having a conversation on one of those topics on Thursday evening at 6 PM.."

"I've told you I don't know these things. I don't know how to talk about..."

"Please. I'm not blaming you. It's okay that you don't know how to—or want to." My throat feels tight. "And it still makes me feel alone in the marriage."

There, I've said it.

"I'm not sure we'll ever move beyond that. I don't even understand the kind of stuff you read, teach, and speak about. Conversely, you don't care about the stuff that I think about."

My tears breach the dam and slide down my cheeks. I try to find the words, my voice trembling. Words that will help me own, not blame. Words that will make space for both our humanity. A tough task.

"I can't go back to who I used to be—and a part of me is sorry about that. On days when I'm deeply frustrated, I get angry with Amma. Of course, it's not much use being angry with someone who's dead because they say nothing. But the work I do today wouldn't be possible if I hadn't become this person."

G stares at his plate, his expression cloudy. "Just because I don't show it or talk about it... doesn't mean I'm not lonely."

Utterly self-absorbed in my marital isolation, the possibility of *his* loneliness hasn't even occurred to me. After all, I married an introvert-doer who never gets off the hamster wheel of his corporate job. Who desperately craves silence and an absence of human connection after a day of endless conference calls and online meetings. Which has led me to presume, incorrectly, that his life is full, not empty—and therefore, not lonely.

"Just because I don't show my feelings doesn't mean I don't feel things," says G.

A giant space of illumined truth opens up inside of me.

He doesn't get what he needs either. It's not just me.

"But I don't dwell on it," he continues. "There's so much that's working well in this marriage. We get to travel, see new places, we're both healthy, you love your work... and even if my job is a grind, it makes all this possible," he gestures, his wide-open arms encompassing the abundance that is our lives.

It's true. No matter what, he wakes up to an alarm every morning, showers, gets dressed, and drives to work.

Whether he feels like it or not.

Whether his heart is in it or not.

Whether it's a gray and gloomy or cold and foggy day.

Whether he wins the next piece of business or loses it to competition.

The golden glow of gratitude radiates a warm feeling in my chest.

He sets his fork down, looks at me. "I love you. I just want you to be happy. Whether or not I understand what you do these days. As long as it makes you happy, I'm happy for you."

"What about you?" I ask.

"I have my good days and bad, but I try to count my blessings. We're both in a challenging season of life. You're following your path, and I'm trying to secure our financial future. That's part of life. I work hard... the rest is up to God."

I listen, inspired by his self-awareness and commitment to stay the course. What he says next takes my breath away. Only a real man who's comfortable in his own skin would express such a selfless sentiment to his wife of three decades.

"It hurts me to see you so unhappy. I've tried my best to give you everything I can. This is all I know. But if you want to find something more, something I don't know how to give you, I'll accept it if you want to look for someone who *can* give it to you." He pauses. "Even if... if it's another man."

Stunned into silence, I stare at my husband.

Another woman may have interpreted these words to mean her man was giving up on her, on them. An abdication of responsibility. To me this feels like the purest love ever. Because if you know anything about my husband, his middle name is Commitment.

"That's... that's not at all what I want. The thought of another man has never even crossed my mind. There's only you. It's always been you."

G shrugs, his palms open to the ceiling. "Then, this is all you've got."

LIFE IS NOT A CABARET

Four months of remote working later, we're finally given the green flag to travel. Relocation plans swing into action, and we arrive in Germany in August 2020. As heartbroken as I was to close the door on our life in magical Marin, I'm enchanted by the landscape of our new country: quaint houses, cobblestoned paths, and ancient churches every direction I look. Church bells ring delightfully all through the day, and I'm happy to be reacquainted with onions and tomatoes that are normal in size, not genetically modified monsters.

We're assigned temporary accommodation in Essen where we will live until our possessions arrive from California. Weeks into our settling-in, the pandemic moves into a new phase of risk. Germany's lockdown is severe. All museums, restaurants, and public spaces are closed. There's nowhere to go, nothing to do.

Except for grocery shopping.

I'm at a local store looking for a bottle of pasta sauce. Grabbing one off the shelf, I stare at the ingredient list, and sigh. Every aisle, every label on every product is in German. Tentatively, I approach the salesgirl and begin to ask, "Could you please..." She shakes her head vehemently to let me know she doesn't speak English; I know about five German words. Not enough to frame a question. I whip out my iPhone, and type each word into Google Translate, carefully spelling every letter out loud so I get it right. Twenty minutes of this and I've only shopped for three of the eleven items on my grocery list.

Living in a foreign country adds another layer to the complexity of pandemic living. G and I have been thrust into each other's company for months on end, all the distractions of work travel and fun trips melting away, no new friendships on the horizon, and old friendships having to recalibrate to screen mode. Lockdown ensures I can't go to a library, not even a German one which has less than half-a-dozen shelves of English books, mostly pop fiction.

When will this pandemic release its tight grip on our world, I wonder.

✤

My copy of *The Buddha's Wife* pulls me to it. Maybe it has a new message to reveal in this season of my life. I pull it off the shelf and start to read it a second time.

The book tells the story of how Yasodhara's—Buddha's wife's—life unfolds after her husband Siddhartha leaves the palace as an awakened being determined to heal the suffering of the world. I marvel at how Yasodhara found soul medicine in the sisterhood she gathered around her at the lowest ebb of her life. Once again I'm reminded of my longing for a sisterhood.

In trying to find a solution to bridge the distance between G and me, I meet an African shaman on a Zoom call and share a summary of our relationship using the book for context. I share how Siddhartha's abandonment of Yasodhara strikes a chord with me, and draw a parallel to the story of my own marriage.

The first words she speaks hit me so hard they rearrange the narratives I've carried for so long. "Uma, have you considered that *you* are the Buddha in your marriage? *You're* the one who left."

My face crumples with emotion. Unable to tear my gaze away from hers, I feel the wisdom of her words pierce my entire being. "Oh, my God. I never saw it that way. *I'm* the one who left, not *he.*"

When G comes home in the evening I wrap my arms around him. My tears drench his shoulder. "I'm sorry I left."

"But you didn't. You're still here," he smiles.

I laugh through my tears. "No, I mean...well, back in '09 when Amma died. When my life fell apart, I took the fork in the road. I made the decision to follow my calling which meant I had to give up some parts of "our life."

"It's okay. You're still here. With me. That's all that matters," he says, his arms tight around me.

MANY FLAVORS OF LOVE

In one of my favorite podcast episodes on Glennon Doyle's *We Can Do Hard Things,* co-host Amanda offers an idea that stirs something in me. It's the idea of *lightning love* versus *summer rain love.*

Lightning love is the Hollywood version of romantic love that we women are especially addicted to. It's the kind of light that dazzles the entire sky. Love that sizzles and steams. We commonly dismiss anything that's not lightning love as *less than.*

"Lightning love can also burn and destroy your entire house and everything that you love inside it," explains Amanda. Sharing from her life, she describes her second marriage as a comforting warm summer shower.

Inspired by this powerfully articulated distinction I grab my phone, launch the Instagram app, and write a heartfelt amen on Glennon's feed. *"I've only listened to 8:50 minutes of this episode and I'm blown away. Yes. Yes. Yes. I've been married thirty years to the same man and our marriage has so much kindness, caring, warmth, and summer rain in it. But this message of wanting lightning love is so loud in western culture that there are times when I question stuff. I'm so grateful to you for normalizing the extraordinary in the ordinary."*

I know this version of me, the one who craves a lightning love relationship. My younger self *was* that woman. I still am, on days when my feelings swell and swallow the part of my brain where logic lives.

I'm a wild romantic. I'm a sucker for sweet nothings, roses-for-no-reason, and pillow talk. My husband is the practical guy. He doesn't know how to gaze into my eyes with smoldering passion. Smoldering passion is great, but it doesn't take out the trash. Heat and passion can also overcook a relationship.

What G brings to our life is good, old-fashioned, wholesome commitment. He takes out the trash. Boy, am I glad he does, especially in Germany where stuff has to be sorted between sixteen bins! He changes the sheets. He builds bookshelves for me. He shops for knickknacks and knows just where to place them and make invisible nooks in our home turn into alive spaces.

For many years, the words *we need to talk* would send him scurrying for cover. And with good reason. I didn't know how to 'talk.' *We need to talk* was code for *let me pull out my laundry list of justified complaints.* These days, we're doing a better job of talking *with* each other instead of *at* each other.

It's also taken me a long while to travel the entire emotional spectrum, from *wanting* the fantasy of lightning love to making myself wrong for wanting it. Neither end of that spectrum serves me. The middle space feels far more peaceful. Acceptance is the middle space. Acceptance of me, acceptance of him, and acceptance of us. I no longer believe that acceptance means having to arrive somewhere. Acceptance is a long walk with no specific destination.

But that doesn't mean I'm all healed and whole and can live in the land of incense and love and light, the flame of eternal forgiveness burning bright in my heart.

Some evenings are still hard. G walks in the front door looking like a thundercloud that is about to rain all over my parade. Maybe he's had a tough day of customer meetings. Or a discussion with his boss that went south. Maybe it was the frustration of a deadline thrust upon him against his will. It could be that traffic was murderous on the drive home.

My mind is busy conjuring up many possible reasons to interpret the look on his face. What I meet is a wall of silence.

A furious seething starts inside me, a reflexive reaction I've felt a million times. I have a habit of taking his silences personally.

He's upset. He's always upset when he comes home to me. Why? Why? I didn't do anything. This is not my fault. Why am I never enough?

When my mind can't come up with a specific reason to explain his behavior because we've spent the past twelve hours in different universes, it switches to blame mode.

Why must he walk in the door looking so grumpy? Damn his job. It's the thing that steals the best parts of my husband leaving me with the stale leftovers.

"You're... upset about something?" I venture timidly.

"Hmmm."

"What hap--?"

"I'd rather not talk about it."

I take a beat before I speak. "Okay, that's fair. But can you just tell me it's not about me, so I'm not making up stories in my head about your silence?"

"It's work. Not you. Just a very... stressful day."

It's a small win. Instead of jumping to conclusions about how he 'never' comes home looking forward to seeing me, giving me a hug, asking about my day, I've detonated the storyteller in my head by asking a clarifying question.

A clarifying question that saves an entire evening. One wobbly step at a time I make the U-turn toward a small measure of inner peace.

Some days I stride purposefully; other days I falter and stumble. But I know this. My husband is walking beside me. When I miss a step or struggle up a steep slope, he holds out his hand. He reminds me that slipping and stumbling are part of navigating the terrain of a three-decade-old marriage.

SEX TALK

Christmas Eve, 2021. The day we return from our 2800-km road trip to Lyon and Barcelona, I wake up with a scratchy throat which soon progresses to a dry, hacking cough. My body has forgotten the right sequence of things, it appears, because the cough is followed by a bad case of the sneezes and sniffles. As a precaution I get a Covid test and, thankfully, test negative.

My runny nose is a bothersome blight on the holidays.

Vicks VapoRub has been my go-to since the congested colds of my childhood. Amma would rub the sticky gray gel on my back and chest, its pungent vapors rising up and tickling my nostrils.

Ever since I became a wife G has faithfully taken over this ritual.

"I'll give you a Vicks rubdown before you go to bed," he says to me as I mangle tissue after tissue in a desperate bid to stall my runny nose.

"No, thank you," I say, wiping my watering eyes.

"Why?" Confusion creases his forehead.

"I don't want it." And I don't wish to offer any further explanation.

Throughout the day, he continues to remind me that VapoRub will help me get a good night's sleep. My stubborn refusal confounds him, but I skillfully evade his persistent why. Ruki is visiting for the holidays, and I don't want to get into a big argument-justification back-and-forth which can quickly go south. It's easier to deflect G's question and change the subject.

Later that night I walk into our bedroom after brushing my teeth to find my husband waiting with the familiar midnight-blue jar of Vicks VapoRub in hand.

"Come on, get into bed," he says.

I start to unfurl my comforter. "No. I said I don't want it."

"Why are you being so stubborn?"

I stretch and shake the comforter taking longer than I need as I search for words to soften what I really want to say. "I just... I don't want you to. I'll do it myself."

"But, why Umsie?" The hurt in his voice cuts to the bone.

He closes the door to our bedroom. "What's really going on? Tell me. Why are you refusing me?"

"Because I don't *want* it." *It* sounds kinder than *you.*

He remains unconvinced. "Talk to me. Tell me why."

So, I break down and speak the words that I know will pierce his heart. "I don't want you to touch me... like that." I stare at the floor, lacking the courage to look up at his face and witness the pain I've caused.

He places the Vicks bottle in the palm of my hand, turns on his heel, and leaves the room.

I open the bottle, inhale deeply. The smells of mentholated shame and guilt. Then I slip my index finger inside, scoop up a gob of gel and rub it on my chest, temples, and back as best as I can. I slide under the comforter, pull it up to my chin, and try to calm my racing mind. I know I've hurt G terribly, but I didn't know how to sugarcoat this bitter confession. My words were brutal; also I was pushed to the brink by his unrelenting insistence. I turn on my right side, then my left, but sleep is far away.

Minutes later, I hear him tiptoeing back into our bedroom. I stay still, my eyes closed. The room is dark. I wait to feel the mattress give as he slides into bed, but nothing happens. I peek, see him leave the room pillow and comforter in hand, taking care to close the door softly behind him.

A deep inhale fills my lungs. Instead of the tears that come predictably, my lips curl in a smile. Not because I'm gloating about getting my way, but because I've *chosen* myself. Owning my power feels new and unfamiliar in the landscape of our shifting marriage dynamic. My default has been a hollow ache.

A week ago, we sat at the dining table and skirted the serrated edges of a strenuous subject: sex. Or the lack of it. Like most things left unattended, it had become rusty, time doing its work of erosion.

Our twelve-year journey of aridity since Amma had died is layered and complicated. Not easy to unpack.

Reeling from Amma's death in 2009, sex was the last thing on my mind. My body was overburdened by the enormous weight of grief. Guilt poked at me from many angles. I'd lived ten minutes away from my parents for an entire decade but had chosen to relocate and live an ocean away, not knowing Amma's cancer diagnosis was coming. I hadn't been in the room when she died. I'd left my little sis to deal with the aftermath of Amma's loss and Appa's care all on her own.

Pleasure had become a dirty word. I couldn't allow myself to feel *pleasure*. I'd lost my appetite for it. The only kind of affection my body opened to was warm, loving hugs that translated to *I'm so sorry you're hurting. I want to help.*

To his credit, G has made no demands on me. He sensed my need to turn inward, burrow into my bewilderment, and stay there.

Grief leading to the path of my radical awakening befuddled him. He didn't recognize the new me who rose from the ashes of Amma's death. He felt abandoned when I embarked on my existential excursion. An adult abdicating adulting, choosing instead to commit to some crazy woo-woo agenda.

Sex, it occurs to me, is like regular exercise. If you fall off the wagon, it's easy to find a bunch of excuses *why* you don't have the energy, or can't make time for it. We made a few half-hearted attempts every now and again, but it quickly became clear that we were unable to recapture the joyful melding our lovemaking used to be. Over time, it was easier not to try, easier to turn to books and iPads as more satisfying bedtime companions.

Yet a part of me misses physical intimacy. In the absence of other intimacies, the ones we'd shared *Before AD* (Amma's Death), like easy conversations, debates about plays and sports, commonly held and supported grouses and grudges, the loss of physical intimacy seems the hardest.

I didn't know how to talk about it. I only knew how to relive the pain of rejection. On the few occasions when I plucked up my courage and voiced a tentative why, his party line—*I don't know*—felt like a door slamming in my face.

Until the day my husband said something that astounded me. "I didn't understand any of it. You'd become this... this elevated person. You were talking about God and spirituality and service all the time. You were so holy. You were like this... this goddess. I didn't feel that I could look at you like a regular woman, much less touch you that way."

"I wish you'd shared this with me," I said. "I would've explained. This journey I'm on doesn't make me less human. In fact, it makes me more human. My spirituality doesn't ever ask me to shun sex. Sex is the sacred union between two humans, and nothing could be a more beautiful connection."

His look of confusion spoke volumes. The perplexed look on his face told me that he didn't understand how to marry the two foreign ideas. As important as it was, this conversation didn't ease our path back to each other. We continued to drift, unmoored from the safe, familiar world we'd once inhabited.

I think back to a few months ago, the night we were sitting at the dining table, dregs of red wine in our glasses, and the detritus of our meal on our plates.

It was the first time we had traveled there together: to the land of honest conversations that hurt before they heal.

I go there, back to that night, one more time.

I start by saying, "It just feels like... I never had closure. This question of *why* we stopped... you know, it had never been answered in my head. Because we could never talk about the why." Even as I speak the words, my body recoils with unnamable shame.

His eyes touch mine for a brief second before he looks away. "When Amma died and you had this... transformation, as you call it..." he pauses, clears his throat. "I didn't even *like* you for some time."

Words that might have caused me to flinch or cringe instead open my body, like an endless vista. Strangely, what I feel is gratitude for honesty—over not knowing.

He continues. "And then, as time went on, there were more and more layers to get through. It was easier not to try. Are we going to move past it all? The honest answer is, I don't know."

I take a deep breath. "I feel better just hearing you say this."

Even when things are hard to hear, the truth has mostly been comforting to me. Vulnerability is a beautiful thing, especially when it is offered to you by a man who has only learned armoring and defending as ways to meet the world.

The grand irony of the moment: in acknowledging the truth, we've just shared a moment of deep connection, true intimacy. The awkward confessions of two flawed humans who didn't know any better and were too scared to try—until right now.

That was as far as we could travel that night. The path ahead was much too dark. We couldn't see beyond this step.

Lying in bed and reflecting on that conversation, my heart feels tender toward G. He is tossing on the living-room couch, squirming under the awful stab of rejection. No part of me wants that for him, to feel what I've lived with all these years: wondering, endlessly analyzing, manufacturing nasty narratives in my head.

You're repulsed by the menopausal fat I'm carrying in my belly, thighs, and hips.

I've become boring, stale, irrelevant.

I no longer turn you on.

Sleep teases me for many hours, but eventually drapes over me and takes me under. I'm dead to the world for nearly eight hours and wake up to G calling my name, his hand on my shoulder.

He is sitting on the edge of our bed. "Did you know I slept in the living-room last night?"

As sleep drugged as I am, I register the absence of a defensive tone in his question. "Mmm-hmm," I say. It's all I can manage, still rising up and out of sleep's deep embrace.

"I just want to say that what happened last night was about *my* stuff. It had nothing to do with you. In fact, what you said... I probably deserved it. I don't blame you at all."

Sleep vanishes in that instant. A wave of affection washes over me, soft feathers brushing my skin ever so gently. Finding the right words is too much of an effort when my brain is still doing its wake-up stretches.

"I just said a lot," he smiles. "And you just woke up. We'll talk about it later," he says, kissing me on the forehead.

It will be three days before we carve out a window of time and privacy to navigate this delicate conversation sitting in our living room armchairs.

G opens the conversation. "My offer to rub Vicks came from a place of affection. I just wanted you to feel better. So, I was confused and hurt when you refused me. But I get it now. I probably deserved it."

I pause for a few seconds to choose my words. My intention is to pick words that are kind but not enough to blur the truth. "I never doubted that your offer came from a genuinely caring place. But... I haven't been naked in front of you for, I don't know. I don't even know how long it's been. A very long time." I take a beat. "So, it just didn't feel right to me to allow you to touch my body *clinically*. What I told myself was that if you didn't want to touch me, you lose access to my body. This is *my* body—and I get to choose. That's just the way I feel."

I lean back in my armchair and indulge in a long, slow exhale.

He nods. "I can't argue with that. It makes sense. But I decided to sleep on the couch because I was hurt..."

"I know. You felt rejected. You felt the pain *I've* felt for many,

many nights—until I made peace with the reality that that door had shut for us. Just so you know, what happened last night wasn't my idea of revenge or anything. It was me saying a loud and clear no because it just didn't feel right to me."

I value other kinds of intimacy even more these days and I want to share that with my husband. "I mean, sex is one way of being intimate. But there are other ways that seem more meaningful to me now. This conversation, for example. Us talking about all this with such openness means a lot to me..."

We don't say anything for a few minutes but the silence between us holds us, bridges the space instead of creating a chasm as it usually does.

"I'm glad we talked about this," he says.

"Me too. It felt important to address—and it feels right that we did."

Strangely, in the aftermath of an extremely sensitive exchange which we both handle with care, a quiet kind of intimacy enfolds us. To feel safe enough to give voice to something which is beautiful and ugly and shame-triggering is an act of deep soul connection. In the telling of it, we hold each other in such a deep and naked way that feels so much better than the best sex we've enjoyed.

FOUR PILLARS

Many years ago, I was assigned to interview a couple who traveled the world hosting seminars on how to keep a marriage healthy. One of the main tenets of their teaching was this: a healthy marriage is built on the four pillars of love, trust, respect, and intimacy.

The first three pillars of our marriage are intact.

Amma's death, my inner rearranging, and the ways in which my husband was forced to adapt have certainly hit our fourth pillar hard. Our views on life and living have shifted. My new lens on life offers a spiritual perspective while his life is firmly rooted in 3-D reality.

As I look back, it occurs to me that my biggest fear has been loss of connection. I was born and raised in Southern India, a 'collective' culture where home, family, and community are at the epicenter of everything. My father's descent into alcoholism was a sharp and shocking whack into the nest of safety and connection. When that nest blew apart leaving me shaky and disoriented, my nervous system locked into the message *I'm not safe when I'm not connected.*

Appa's preoccupation with the next drink (which turned into the next binge) reinforced the message *I don't matter.* If I mattered he wouldn't seek to escape into a bottle of amber seduction. My innocent psyche anchored this defense mechanism in place as my father drank the nights away.

I have faithfully transferred the neurosis to G. If I mattered he'd choose me over work, his constantly pinging cell phone, or the need to disappear into himself.

I wasn't enough for my father. I'm not enough for my husband. *I don't matter.*

The wounded child trapped inside my grown woman body is throwing a mighty tantrum—and I have no idea how to calm her.

The clock doesn't stop ticking. Calendars don't freeze. Time keeps moving forward. Whether we feel it or not, like it or not, we keep growing but to evolve the soul is a choice. When that moment of satori clobbers us, we come to a crossroads: awaken, or choose to go back to sleep because what your soul is asking scares the bejeezus out of you.

As long as my frightened inner child holds the reins, I suffer and struggle. Her all-consuming fear is that no one is going to love us, that we'll be abandoned and alone. My *sadhana* is to hold her in my arms, comfort her, repeat the words she's longed to hear, and create safety.

It was so much easier to blame G for not loving me the way I *wanted* to be loved. But I have to tell the whole, unvarnished truth about my inadequacies and take ownership of my fears, insecurities, and unmet childhood needs—or nothing in my adult life and our marriage is going to change.

Taking responsibility is hard. It means facing all the parts of me that I've pushed into the shadows. My neediness made me feel broken in some way. I poke around in the nooks and crannies and gently tease out the scared, confused, shamed, hurt, and sad parts of me I've turned away from.

I grasp, I let go. I cling, I let go. I attach, I let go. It's a constant practice. The universe uses everything it can to gently pry my fingers from the very thing I can't seem to let go of: my fear of losing connection. The toughest lesson in my soul curriculum this time around is self-love. *I couldn't have picked a better soulmate to be my teacher.*

It takes a village to heal a wounded soul. My village includes awakened guides. Tara Brach, Pema Chodron, Eckhart Tolle, Kristin Neff, Tosha Silver, Janet Conner, and Anita Moorjani. Every book, podcast, and course points the way to a new truth, a new beginning. Me, my heart, my true refuge. My spiritual explorations move me toward the possibility that G and I came here to heal our relationship dynamic. Not by breaking it but by *staying and honoring each other's path.*

So, I start over, try again. When I'm triggered by his distracted self, I place a hand on my heart and offer myself words of compassion: *This human journey is hard. I'm the one I've been waiting for. I am safe. All my needs are always met.*

I grieve what's no longer available in our marriage.

I fling open the doors of my heart and invite every emotion to take a seat at the table.

Grief, I see you. Anger, I'm open to hearing what you have to say. Guilt, come, sit beside me. Fear, let me hold your hand. We can be in this together.

In the invitation is an immediate softening, listening, curiosity.

Grief says, *what used to be is never coming back. It died.*

Anger says, *speak your truth even if it's hard—or you'll feel bitter.*

Guilt says, *reassess your values before you make yourself wrong.*

Fear says, *it's scary to embark on a solo path but you're held.*

Finally, my Wise Woman speaks up. *You are Love. Why do you search for what you're made of?*

I've been searching for my one true love all my life. And she has been right here inside of me all this time. *She is me.*

What my younger self didn't know—and I do—is this. Whereas she looked outside of herself and silently screamed *See me, love me* to anyone who cared to stop and look and listen, the job of loving me is mine and mine alone. Also, I need trusted friends—my tribe—for conversation and companionship because I'm a human hardwired for connection. *Both/And.*

❧

Some mornings the tears come. The salt of sorrow. I cup my palms and catch them in the sacred bowl of self-acceptance. For so long the world has forced me to attach a *why* to my tears.

The world loves justifications, reasons, neat little boxes. The world is impatient with *I don't know and Maybe I don't have to know.*

Often my *why* has been attached to blaming the other. *You didn't... You made me feel... You never...*

Now I cry without feeling the need to fit my tears into a neat story of what was done to me or what I didn't receive.

I cry because Sister Sorrow shows up, sits beside me, and says: Feel me, then release me. I silence my mind and let my body take over and do what it knows to do. I let the tears fall because they want to come. My mind is not invited to fashion a narrative around it.

I feel because my feelings are real.

I feel because it's healthy to feel.

I feel because I'm a sensitive human.

Good enough reasons without watering the garden of self-righteous thoughts and demanding things others don't know how to give me.

And then I forget. I fail. I blame. I'm unkind. And that becomes the perfect sacred ground to practice forgiveness over and over. I forgive myself for every time I'm unable to break free of a lifelong pattern, for making another human responsible for what's mine to take care of, for using my wounds to wound.

I have needs—and that doesn't make me needy. You have needs—and that doesn't make you needy. We have needs because we're human. We have needs because we're meant to meet each other's needs and take care of each other.

When we ignore our needs and isolate, pretending that we're strong and self-sufficient, we suffer alone. When we suffer alone we feel the need to don a false mask and pretend that all is well. We create layers of narratives, most of them useless and untrue.

When the tears come and I need a conversation to feel better, I take my need to G.

"I need to share something," I say.

"Let's find a time to talk today," he offers.

I pause at the doorway of the conversation and enter with intent. The desire to blame or prove my rightness, I know, will only create separation and suffering.

My tears are signaling to me that I need connection.

As the words begin to pour out of me, he listens, nods. Then he shares his current emotional weather. We create space for what is hard to exist between us. We're two imperfect humans who are not willing to give up.

In the shared acknowledgment of our individual reality, new threads of connection and intimacy are woven.

Sometimes, just nodding to a need and letting it be is an act of healing. I've learned the wisdom of letting my body speak. All I need to do is show up and listen.

Self-compassion gets me through the days when what I need is unavailable. On such days I let my breath guide me to gratitude. Gratitude for the perfect circumstance that help me learn how to *be here* for me at all times. When my husband doesn't know how to comfort me or can't find the words, when I felt lost and friendless in a foreign country, when a virus pushed all my social connections far out of reach.

One of the most transformative tools in my spiritual toolkit is *paradox.* The idea that two opposites can be true at the same time and held together. I feel loved and supported by my husband *and* I desire a level of connection he's unable to give me. But I no longer want to punish a human for not knowing—especially when he supports everything I do and loves me for all that I am *right now.*

Is G a committed, caring, loving husband? *Yes.*

Is he capable of loving me in all the ways I want to be loved? *No.*

Is it my responsibility to love me? *Yes.*

Am I always good about honoring self-love? *No.*

He can love me in the deepest, most beautiful ways *and* I still need to cherish myself. I can love myself deeply *and* still need the gifts of companionship and connection he offers.

Both/And.

INTIMACY

*I*ntimacy. It's a word I've mostly had a challenging relationship with. I've loved intimacy, longed for it, craved it, and felt the powerlessness of grasping for it when it seems out of reach.

If I'd known about intimacy what I know now, I'd have saved myself a ton of heartache. No human being knows how to love us the way we want to be loved.

For many years I lived my life anchored to the belief that intimacy and scarcity are a couple. Always afraid of losing connection, being vigilant of squandering connection because of a wrong word, a wrong look, an incorrect assumption. Questioning G's motives, investing his behaviors with meanings derived from the disempowering stories crowding my head.

We don't talk enough.

We don't have enough sex.

We don't do stuff together anymore.

My nerve endings were on fire. My primal brain scanning for danger and making split-second decisions about whether I was on the cliff-edge of losing connection and risking the deep drop into loneliness. It is not a healthy way to live.

It has taken me the fifth decade of my life to unravel this storyline. There's nothing wrong with me. There's everything wrong with the story I'm telling about how I'll never have intimacy, that I'll end up alone and lonely.

I've been so scared of losing intimacy that I had to lose it, learn to breathe through it, and make the U-turn home to where true intimacy lives: within me.

Culture and society dope us on the big fat lie that intimacy has to be earned, fought for, deserved. Traditionally, most women have learned to love their body through the male gaze. The ability to make male heads turn, being the coveted one in a crowd, knowing male attention is a given because of your beautiful architecture. As the assaults of time leave their mark on the body and cause the male gaze to shift away, a woman carries the shame that her body is no longer worthy of lust and love.

I've been that woman.

So, when my body was no longer able to hold my husband's gaze, I made it my fault and gathered enough evidence. Gravity. Menopausal fat. Age spots and scars. The softening and wrinkling of what once used to be firm and smooth.

I was blind to the miracle of my beating heart and breathing lungs, functions that kept going even as I slept.

Here's what I know now: Reclaiming body love is only possible when I live with soul awareness. My body is the vessel my soul travels in and worthy of my greatest devotion. This holy home of mine helps me walk my earthly journey. It's my reason for being here.

My redefinition of intimacy begins here.

Safety in my body and intimacy with my own experience are the only truths from which true partnership-intimacy can be created.

Can I meet my most intimate needs?

Can I be my own best friend?

Can I hold myself with tenderness, listen deeply, and love myself especially when I'm in my lowest low?

Intimacy is on the table when I love *all* of me, not just the best parts of me.

The burden of a partnership is the expectation that we be loved *as we love the other*. But how can someone give you what they don't know how to give themselves? Until G learns to befriend his own feelings, he won't know what to do with mine.

It's my job to be intimate with me.

As I return home to my own belonging, I open to a deeper, more sacred intimacy with the Divine. For I am the Divine and the Divine is me. The sweetness of this forever love is the one constant in my life.

Intimacy is dialoguing with the divine.

Intimacy is placing a hand over my heart and affirming myself for being enough right here, right now.

Intimacy is being okay with all the parts of me that live within me: my guilt, grief, anger, envy, resentment, and bitterness.

Intimacy is cradling the sacred chalice in my palms and catching my tears.

Intimacy is saying *I love you; I'll always be here for you* over and over, especially on the days when I'm unable to rise up to the highest vision I hold for myself.

When I'm intimate with myself, I'm able to be intimate with my husband. The conversations we have are rich, real, and resonant with truth-telling. Deeply difficult, yet profoundly meaningful.

Unfortunately, most of our scripts for intimacy are borrowed from the worst sources: Hollywood (and Bollywood, in my case). A version where heroes and heroines cavort in fields of sun-kissed flowers, their adoration of each other choreographed in song and dance.

In real life, the shape of intimacy shifts over the lifetime of a committed relationship.

My husband's acts of intimacy are many. It's taken me a new lens to see them, appreciate them, and bless them.

He leans down to lace my sneakers when my back is sore.

He reaches into his pocket and pulls out a handkerchief to mop my streaming eyes—when he doesn't have the words.

He reschedules a work meeting to drop me off at the airport and kiss me goodbye.

He knows how I like spaghetti drenched in red sauce, the strength of the coffee I drink. He creates space for my wake-up rituals and brings home a slice of bakery pie when I'm having a rough day.

Self-honoring and honoring the other expands the container of intimacy. We walk hand in hand even when we don't see eye to eye.

HEALING THE HEALER

O ver time the real meaning of the word *broken* reveals itself to me. To be *broken* means something that cannot exist in the form it once used to. It is a shattering of the old self, the self that needed to die so that a new version could be born. Shattering begins with a summons from the soul.

To be broken is to be reconfigured. It is our brokenness that lets life and light in and illumines what once lived in the dark. It is in the new seeing of things that our interior lives are rearranged into a brand-new mosaic.

The work of excavating what's hiding in the dark—shadow work—and meeting it with love and acceptance takes courage.

Now that we're in Germany, I like visiting my daughter in

Chicago during the summer. In the summer of 2021, I put a deposit down on an Airbnb in Evanston, IL. The leafy suburb feels like the perfect place to honor my intention: alone-time to do Shadow Work. I'm ready to welcome home all the parts of me I've exiled because they made me feel bad about myself.

Creating boundaries around my solo sojourn feels important so I request G and Ruki to honor my wish for complete solitude that entire week. I know my husband will be uncomfortable with this boundary. He likes it when I text to let him know I've arrived at my destination; it's important to him to know I'm safe and have everything I need. But he generously honors my request not to text or call. To embrace the discomfort of not-knowing.

When I arrived at the Airbnb I'd booked for this private and sacred ritual, I was dismayed to learn that my room was in the basement. My knee-jerk reaction was utter frustration. As I wrestled with the unfairness of it, the wisdom of the universe gradually dawned on me. I'd been sent to the bowels of the building where the deepest shadows live as the perfect setting to begin the work of excavating, blessing, and releasing my own shadows.

My copy of Debbie Ford's *The Dark Side of the Light Chasers* was dog-eared and marked, with notes scribbled in the margins by the time that week drew to a close. As I excavated deeply buried selves and dialogued with them, I took plenty of long walks in nature, spent time in meditation, and journaled pages and pages that resulted from inner inquiry.

I cried. I apologized. I offered deep forgiveness. I showered love and light on all that I'd rejected. I called a Conference of My Shadow Selves. Each part spoke as I listened to its truth—the energy it was holding, why, and what it needed from me to feel safe and accepted. I made a commitment to never exclude any of them but honor them and their precious roles in my life, to hold a place at the table where they're always welcome and have a voice.

Often we walk on eggshells around the people we love because we fear something we say or do might upset them. That's a hard way to do life. We *are* going to hurt the ones we love.

It's not what causes the hurt that matters as much as *what happens next.*

When this wisdom lands in my heart, it feels right.

G and I are sipping coffee at a street café when we cross wires over something trivial. He starts to beat himself up for that moment of thoughtlessness when I share this truth with him. "You're human, just as I am. We're going to say stuff in the moment and hurt each other. But if we can take care of what happens next, it can be the best way to make amends."

Can I be more understanding of his crabbiness when he walks in the door after a rough day at work?

Can I be kind in the moment?

Can I bite my tongue and say nothing instead of reacting with a barb?

Can I choose to forgive?

It's always *what happens next* that determines whether we

continue to propagate the hurt or heal the rift.

Many of us are addicted to the self-image of 'the healed healer.' We believe that we *must* bring our perfectly healed self to the person we're guiding. This stems from the mistaken notion that 'Healed' is a destination. Arriving at this destination makes us worthy enough to hold space for the people we're here to serve.

But this is what I know to be true for myself. Healing is a spiral. Every time I travel the loop it feels as if I've arrived back in the same place. The truth is that each time I've gained a higher perspective.

I'm never done. We're never finished. That doesn't mean we make healing an endless obsession, chasing one modality after another. That's just another convenient and 'responsible' distraction from what we simply need to *be with*. Our job is not to feel good all the time; our job is to feel what wants to be felt in the moment.

The most healing thing I've learned to do is to 'catch' my own tears, hold my inner child close to me and whisper the words: "I'm here with you. I love you. I'll never leave you. I'll stay with you for as long as you need me to."

It took some time, but I finally got it. I was the one I'd been waiting for the whole time. Not my father. Not my husband. Not my therapist. Just me.

My client Sandra's eyes are closed. She's breathing and grounding as I create a sacred space for us to begin our session.

"Everything is welcome here," I say the words softly. "Your grief, anger, shame, guilt, and rage. All of you is welcome here. Everything is allowed, embraced, and loved. It's safe for you to arrive here just as you are."

This is an invocation I speak at the beginning of my sessions, the scent from my sacred candle and the smoke curling from a stick of palo santo blessing the space.

It wasn't until I made it okay for all me to exist in my glorious holy human messiness that I could call it forth from my clients.

I no longer chase after the next bright thing on the holiness wagon. My spirituality is simple. When I'm able to be with what is, my body and mind follow, and I heal. Tending to the softness and sensitivity of my being. Cradling my tender emotions and loving them until they move through me.

My only intention these days is to hold and honor my humanity and my divinity together.

The oneness I feel with the Divine is a brand-new experience in devotion. Hymns and prayers move me to tears. The Divine doesn't need me to do, be, or have anything in order for me to be worthy of Her Love. I am eternally and perfectly loved because I am. This love begins to feel far more nourishing than earthly love which, by definition, is mostly flawed.

As my awareness deepens, separation dissolves. I am the Divine; the Divine is me. I *am* that eternal love. It is in me. I am it. What muddies this pure love is my humanness. My judgments, expectations, fears, and insecurities. Boundaries and barriers I erect because I am unable, often unwilling, to love without limits.

My eyes mist at this realization. A wellspring of compassion flows out of me. Flawed love is what we all know to give and receive. No matter our best intentions, G and I are wounded humans who, in moments when our pain overpowers our sanity, lash out at each other.

My primary responsibility is to tend to my own pain and pour loving kindness all over it. That is how I will heal. I know that love is the home of my soul. My job is to return home as the most abundant source of that which I seek from G. As long as I place my needs and expectations on my husband and depend on his validation for my survival, I will, forever, be at the mercy of flawed love.

Soul journaling saves me time and again.

I've never been fond of the *Dear Diary* routine. I've found it to be boring and bland.

Soul journaling requires me to poke around inside me and dig up honest truths. Instead of blaming (If only he would…) and begging (See me), I turn into a detective of my inner dialogue.

What was I unwilling to give in this situation?

What was I afraid of losing?

What is mine to own?

Every time I pose these questions to my soul, She offers me glimmers of insight. Even if my reactive self has her hands wrapped tight around the steering wheel of my life, wisdom gently pries my fingers open every time. My rigid stance softens as words pour from my pen.

They say, "Don't go to bed angry." It's one of those rules that hasn't served us well, so we ignore it. Trying to find the right words to build a bridge between us when we're both locked into our positions is an impossible task. We do much better when we come together twenty-four hours later. The heat of righteousness has dissipated, and calm reasoning usually prevails. We're both more open-hearted, compassionate, and forgiving of the other's humanness.

SOLO VACATION

Sitting in the living room, G fires up his laptop. I'm sitting beside him, eager to see the pictures of Madeira in Portugal off the northwest coast of Africa.

We've talked about this, off and on, the idea of taking solo vacations aside from the ones we take together.

Six months after my solo sojourn, G is getting ready to embark on his solo vacation. As much as he craves a week of peace, quiet, and alone time, the reality of planning it brings up big feelings. It's the first time since we've known each other that he will be taking a vacation without me. The prospect triggers a large dose of guilt.

As the website loads he turns to me. "Please. Try not to be wildly excited when you see the location. I won't be able to go through with it if you do."

"I won't say a word," I promise, moving my fingers across my lips to suggest zipping them.

The laptop screen fills with ocean blue. The view of the Atlantic Ocean from the outdoor patio of the Airbnb, a weathered wooden table and a slatted chair waiting for G. A single white cup sits on the table (imagine your favorite beverage in it).

I can see him leaning back in that wooden chair, a glass of Pinot in front of him, gazing at the aquamarine waters, drinking in the peace.

I want to be there.

The images shift as he clicks through. Well-appointed rooms to eat, sleep, and shower in. A small, efficient kitchenette. The blue waters stretch to an endless horizon. It is all sky and sea.

G glances at me. "Just say the word and I'll book your ticket."

I work hard at maintaining a neutral expression. "No. We've talked about this. You need to do this *for you.* God knows you deserve it more than anyone I know."

"Come with me, Ums," he says, taking my hand. "Let's go away for a week."

I shake my head no. "You'll feel so much better on the other side. I know you will. Imagine all that peace and quiet. Just you and the sea and the hiking trails."

He's lived his entire life pouring into everyone he cares about, including me. Especially me. To seek solo pleasure has always felt selfish to him. But I know his soul longs for alone time, an open calendar, away from the relentless pressures of his corporate job.

"Want to go with me?" he tries one more time.

"No, not this time. Tell you what. If you love this place enough we'll make a trip together some other time."

Spending time without an agenda is a gift I know will be a balm to his soul. He knows it too, but he's struggling with the rightness of his decision. There's only one way to find out—by doing it.

∽৵৹

I, dear reader, am as human as you. There are days when I, as I'm sure you do too, read or hear about couples who hold hands at bedtime and speak their gratitudes out loud before they go to bed. Or who travel to meditation retreats and share their journal entries with each other. I'm hit by a wave of longing when that happens.

There used to be a time when I made myself wrong for my longings. How dare I long for anything when I have so much goodness going for me in my marriage!

No longer. My desires are mine to own. They come and go.. The doors of my heart swing wide open to let these longings in. They're mine and they have a place inside of me. It's not wrong to long.

There are days when I can detach from those moments of longing. I remember that my soul path and the karma G and I came here to clear are as unique as our sacred union.

Grief and gratitude sit on the weighing scales of my marriage. Some days, grief is heavier. Other days, the rosy glow of gratitude suffuses everything. I'm no longer seeking a destination called "healed." I'm not even sure what that looks like. But my heart's capacity to meet myself and all the complexities of being a human has grown.

Feel the longing, honor the grief, and allow the warmth of my gratitude for this life, for this beloved man, to be present and alive.

This is my spiritual practice. I'm not trying to become the best version of me; I'm deepening my love for the not-so-lovable versions of me.

∾

Loneliness is a universal condition. Being a human and having a nervous system is a complex experience. I'm blown away when I hear best-selling author Marilynne Robinson reframe loneliness as a *privilege*. I can live with that definition.

According to Robinson, we're given this time to ourselves to do our own thinking and have our own experience of being mortal in the world. We fear loneliness. We misdiagnose it. As failure, pathology, inadequacy. It's none of that. It is about having a tremendously powerful consciousness isolated in the specific circumstance of one's life. That is what makes my life, and yours, a privilege.

MAY 19, 2022

I wake up and see G sitting on my side of the bed. It is our 31st wedding anniversary. He leans down and kisses me.

"Happy anniversary, Umsie."

"To you as well, my love."

"I'm sorry I haven't bought you anything this year," he says. "But we're driving to Paris. I'm going to stay away from all work emails and calls today. We have five to six hours on the road. We can talk, just be with each other."

"That sounds like the best gift ever." I smile at him.

Hours later, our bags are stowed in the trunk for our week-long vacation to Paris, Arcachon, Bordeaux, and Lourdes.

Before we set off we stop at a gas station for a car wash and fuel top-up. It's summer and the windshield is splattered with dead-bug juice.

G goes inside to pay for gas. When he steps out, he's holding one beautiful crimson rose, its long thorny stem wrapped in a paper towel.

"Happy anniversary," he says, handing me the rose. "Sorry, the guy didn't have a pair of scissors to snip off the thorny stem."

We click our seat belts and drive onward. An extraordinary milestone. A perfect moment. A reminder that roses and thorns always go together.

~ THE END ~

With Gratitude

My deep devotion and gratitude to the Divine for all the abundance You sent my way so this book could be born.

To my beloved Co-Hearts: Elan, Jen, Mary, Meredith, and Zoe for critiques, unwavering support, and encouragement.

To my beta readers: Lisa, Ruki, Amy, for your time and generosity in helping shape this book.

To Marisa, for your abiding friendship and for introducing me to Michelle.

To Michelle and Lucie, the book doulas on my team.

And last but not least: You, dear reader, for receiving my words.

You are the reason I write.

About the Author

UMA GIRISH is a spiritual mentor, award-winning author, and Human Design guide. She mentors women who are grieving different kinds of losses to find the bigger meaning and purpose in their pain and embrace authentic living. Her previous books include **Understanding Death**: *10 Ways to Inner Peace for the Grieving;* **Losing Amma, Finding Home**: *A Memoir About Love, Loss, and Life's Detours; and* **Lessons from Grace**: *What A Baby Taught Me About Living and Loving.* She hosts a podcast *Being Fully Me* to share stories and reflections about her journey, work, and life. Uma lives in a Chicago suburb with her husband of 34 years. Connect with Uma and learn more about her work at https://umagirish.com

Is It Time to Share Your Story with the World?

If this book has sparked something within you—a whisper, a nudge, or a full-blown calling to finally put your story into words—then consider this your invitation.

At Soul Spark Publishing, we believe that every story holds power, and every voice deserves to be heard. If you've been dreaming of writing a book, whether to share your expertise, inspire others, or cement your legacy, we are here to guide you.

Our bespoke, high-touch publishing experience ensures that your book is crafted with intention, excellence, and artistry. We work with authors who are ready to create something extraordinary—a book that resonates, lasts, and leaves an impact.

If that sounds like you, let's begin. Visit soulsparkpublishing.com. We cannot wait to help you bring your story to life.

OTHER TITLES FROM SOUL SPARK PUBLISHING

The Me I Didn't See

The 6-Figure Creative: Heal Your Relationship with Money Doing Work You Love

Beautiful Chaos: Embracing the Unexpected

Insights from the Soul: Gentle Conversations With Your Inner Self

The Seeker Within

Whole Wisdom: Trusting the Connection of Mind and Body

www.ingramcontent.com/pod-product-compliance
Lightning Source LLC
Chambersburg PA
CBHW020429130626
46549CB00001B/53